February 1, 2017

Dear Sandy,

I hope you enjoy this book written in memory of my Dad in hopes that we never forget the price of freedom.

For you in memory of your Uncle Lawrence Breckbill, Pilot of "Scrappy Mike."

With Best Wishes,

Candy Kyler Brown

WHAT I NEVER TOLD YOU

*A Daughter Traces the Wartime
Imprisonment of Her Father*

Candy Kyler Brown

authorHOUSE®

AuthorHouse™
1663 Liberty Drive
Bloomington, IN 47403
www.authorhouse.com
Phone: 1-800-839-8640

First published by AuthorHouse 8/17/2010

ISBN: 978-1-4490-0887-1 (sc)
ISBN: 978-1-4490-0888-8 (hc)

Library of Congress Control Number: 2010906446

Printed in the United States of America
Bloomington, Indiana

This book is printed on acid-free paper.

Cover drawing by Carolyn Councell.

Scripture taken from the King James Version Bible.

For my Dad: One of a noble group that was part of the history of the United States…

May that group's sacrifice never be forgotten.

Table of Contents

Pre-Enlistment

The Phases

Arrival In England – 8th Air Force

Stalag Luft IV – Camp #2

The Move To Stalag Luft I – Camp #3

Foreword

World War II changed the lives of people throughout the world, among the Allied forces and the Axis powers, and the thousands of innocent victims who had nothing to do with either. In the United States the apron strings of the American housewives were untied and a new and powerful industrial might was created. "Rosie the Riveter" was born. The Eighth Army Air Corps was also born and became a mighty force to be reckoned with. Staff Sergeant John Roland Kyler, a ball turret gunner on a B-17 Flying Fortress, POW #1277, was a part of that mighty force.

This is the story of Sgt. Kyler's combat experience with the 92nd Bombardment Group (H) that flew the famous Boeing B-17 "Flying Fortresses" from Podington, England. It tells the story of his training, the destruction of his aircraft, and his capture, treatment and struggle to survive as a Prisoner of War in Nazi Germany. Candy Brown, daughter of Sgt. Kyler, wrote this book to remember and bring recognition to our American ex-prisoners of war by telling Sgt. Kyler's story, and by keeping these little-known war experiences alive.

This journal is a must-read in all American communities, for both the young and old. As veterans from this era pass on, these stories must be recorded for posterity, or the oral history of these POW experiences will be lost forever.

Joseph P. O'Donnell
Robbinsville, New Jersey
April 19, 2009
(POW# 1414, Stalag Luft IV)

Sgt. Joseph P. O'Donnell
Courtesy of Joseph P. O'Donnell

Introduction

As I awoke from a restless sleep on the morning of May 4, 2004, I hoped that the unsettling feelings that came over me were the result of a nightmare, and that the pictures so clear in my mind and the pain that I felt in my heart were products of my sleeping imagination. I so wished that the awful vision of my father's death, borne on my dreams, was not real. I lay there, fully aware that I had not been dreaming, and that my father was indeed gone. Still, the images flooding my mind were not figments of my imagination, but real events that I had witnessed hours before. I could not stop crying, and I wondered if the tears would ever subside. I had no control over them. I wanted my dad. How could I go on – how could *we* go on without him? What was next? I had no choice but to shower, get dressed, and drive over to my old home that I always referred to as "Mom and Dad's" house.

That home was to be the gathering place. My oldest sister Sandra, and my brother Buster, who no longer lived near home, had been notified of dad's deteriorating condition the previous evening. Then the final phone calls were made, notifying them of his death. They would soon be joining us to share our grief.

Many kind family members and friends arrived at my mother's to extend their condolences and to bring food to sustain us during the painful days that would follow. Along with my mother and sisters Dawn and Angel, I drove to the funeral home at noon. We picked out Dad's casket, and gave information for his obituary. We were all just going through the motions of doing what had to be done. The obituary would contain dad's military information, of course, which was not difficult to find at the house. It was readily available as a result of his recent dealings with the Veteran's Administration when gathering documents for his award of the Medal for Merit and the proof of compensation eligibility. More detailed information would be obtained from the Veteran's Administration by the funeral director. We had taken with us a small piece of paper on which dad had written significant dates and information concerning his wartime experience. That tiny piece of paper summed up data that would fill many volumes.

Returning to my mom's house, we began looking for pictures and articles to take to the funeral home to display during visitation hours. It was during this time that I became riveted by what we found, and so was inspired to learn more about my father and a part of his life that I did not know.

Dad lived most of his life without any mention of the hardships that he had endured during the war. But his abrupt and unexpected death in 2004 brought his involvement in WWII to the forefront, as we family members now freely looked through the memorabilia that he had kept stashed away all these years, and we were in awe of what we saw.

Although it appeared to us that he wanted to forget most everything about his war years, he had saved his precious belongings from that critical time, which indicated that this part of his life had not been insignificant to him. His memories were indelibly etched on his person. He had hung onto these mementoes even though he had never exhibited them. They were at one time private items, personal to him, but had become treasures to those he left behind.

The worn and faded pages of the notebooks that my father had so carefully written when he was a POW bespoke the significance of a life that none of us knew. These pages brought to light the critical role Dad played as a ball turret gunner on a B-17; the role that would change to "POW" when he was shot down and captured. I leafed through these notebooks, and each turn of a page took me back further in time. I was not satisfied to just fleetingly skim over those magnificent poems and sketches and then return the notebooks to the place they had been kept for nearly sixty years. Remnants of my father's past had been unveiled upon his death, but it was clear to me even then that they could become the foundation on which to build his story. The moment I examined them I vowed to retrace his journey as an airman and POW; to assemble the pieces of his past the best way that I could without having him there to help with the many questions that would arise. These pages inspired my dedication to seek the life of young Sergeant John Roland Kyler.

It is this young man that I dream of – his life before marriage and children – that I wonder about. That life was hidden away by the time, and probably well before, I knew him…at least there was always a shared silence about it in our household. My mission became the revelation of that young man's story, to learn of the life that most certainly laid the groundwork for the wonderful human being who became my father.

Candy Kyler Brown
Kill Buck, New York
March 2010

Acknowledgments

Over the course of this six-year endeavor I developed many treasured relationships with individuals to whom I am forever grateful. Without their knowledge and input I would never have achieved my goal...

WORLD WAR II VETERANS – MY HEROES, MENTORS and FRIENDS...

Jetty Cook – Flight Engineer/Top Turret Gunner/Evader
Lawrence Cook – "My Pilot," and adopted Father
Bob Elliott – 92nd Bomb Group Historian
Ellis "Gib" Gibson – formerly Third Army: liberator, tour guide (Travel Designs)
George Guderley – Waist Gunner, Ex-POW
Joe O'Donnell – B-17 Ball Turret Gunner, Ex-POW
Paul Schultz – Amateur Historian, Enthusiastic Adventurer, Believer
Oscar "Mick" Wagelie – B-24 Ball Turret Gunner, Ex-POW

MY KIND FRIENDS WHO CONTRIBUTED TO THE MEMORABLE JOURNEYS INTO ENGLAND, BELGIUM, POLAND, GERMANY AND LITHUANIA ...

ENGLAND
Gerry and Audrey Darnell

BELGIUM
Guy, Willy and Raimond Wendelen
Louise Wendelen and daughters, Vera and Olga

Nils & Bente Baaring
Richard, Suzanne, Robert and Ann Heyligen
Jules Heyligen Family
Ludo Bobbaers, and his organization, *Hell on Wheels-Belgium*
Bart Beckers
Dirk Decuypere
Rudy Kenis
Baudouin Litt
Edouard Renière

All witnesses and others in Belgium who participated in an unforgettable day with Mom and me.

POLAND
Jupi Podlaszewski
Zygmunt Wujek
Amy and Maura
Everyone who participated in and attended the ceremonies.

GERMANY
Helga Radau, dear friend
Dr. Martin Albrecht
DOK Exhibition/Association members, and the many gracious people in Barth.
Peter Gajda
Eb Haelbig
Manfred Kopp
Gerhard Raiss

LITHUANIA
David Ickes, United States Navy
Michael Karpuzovas, Lithuanian Navy
Stasys Melinauskas, Historian
Roza Sikilliane, Historian

Special Acknowledgments

Ejvind and Bjoerg Jensen – My "Private Detective" and his sweet wife. Sadly, Ejvind passed away November 30, 2006, shortly after returning home from our unforgettable adventure to Belgium.

Beulah "Bea" Joyce – For her faith and support in my endeavor aimed at remembering our heroes, Jay Joyce and Dad.

Lawrence Cook's daughters, Janis and Laurel – For sharing their wonderful father.

Marcel Van Lierde – For his kindness and willingness to contribute to my mission.

OTHER IMPORTANT CONTRIBUTORS TO THE COMPLETION OF MY MISSION
Piet Brouwer – For his generosity and encouragement.
John Schubert – For his interest in my quest & providing direction to a stranger.

MY FAMILY
My Aunt Helen Stephens, Dad's big sister, who believed in me.
My courageous mother, Sara Kyler.
My patient husband, Brad.
My daughter, Lindsay (my jump partner).
My tolerant son, Nicholas.
My sister, Dawn, the Proofreader.
My reason for my strong desire to tell the story, Dad.

MY EDITOR

I met Jim Morrin in Berlin in 2005, when we participated in a tour group of ex-POWs and children of POWs traveling to Barth, Germany for the 60th anniversary of the liberation of Stalag Luft I. Jim's father, John R. Morrin, was a B-17 pilot who was shot down over Belgium and became a POW in Stalag Luft I, the camp my father was also liberated from. In April 2009, I was wrapping up this manuscript. I had nothing left to put into it and I considered it finished. Fortunately for me, Jim convinced me to send it to him for editing. Jim Morrin not only had the talent and the knowledge to oversee my writing, but he had the heart and drive to enhance it, owing to the pride he felt in our fathers. Of course, I would have finished this work, but I would not have been as proud of the result as I am today; nor would my dad have been. I am forever indebted to Jim for his interest and desire to ensure that my book is the best that it could be. Although it was painful at times (mostly for him), I am grateful to him for his patience and honesty in this undertaking.

EVERYONE THAT I HAVE INADVERTENTLY FAILED TO MENTION....
Over a six year period, I am bound to exclude someone, and I apologize!

Prologue

It appears to me that few World War II veterans have written their stories or shared their experiences, especially their experiences as prisoners of war. My father's perceived good fortune of surviving the extremely adverse conditions after his capture may be the reason he did not write or communicate his memories of this time. He was one of the lucky ones; many of his comrades did not return home. Only someone who was there could possibly understand, and among those who were there, there wasn't a need to say much about it.

The majority of the returning POWs, like my father, buried their painful memories deep in their subconscious, desiring only to put away that part of their lives and move on. For a few, it was therapeutic to tell or write their experiences, and fortunate for us that they shared their recollections. My father spoke only briefly to his sister Helen of the fifteen months he spent in German prison camps, and that was on the day he returned home. My Aunt Helen has a vivid recollection of her baby brother walking down Elm Street after being dropped off at the bus stop in downtown Salamanca, New York. There was no hoopla, and none was expected. Our brave fathers were a generation of heroes, but they simply did not see themselves as the distinguished and admirable individuals that they were.

I feel strongly that if my father had kept in touch with any of his crew members or roommates to reminisce, it would have helped him, knowing that they were there, and that they did understand. It may have made it easier for him to open up, or I'd like to think so. And we would have reaped the benefit of his openness. As it is, never having spoken to my father about his time served, but being extremely interested ever since I became aware of his role as an American Airman and Prisoner of War, I ran out of time when he abruptly passed away. I was left to fill in the gaps myself, assembling this puzzle one small piece at a time, searching for the answers to the questions that arose.

As the daughter of one of the many men who risked their lives for our freedom during World War II, I am compelled to share what I have learned of my father's history. His life in the war years has been revived by learning from others who were there, by "reading between the lines," of his notebooks, and by revisiting the areas of his past. My heartfelt motivation led me on a sentimental journey – a journey to live and feel my father's experience by retracing his own journey from his air base ("Station") in England, to the field into which he parachuted in Belgium, through his place of interrogation, across the area of the POW Camps where he was held captive, and ending with his flight from a German airport after his liberation in the Spring of 1945.

This account is being told in the voice of my father, John Roland Kyler. He passed away before he had a chance to tell his wartime story, and I believe he was stuck in some sort of Limbo because of this unfinished business – this untold episode of his life. In this tale, he was given one last chance, before moving on to the afterlife, to walk along with me as I retraced his path so that I could tell his story through him. This narrative is my way of remembering and honoring the unsung heroes, like my father, who quietly went on with their lives after the war. In this journey, he traveled with me as I retraced his steps through foreign lands. There was never a time that I didn't feel his presence.

I have written, but also imagined, my father's history based on facts that I've gathered since his death. This depiction could apply to a multitude of men. My hope is that it serves, in some small way, to carry on the memory of our brave and honorable fathers.

My father's tale begins with the years leading up to his enlistment. He writes of his experience as a ball turret gunner and prisoner of war, and describes the current undertakings that parallel his journey as he returns with me to the present. At times, he speaks as "we", instead of "my daughter and me", or place of "my wife, daughter and me", for he was with us every step of the way.

His experience is imagined based on facts, and the presentation throughout is as a story written by him.

John Kyler – My Story

In a bar I could shorten it to a few short sentences: "I was with the Eighth, at Podington. I sat ball turret gunner on B-17s. Three missions in 1944, shot up over Belgium, bailed out, picked up by the Germans, interrogated in Belgium, then in prison for fifteen months until liberation in 1945. I was held at three prisons: Stalag Luft VI, then Stalag Luft IV, and finally, near the end, at Stalag Luft I. The treatment was poor, then got much worse. But I made it."

That was it – neat, and sweet. No questions, please.

Frankly, I rarely said more than this to anyone, including my wife Sara and my five children. What could I say to ever make anyone understand? It would only sound like I was looking for sympathy, and I had no need to be felt sorry for by anyone, my wife, kids, or anyone else. So, I kept it to myself. They didn't understand at first, but over time I taught them to *leave it alone.*

Then, two things happened. I died an untimely death, leaving all this untold. And one of my daughters, Candy Brown, just couldn't let it go. She started digging up the past, digging really deep. And one day she left her home and traveled to Germany to see one of my old prisons. When she came back, she was a changed woman – a woman on a mission. And before I could think about it much, *I was back.* Back with her and back with my wife Sara, and setting out on a bunch of different journeys, some in America, and some to England, Belgium, Germany, Poland, and Lithuania. We were all of us – the three of us, Sara, Candy and me – bound to experience my old experiences, but also to meet some new people and learn some new things, sixty years after I had carefully perfected my history down to just a few sentences...

Two Time Lines

JOHN R. KYLER'S TIME LINE

1943

January 27	Enlists, Niagara Falls, NY
February–March	Basic Training, Miami FL
May 29	Completes Aircraft Armorer's Course, Lowrey Field, Denver, CO
August 7	Receives wings, promotion to Sergeant, Laredo, TX
August–October	Completes crew training and ball turret gunner training, Ephrata, WA and Redmond, OR
November 12-15	Departs Presque Isle, ME to Meek Field (Iceland) to Prestwick and arrives at Stone, England
November	Assigned to Lawrence Cook Crew, 407th Squadron, 92nd Bomb Group, 8th Air Force, Podington, England (Station 109)

1944

January 21	Mission: to Le Plouy Ferme/Bellevue (France) [aborted: weather]
January 30	1st Mission: Waggum Airfield, Brunswick (Germany)
February 3	2nd Mission: Wilhelmshaven (Germany)
February 4	3rd Mission: Frankfurt (Germany)
February 4	Shot down over Belgium/John Kyler captured
February 7-14	Transferred and interrogated at Oberursal, Dulag Luft, near Frankfurt (Germany)
February 14-21	Enroute to Stalag Luft VI, Hydekrug, E. Prussia (via railcar)
February 21-July 15	POW, Stalag Luft VI

July 15-18	Enroute to Stalag Luft IV, Kiefheide Railway Station, Gross Tychow, Poland (via railcar, boat, railcar, forced march)
July 18 – January 29, 1945	POW, Stalag Luft IV, Gross Tychow, Poland

1945

January 29-February 8	Enroute to Stalag Luft I, Barth Germany (via forced march, railcar)
May 1	Stalag Luft I prisoners liberated by Red Army
May 13	Enroute to Lyons, France via B-17 airlift from Stalag Luft I
May 14	Enroute to Camp Lucky Strike, Le Havre, France (via truck)

THE AUTHOR'S TIME LINE

August 27, 2005	B-17 Ride over Niagara Falls
September 20, 2006	Podington, England
September 23, 2006	Koersel, Belgium
April 26, 2005/October 6, 2007	Frankfurt, Germany
April 27, 2005/October 6, 2007	Oberursel, Germany
September 24, 2007	Silute, Lithuania (f/k/a Hydekrug)
October 1, 2006/September 29, 2007	Tychowo, Poland (f/k/a Gross Tychow)
May 1, 2005/September 29, 2006/September 27, 2007	Barth, Germany
January 14, 2007	Meet Lawrence Cook (CA)
May 28, 2006	Skydive in Pennsylvania
October 25, 2006	Meet Bea Joyce (Pennsylvania)
July 7, 2007	B-17 Inspection, New York

Pre-Enlistment

1

JOHNNIE

I, John Roland Kyler, was the youngest of five children born to David and Grace Kyler. My oldest sister Kathleen, and brother, Morris, were born in Otto, New York, in 1912 and 1914 respectively; Helen, next oldest, was born in 1916 on River Street in the City of Salamanca, NY; and my sister, Jean, and I, the "babies," were both born in the house that would remain my address my entire life at 197 Elm Street, in Salamanca. Jean arrived in 1920 and I came along in 1923.

I've been told by my sisters that I was a quiet, shy, freckle-faced little boy. I was affectionately called "Johnnie" when I was young, and my sisters made me feel that they idolized me, always letting me tag along and looking after me. "Roland" would become the prevalent name that I would be addressed by in later years, with my brother-in-law, Tony Bizzaro, shortening it to "Rollie" or "Roro."

Because of my high regard for my mother, I was a well-mannered and obedient boy who was respectful of my elders. My fondness of my sisters resulted in a good relationship with them throughout my life.

It was not easy growing up in the early days when money was scarce. The combination of the lack of money and the marital problems of my mother and father created a scary childhood. Kathleen and Morris, my oldest siblings, left when I was about 6 years old to take jobs out of town.

I remember the day that my sister, Helen, called my mother to tell her that my father had left and he wasn't coming back. It was a short time after this desertion that my parents went to court. Then, my life grew especially difficult when the judge placed me into my father's custody. I suffered the pain of being separated from my mother and sisters when I was 8 years old.

It was like a nightmare when the social worker came to the house right away to take me away from the environment that I was accustomed to. My arms had to be pried from around my mother as I cried desperately that I wanted to stay with her and my sisters, and didn't want to live anywhere else.

I wondered why this was happening to me and why I had to leave those who I was closest to. My mother and sisters were helpless as they watched me being taken away through their own tears. I belonged with them. That was where I was contented. I should have been asked about this decision but I wasn't. I had no say in where I wanted to be. My heart was broken and I felt that I was being punished for something, but what could it possibly be? I was too young to get into any serious trouble, so how could it be that I had to leave the people who had been the focus of my attention from day one, and I the focus of theirs? I knew that they still loved me because they were always fussing over me, and I saw them crying as I left. I was sure they didn't want me to go away either. I was so afraid that I would never see them again. It was frightening for the young boy that I was, and sad for those I was forced to leave – those who had cared for me for 8 years.

I was taken to a farm to live with my grandparents and father on Kyler Hill Road, in Little Valley, New York. I attended a small schoolhouse, not far from the farm. My dad worked on the railroad and was seldom home. I tried to run away from the school twice to return to the family, but each time I was caught and returned to the farm. I longed for my mother and my sisters who always looked out for me when my mother wasn't there. Helen was like my second mother, being 6 years older than me. They couldn't even come to visit me because they didn't have a car and it was too far to walk.

After a period of time, which seemed like an eternity, my parents reconciled and we were all together again. My grandparents obviously loved me and were good to me but it was a joyful time when I was reunited with my mother and sisters. I was happy to visit my grandparents but I wanted to live in the same house with my mom and sisters as a family. I hoped that I would never know such homesickness again.

Now in the comfort of my home, where my life had begun I thrived in a neighborhood full of kids to play with – in the good old days when a pick-up game of baseball, football or hide and seek was played until dark. I remember having many friends. Some members of the old gang still refer to me as "kicker", a name acquired from some of my kicking experiences in the local sporting activities.

As a typical kid, I enjoyed the days of playing and attending school with my neighborhood friends. During those early years I recall noticing that one of my best buddies, Joe, seemed to receive special treatment, and I thought him to be spoiled. He could have anything that he wanted. He'd just tell his parents and they would get it for him. He was always so lucky. He and I traveled a lot with our older sisters, Helen and Mac, and I used to pout sometimes when I felt left out. This friend was catered to and I was feeling envious of him. It didn't seem fair that he was treated so special and that he had so much more than I did, things that I would have liked to have, too. I was taught one of the hardest lessons as a teenager. I began to notice that my friend wasn't allowed to run or participate in the activities that all of us did. I'll never forget hearing him ask my sister, "It's hard not to run, ain't it, Helen?" I discovered just how unfair that life could be, and how little material things meant, when I learned that my friend was terminally ill. He would lose his life at the very young age of 16 years to what was termed then as "leakage of the heart," and I would lose a good friend. That explained his special treatment and I felt ashamed of my jealousy for I was the lucky one – I had my health.

High school ended for me when I completed tenth grade. I didn't like school and I was not getting paid to learn. It was more appealing to me to seek employment and be compensated for the hours that I was putting in during the day. I was getting nothing for my efforts in school, which were becoming less with time because of my disinterest. It became more important to me to earn some much-needed money during the tough financial times. If I had applied myself I feel that, more than likely, I would have excelled in my studies, but my mind was not on my schoolwork. All I could think of was seeking employment. I toughed it out through my sophomore year and at 16 years of age I was in the market for my first job.

I felt that having money in my pocket would make life much easier for me and my family.

Me at the farm on Kyler Hill Road
Courtesy of Sharon Jusko

Me with my sisters, Helen and Jean, on Elm Street
Courtesy of Sharon Jusko

Family on Kyler Hill Road
Courtesy of Sharon Jusko

Front Row – Marg Higgins (cousin), sister Jean
Kyler Bizzaro, Brother Morris Kyler
Middle – John Kyler, Della Kyler (step-grandma), Aunt
Julie Murray, sister Helen Kyler Stephens, Julia Higgins
Tenhagen (cousin), sister Kathleen Kyler Sullivan
Back – Aunt Eva Fitzmorris Higgins, Uncle Elmer
Higgins, father David Kyler, mother Grace Fitzmorris
Kyler, Grandfather Rowland Kyler.

2

JOINING THE WORK FORCE

I worked a short period of time on the Baltimore and Ohio Railroad. My job was short lived; my friend Willy found out about another job prospect in a factory in Olean, NY, that was more appealing to me. Olean was about 15 miles from Salamanca. I was feeling pretty good about myself with this new found independence. I could buy whatever I wanted, within reason, but it was just a good feeling to have a little cash, and I'm sure it had to be a relief for my parents.

I will never forget hearing the shocking news of the Japanese bombing Pearl Harbor – the start of World War II. I was at work with my friends in Olean when the announcement came on the loudspeaker and it sent shock waves through all of us. We all knew that our lives would never be the same, and the uncertainty of exactly what this meant for us was very alarming. We would certainly all be affected by this blatant attack. This bold assault enforced the necessity of aerial bombardment and, thus, began the manufacture of the B-17 bomber in great numbers, which in turn created job opportunities.

The bombing of Pearl Harbor initiated what would become the beginning of a lengthy love affair for me with the B-17 when I began work at Bell Aircraft in Buffalo, New York. I heard of the employment prospect through my friend, Willy, and once again I was happy to apply for a more attractive position. The two of us almost immediately quit our jobs for this new exciting opportunity and rented an apartment together.

It was thrilling just to be going to the big city where things were buzzing. I was enjoying nights out with the boys so much that I would not always travel home on the weekends. I didn't want to miss anything. I was a normal teenager for the times and getting a taste of freedom gave me an adult feeling.

I was beginning a responsible profession that was very alluring to me, and I felt it to be more important than any of the jobs that I had held up to this time in my young life. I assisted in the assembly of what I considered to be beautiful works of art. I would excitedly explain to my family that I was building planes – not just planes but bombers – to be used in the war. I respected this aircraft and to be able to participate in its assembly was thrilling to me. I always liked to tinker with things so this was a great challenge. I had a knack for figuring things out and this required a skill I knew I possessed. I was happy in my new job as an "Aircraft Assembler."

I wanted to know everything about this machine and I became consumed with my job. I realized the importance of my new occupation and I would execute my tasks responsibly, knowing that there were lives that would depend on the performance of what was to become a prestigious bomber. These distinguished masterpieces would prove to be a crucial weapon of the US Army Air Corps during WWII.

3

THE NOTICE

I knew that it was just a matter of time before I would receive my draft notice. The way things were going in the war, it was inevitable that anyone my age would be called up. I have to admit that I was concerned and worried about it, but I was also motivated to do my part. My job as an aircraft assembler helped to prepare me for the draft in that I was already hooked on the desire to be involved in the war effort.

We'd go out at night and it's all that anyone was talking about. Things were getting scary. The Germans were wreaking havoc and their aggression needed to be stopped. In a way I was anxious to go. One by one, guys that I knew were getting their notice. I was getting to the point that I just wanted to get it over with so I could quit wondering. Finally, the day came and the Army Air Corps fell in line with what I, without realizing, had been preparing myself for during the past months. It would be a continuation of my attachment to the aircraft that I had been so involved with.

I would think, at times, about the day I left school, having made the decision to find employment and not return. I always hoped that it was not a mistake and I would not be sorry. My move to Buffalo, in particular building aircraft, helped to better prepare me mentally and physically for what was ahead. I could easily rid my mind of any doubt, and justify totally, that leaving school was not just the only choice to me as it seemed at the time, but it was the right one. The feelings and thoughts that joining the Army Air Corps brought about solidified that fact to me.

Of course, I had mixed feelings about what my new role would entail. I was only human. When I broke the news to my family they found it upsetting but they, too, knew that it was to be expected. I tried to make them feel better by acting more excited about it than I was. They believed that I had no reservations grasping this new opportunity – to broaden my horizons and see places I may never have had a chance to see otherwise. And, I would explain how I had learned the workings of the aircraft that, perhaps, I would maintain or even fly in.

This piece of paper, this notice, would be the beginning of my questioning myself, as well as learning more about myself than I ever had at home, in school or in any of my jobs. I would be put to the test of my life, and hope that I was up for the task. My career at Bell Aircraft would come to an end, but I knew going into it that it would not be a long lasting employment. Once we had built all of the bombers that were required, the jobs would end. I was soon to embark on a new career where I was needed the most that would take me to a different level and to places I'd never been. I would soon find out what I was made of. A Salamanca boy, Johnnie Kyler, would be going to war. I would see and do things I never thought of before, and really couldn't fathom. I would focus on the present and enjoy the days before January 27, 1943, my scheduled date of induction into the US Army Air Corps.

4

THE ENTRY

I gave my notice at the plant, and so did others who also received their "invitation" to enter the service; but there were boys and girls waiting to take our places and soon it would be their turn to enlist, as replacements would be needed in this growing war.

As my time grew short, it was not quite as much fun to frequent the bars. The times weren't as lively and carefree as they had been in the past because I had other, more pressing things on my mind. I would say my goodbyes to my co-workers and friends. My apartment would not be empty as one of the new hires was taking over. And now, the time had come to bid farewell to my family. This would be the hardest goodbye of all.

I sat in my home with my mother and sisters the day I was to leave. It was hard to know what to say and I remember sitting on the floor in silence, in a daze, staring into the furnace grate, and contemplating about what the training would be like and where I was going to end up. Certainly, I would eventually be leaving the country, and the wonder of whether I would ever see my loved ones again entered my mind. I tried to hide all of these thoughts, but when I looked up at Helen, her eyes told me without her saying a word that she knew what I was thinking about. She understood me better than anyone, and we both knew that. I couldn't hide my worries from her, nor could she hide hers from me. It was as if we could read each other's minds and we shared the same thoughts and uneasiness.

When it was time to go, I rose to get my things trying to smile confidently. I said something similar to "I guess this is it," and I proceeded to hug and kiss everyone goodbye. There were some tears and I laughed a nervous laugh asking why they were crying as they knew that I would be back. I promised that I would write as soon as I could to let them know where I was and what I would be doing. But deep down I felt like crying – it was the realization that I was going to miss everyone and wouldn't be close enough to come home for weekends, or any other days, for that matter. It was the fear of the unknown chapter of my life that I would be entering that was weighing on me as well. When would I actually be able to see everyone again? I had no idea.

I walked to the door and turned for one last look, as if to embed this image permanently in my mind so I would never forget. I smiled and waved and was off on my route to Fort Niagara, where I would be inducted into the Army Air Corps for a yet to be determined destination and position.

My induction took place on January 27, 1943, at Fort Niagara, in Niagara Falls, New York. My date of entry was February 3, 1943. This is where I would begin my adjustment to my new role, as would hundreds of others. It helped to be with young men who shared my feelings. For many, it was their first time away from home and they didn't know what to expect either. I always felt in everything that I'd done in my nineteen years that whatever my job would be I would perform it to the best of my ability, and that would not change. I knew that there were people depending on me and it was with this drive and determination that I began my service to my country. Maintaining this strong attitude would help to protect my loved ones and those I didn't know. I was there, and I couldn't change it, so I would work hard at whatever my assignment would be. I wanted to think positive and make my family proud. I was not going to dwell on how much I already missed everyone. This was a new experience and I vowed to make the most of it and not look back. It would be easier that way. I would adjust.

Fort Niagara
Courtesy of James Pedacchio

Fort Niagara
Courtesy of James Pedacchio

The Phases

5

THE TRAINING

Our group of new inductees was sent to Miami, Florida, for basic training, arriving on February 8, and finishing March 13, 1943.

I completed an Aircraft Armorer's Course of Instruction at Air Force Technical School at Buckley Field and Lowry Field in Denver, Colorado, on May 29, 1943. I went on to receive my wings and sergeant's rating at a Gunnery Technical School in Laredo, Texas, on August 7, 1943.

Without boasting about my expertise in the area, I have to say that the gunnery training was probably my favorite phase and proved to be one of my greatest strengths. My average of 95% was the highest in my flight.

I had good hand-eye coordination, which enhanced my performance. I understood the concept of leading the target. We shot at clay targets and were taught that it was necessary to fire in front of where the target is flying – at the spot where the target will be. I learned just how much to lead. It would be more if the target was far away or moving rapidly, and less on slow moving or closer targets. This was not the easiest task. It is a proficiency that is acquired only with concentration and practice. I can remember how sore my shoulder would get from the recoil of the 12 gauge shotgun.

Shooting at moving targets to try to get the feel of flying in a B-17, we shot from the back of a moving truck. This segment of the training, skeet shooting, was fun and I remember thinking that it would not be so much fun in reality when facing the enemy, but I was living in the moment and enjoying it. This is where I learned the knack of reacting quickly. It was extremely important to develop confidence in our gunnery skills.

In classroom training, we were taught the importance of learning about the type of plane we might be assigned to. We attended classes in recognizing both friendly and enemy aircraft. We learned how to react to different types of attacks and about the most common enemy tactics. The offensive and defensive tactics, however, changed constantly with the technology advancement.

We familiarized ourselves with the planes and learned to operate equipment other than machine guns. Gunners had to learn how to fire from every machine gun position on the B-17. We were taught how to operate hydraulic and electrical systems. It seemed that the learning process was endless as there was so much to absorb realizing that one day our lives could depend on this knowledge.

I was involved, as we all were, in an intensive program to learn everything I possibly could about .30 and .50 caliber machine guns. This is where I learned to clean, disassemble and reassemble machine guns by performing these tasks repeatedly. Sometimes during the training, the instructor would slip in a bad part to test our competence. It was important to be expert at making gun repairs if the need arose. I became proficient at handling, adjusting and firing the guns. Being taught the sighting system was another critical and integral part of the training.

We also experienced drills that simulated attacks by fighter planes. These exercises instilled the realization of how crucial it was to learn and study every facet of this important gunnery training. Each portion would provide valuable knowledge that we would, likely, soon take into combat. We all depended on each other to have the same commitment.

I was combined with a crew when I was assigned to Operational Training in Ephrata, Washington, on August 29, 1943. We continued to train as a crew in Redmond, Oregon, from September 7 to October 14, 1943. This training together is where we bonded emotionally as a crew, which helped us through the stress that we endured preparing for, and in, combat. We knew each other's strengths and weaknesses and collectively gained our confidence.

Each member became experienced in their assigned position. I was assigned the ball turret gunner position. Actually, I volunteered for it. It wasn't the most desirable position on the plane. I was pretty thin and felt that someone had to do it, so it might as well be me. My height hampered me a little but I managed to adjust to the cramped quarters. As a gunner, we practiced in all sorts of adverse conditions. We all changed positions should we need to cover another gun position.

Our crew consisted of Pilot, Lawrence Cook; Co-Pilot, Bob Bangs; Top Turret Gunner, John Booth; Bombardier, Emmett Bell; Navigator, Donald Caylor; Radio Operator, Jay Joyce; Left Waist Gunner, Milo Blakely; Right Waist Gunner, John Alexander, Jr.; Tail Gunner, Thomas Mikulka; and me, the Ball Turret Gunner.

Once again, in classroom activity we focused on aircraft identification. This could not be stressed enough and it was vital to reiterate in every phase of our training.

During the days of preparation as a crew, we became increasingly comfortable with each other, and how important that it was to have faith in fellow crewmates. It was during this time that I developed a special relationship with our radio operator, Jay Joyce.

Our parachute training was brief. We jumped from a tower holding onto a handle attached to a pulley. During descent, the instructor pulled a release that dropped an airman to the ground. This training was also a necessity in learning how to land should one be forced to bail out. I was glad that this part of the exercise was brief because I did not want to feel that I needed it.

From Redmond, we began our journey to England. We spent a week in Grand Island. We were in Wilmington, Delaware, from November 2nd to November 5th. Our departure for overseas was from Presque Isle, Maine, where we spent another week from November 5th to November 12, 1943. We did not fly together as a crew in the B-17 to England. However, Jay and I were together for this adventure. We flew from Presque Isle to Goose Bay, Labrador, on November 12th and from there to Meek Field in Iceland. We left Iceland on November 13th for Prestwick, Scotland. Our departure from Scotland was November 14th and we arrived in Stone, England on November 15th. After meeting up with the rest of our crew members, we underwent additional training until November 26th at which time we moved on to Hammond Site 4. I kept track of these places and dates in a small flight training log book.

John Kyler Receives Wings, Made Sergeant

Mrs. Grace Kyler, 197 Elm street, has been informed that her son, Pfc. John R. Kyler, who was inducted Feb. 3, has received his wings and sergeant's rating at a gunnery technical school in Lareda, Tex.

His average of ninety-five per cent was the highest in his flight. On May 29 Sgt. Kyler was awarded a diploma upon completion of a course in aircraft, armorers and bombardment at a technical school in Denver, Colo.

Sgt. Kyler, who was employed at Bell Aircraft, Kenmore, before induction, now is stationed at Salt Lake City, Utah.

6

Position Assignment — Ball Turret Gunner

I'd heard it said many times that the ball turret gunner was the most dangerous position on the B-17. Well, it *was* a dangerous position – a prime example of the application of Murphy's Law. Yet as far as injuries suffered during combat, I believed it was one of the safest places to be. The reason was that when you were curled up in a ball with your back against the armor-plated door, less of your body was exposed to enemy fire than in any of the other crew member positions. The danger of the ball turret position was greatest, at least in terms of enemy airplane fire, when the enemy attacked from beneath the plane or from head on. Of course anti-aircraft fire presented yet a different risk, and then there was fire in the ship, loss of oxygen or interphone contact and, well, there were a lot of ways your life was endangered in the ball, but those risks were also there for the rest of the crew.

The relative safety of each position in the ship was the source of constant morbid speculation among the crew. It did seem that the ball turret may have been most susceptible to things that could go wrong. It was the only position that you had to climb into and climb out of, and it was the most confined space for the airman. Gunners were trained for all positions and then assigned to a crew and a position as needed. I acquired the ball turret spot, I think, because it was the least sought-after position, and therefore the most available. It was usually manned by slightly built men. I was thin, about 5' 8 ½", and pretty agile. Most crew members thought it to be the worst position, but as I previously stated somebody had to do it. Anyone with claustrophobia would never make it in this spot. There were many things that could and did go awry. I recall how frustrating it was that any movement of your arms or legs, or every turn of your head, would unplug something or detach your oxygen mask, throat microphone or some part of your electrically heated suit. The space was so cramped that the parachute could not fit in there with you; you had to leave it lying in the ship, on the deck. That, in itself, was a major concern.

Radio operators, unlike gunners, knew where their place in the ship would be. It seems that the position that you were assigned depended a lot on what you were best at and had the smarts for. I did well in armory and gunnery training, so I was in charge of checking all armaments on the plane – bombs, guns, ammunition, etc.

While on the ground, the guns in the ball turret were facing rearward for takeoffs and landings, and the entry door was facing forward. However, entry to the turret from outside the ship was not permitted, nor was the gunner allowed to be in the turret for the landing, except in an emergency. The ball turret gunner did not enter the turret until after the aircraft was airborne. Entry was then made from the waist gun position. After takeoff, the turret was hand cranked until the guns were pointed down at the ground, aligning the entry hatch with the inside of the plane. Entry into the turret was then possible from inside the aircraft. Once inside the turret, I would fasten my safety strap, turn on the power, and operate the turret electrically from inside.

I remember how lonely it was being shut into my little space in this ball attached to the belly of the plane, separated from the rest of the crew by steel, armor plate and bullet-proof glass. In the cramped quarters, I sat curled up in a fetal-like position. The turret had a full 360 degrees of motion horizontally and 90 degrees of motion vertically, and I could swivel the entire turret as I aimed the two guns. This 360 degree rotation provided an extraordinary vantage point in covering the bomber against attackers from below. I could rotate the ball to go from lying on my back to standing on my feet. I sat between the guns with my feet in stirrups positioned on each side of a 13" diameter window that was about 30" in front of my face. The gun sight hung in front of my eyes and my knees were up around my ears. The only padding that I had was my flight suit.

A pedal under my left foot adjusted the cross hairs on the gun sight glass. When the target was framed in the sight, I knew the range was right. The movement of the ball was controlled by two post handles that pointed rearward and were located above the sight. The firing buttons located at the end of each handle would fire both guns. The empty shell casings were ejected through a port just below the gun barrel.

My role as a ball turret gunner was exciting and frightening both. My job was protecting the belly of the plane. The mobility of the ball afforded a large range of protection. The feeling of terror was not so much from fear of getting hit by enemy fire, but due to the worry about power failure and having no one to manually crank the ball from inside the aircraft so that you could get out. There was the fear of going down with the plane while stuck in the turret, or failing to exit quickly enough to get your parachute on. And there was always the threat that equipment could malfunction. If you were stuck in the ball turret and the landing gear failed to operate, tragedy was inevitable.

I would be no good to myself or my crew if I were frozen with terror the whole time. I had to be confident in my role and my abilities while fighting on the B-17. It was better to think positive rather than focusing on all the negatives that could happen. And it was foolish to invite trouble, but wise to be as prepared as possible for whatever problems might arise. In fact, preparation was fundamental, and it was important to be thorough in running through the necessary checks of equipment and armaments before and after we left the ground. We all depended on the efficient operation of machinery, and no one wanted to die (but some of us did) because they had overlooked the basic safety checks.

Ball Turret

View of Ball Turret from inside of the plane

7

In the present…..

BALL TURRET GUNNER — 62 YEARS LATER

In July 2007, there was news that a B-17 was to be on display and available for rides at Prior Aviation in Buffalo, New York. My daughter Candy and wife Sara decided to take a drive to see *Liberty Belle*. Candy wanted to walk through and study each station of the plane, and she was sure that they would allow tours. She and her mother agreed that they wanted to see the starting of the engines on the mighty Fortress, and watch it taxi and take off.

As they pulled into the parking area at Prior Aviation, they caught their first glimpse of *Liberty Belle* and could not get out of the car fast enough. They both agreed that their love of this aircraft must have carried over from me, because they were so thrilled at the sight of "her." The gate was open, and they walked directly over to the plane and crouched under it to examine the ball turret.

Just as Candy had hoped, visitors were being allowed to walk through the plane! Sara chose not to climb up inside the craft, but she encouraged our daughter to do so. Climbing the ladder, Candy had to crouch upon entering the bomber in order to walk up to the cockpit area and then crouch down to slide into the nose area – she knew this was where the bombardier and navigator sat during the mission. The Bombardier's

Norden bomb sight was there, mounted in the nose. On a mission, the bomb sight enabled the bombardier to actually take control of the airplane during the bomb run to ensure an accurate "drop." Candy sat there for a period of time as she stared out the glass in the nose, catching sight of her mother out on the tarmac and waving to her. Towards the back of the nose cone area there was a machine gun located on the right side of the ship, that she was told was used by the navigator as well as the bombardier during battle.

Candy slid back out of the nose area, returning to the cockpit where she now saw an older gentleman, apparently a former B-17 pilot, sitting in the pilot's seat that he once occupied. It was clearly an emotional moment for him, as he sat teary-eyed, transported back sixty years in his mind, recalling his memories. I could understand that emotion – it had been just as long a time for me, but once I set foot in that ship all of those wartime memories came into mind like a hot wind, blushing my face and making me squint.

Candy's tour continued and she left the old man to his dreams and walked aft to the top turret gunner position and then onto the catwalk over the bomb bay doors, which were closed. She was getting close, and she easily identified my position – the metal hemisphere in the middle of the floor with the small door through which I would pass into my lonely and confined position.

I next saw Candy examining the small table in the radio room – the station that the radio operator occupied during flight – the radio operator was the only crewman to have his own small compartment. Behind the radio operator's space were the two waist gunner positions. Candy was trying to figure what door I would have used to bail out; she guessed that it would probably have been the waist door, and she was right. She mentioned this to one of the guides, and he agreed that this had been my likely point of exit.

Candy continued to the back of the plane, still hunched down, and looked at the tail gunner's station. This was actually quite a little walk for her through this crowded plane – crowded, even though there were then only five people on board. I well remembered how cramped these ships were with a full crew of ten.

Candy finished her inspection, climbed down, and reunited with Sara outside the plane. From a guide they learned that *Liberty Belle* would not fly until the afternoon. They took advantage of the opportunity to talk about me. They were among people with a shared interest who were happy to hear about John Kyler, their husband and father, a ball turret gunner out of Podington. Everyone there had come because of their attraction to this bomber, and all that it meant to them, either as a veteran, former crew member, or as a relative or friend of a former crew member, and of course there were the serious history buffs, just as attentive, just as interested. Sara and Candy were definitely in their element.

In talking to the men who tended to *Liberty Belle*, Candy told one of them—after her third trip inside the plane—that she just couldn't get enough of it. One of the men working that day remarked that his love of the B-17 was why he shows up there every day and does what he does.

Candy explained to him that her father was a ball turret gunner. He told her to wait where she was standing and he'd be right back. She did as he said and he came back with some tools. He opened the ball turret so she and Sara could see the inside. They were noticeably delighted. Candy asked if she could climb in it and the man told her that she could!

Candy first tried sticking one foot into the space, but that wasn't going to work. She had to put both feet in first and pull herself up and in by holding onto the heavy metal frame at the top of the door. She was almost upside down because the stirrups were at the top. Seeing her open the hatch, looking inside, and watching her climb in, brought back to me so many memories that I was a bit shaken. And I experienced amazement that I could ever have fit into that small turret. I always entered from the inside of the plane after we were in flight. The gunner was not allowed to be in his ball turret position when taking off or landing, but it was not something he wanted to do anyway – at those times, the turret was very near the ground speeding past the plane, and any failure of the plane's undercarriage could have a devastating impact on the ball turret gunner!

Candy climbed out of the turret, but then pleaded with the attendant to allow her to climb in "one more time," and have the door closed. The guy humored her, and actually locked her inside for a few seconds. There was no gun sight, and she explained to her mother that there would have been even less room for her dad back in 1943. Candy was kind of overwhelmed by the whole experience – clearly very meaningful to her – and said she was suddenly able to sense, locked in the turret, all by herself, the difficulties I faced as I flew into enemy territory, straddling a pair of huge machine guns, locked in a steel ball hanging from a thin tube suspended 30,000 feet above the Earth. She mentioned how difficult that it must have been with the gun sight right in my face, rotating the ball turret, looking for enemy fighters and trying to protect the belly of the ship from their attack. She remarked on how hard it was to imagine being cooped up for many hours in this tiny space. For my part, I would have reminded her that on top of all that, we were surrounded by freezing, blistering air cooled to Arctic temperatures.

After her unexpected experience in the ball turret, she commented that these few moments "in the turret" made her better understand the bravery that was shown by the men who flew in these bombers, and particularly the men cooped up in the ball turret.

Candy could not have been more appreciative of the kind people who probably had no idea what impact their kindness had on her, and I was proud of the sincere thanks she extended to the men who had made her "moment" possible. It obviously was momentous for her to be able to actually sit in my position on the aircraft. I don't think Candy expected that her day would be so special—that she would be able to "man" my position and, even if it was only for seconds, feel what I had felt.

A wonderful conclusion to this very special day for my daughter and wife ended with the two of them listening to and feeling, the sound of those four Wright Cyclone engines as they coughed, smoked, and roared into bone-shaking life, one by one. Their expressions as they observed the plane taxi, pause, and then take off into the late-afternoon sky told it all: Not just their emotion, but their pride. Those looks were especially important to me because they, and the others present, were remembering history.

So, they had accomplished what they had set out to do, and more. Candy told her mother that she never dreamt that the day could be so special. On the drive home and for a long time after – perhaps forever – they would remind each other how fortunate they were to add to their experience this particular segment of my route, and in many ways, this experience, this being part of a great group of men and machines, was central to all of it – it had to start with this B-17, the Flying Fortress.

Candy in Ball Turret of B-17 "Liberty Belle"

Arrival In England –
8th Air Force

The Eighth Air Force, activated a month after Pearl Harbor, arrived in England in February of 1942. By war's end, more than 350,000 men and women had served on 126 bases in England. Between 1942 and 1945, three famous generals — Jimmy Doolittle, Ira Eaker and Tuohy Spaatz — commanded the Mighty Eighth.

The Eighth Air Force was the largest of all the Allied Air Forces assembled during World War II and in its three-year war over Germany suffered half of all American casualties.

Courtesy of Cook Family

TOAST TO OUR B-SEVENTEEN

Here's to you and the Air Corps in which
We are proud to serve.
In many a strife we fought for life
And never lost our nerve.

If the enemies and his armies
Ever looked upon heaven scene
He'll find the skies are filled
With our beautiful "B"-Seventeens.

(Poem from Jay Joyce's *POW notebook* – Courtesy of Bea Joyce)

8

PODINGTON

In November 1943, our crew was assigned to the 407th Squadron of the 92nd Bombardment Group, of the Eighth Air Force. Our brief training upon arrival in England occurred at a place called "The Wash." This additional training exposed us to various tactics that the British RAF airmen utilized that would be helpful when we began flying our missions. Our new home away from home was the base in Podington. We would begin our participation in the "round the clock" bombing raids from this station – Station Number 109. The British were area bombing during the night, and the 8th Air Force's mission was to attack strategic areas during the daylight hours.

I decided to make the most of my time before we began flying our missions. Life during this waiting time could be boring; in fact, it was always the *anticipation* of each mission that was so tough to deal with. There was the exhilaration you felt to do your part accompanied with the trepidation that you would not survive it. There were many tragic incidents that occurred, but as an "immortal" young airman, I never felt that it would happen to me. This belief is one of the virtues (or curses) of youth.

Our reason for being in Podington was always in the forefront of our minds, and we would visualize and fly those "mental missions" whenever we were not occupied in other ways, which was often. We all did our best to be prepared when our time came.

The night time was the worst. My mind would reel, and I would lay awake thinking about what was in the cards for me. The worst nights were when I saw empty seats in the mess hall or I had learned of a crew not returning. It didn't take me long to conclude that maybe I didn't want to get too close to anyone for fear they wouldn't come back, and this distinctly anti-social reaction, coming as it did so quickly upon me, added immeasurably to the anxiety that one could feel about the whole situation. I wasn't the only one going through these nights made sleepless by the feelings of sadness and despair for friends lost, and everyone's inescapable uneasiness about what the future held. But new as these feelings were to me, this was a normal occurrence in the life of an American airman.

Before we even began our first mission, there occurred a horrible incident: We were all saddened in the second week of January 1944 to learn that a fellow airman had committed suicide. I guess things got to be too much for him. He left no note, but those closest to him said the combination of homesickness and the tremendous stress endured before, during, and after missions contributed to his depression. It was bound to happen, as we were all being pushed to our limits mentally. We are only human, and fear was a constant companion those days. Everyone wished they had seen it coming. The signs that the fellow had shown were all signs that any one of us, at any given time, might display. After the suicide, we all looked at each other differently, talking more openly about our feelings, and taking a greater personal interest in our fellow crew. We were going to look out for each other – we had to. The suicide was such a waste of a young life and was a rude reminder of the great toll that our missions can take on a man. We realized that we must try to get better at detecting the feelings of our crewmen before they erupted into something so…final… right at the airfield, in broad daylight. This was unsettling to all, but it was bound to happen.

To my novice eyes, there seemed so much activity at times that you could wonder if you would ever get your chance in the sky or if, perhaps, by some twist of fate, you would never leave the ground because of a mistiming over which a plane's crew had no control. The timing of the takeoffs and tight formations that followed meant that clear communications were of the utmost importance, yet the real possibility of a small mistake and the horrible consequences were there for all of us to see…and ponder.

In contrast to the nervous tension that permeated the operations at the base itself, I saw Podington as a charming and friendly village, and one of my first orders of business in my free time was to purchase and register a Bendix bicycle. Having a bicycle would allow me to easily travel to the Village whenever I could acquire a pass. My fellow crewmen and friends, Jay Joyce (our radio operator) and John Alexander (one of our waist gunners), followed suit and soon all three of us were bi-wheeled and mobile.

What a peaceful ride it was on the road from the base to town – a ride that I remember being about five miles. The narrow road was flanked by trees on both sides. This well-traveled route could be full of bicycles at almost any time of the day or night; it was a great ride and grand way to enjoy the surroundings.

By obtaining a pass and leaving the airfield to mingle with other folks, I could almost forget my worries for a period of time. The pubs were especially welcoming. We were treated well by most of the people that we came in contact with. However, it was obvious at times that we were not extremely popular with the British men when it came to their women. Many of them thought that the Americans were "over paid, over sexed, and over here." I didn't know about the "over-sexed" part, but there was no doubt that our pay was vastly better than that of the British soldiers and airmen. I spent little time worrying about this! The majority of the time, though, our fine treatment by the villagers made for a comfortable environment for young men so far away from home. The women were a welcome sight, and friendly to us GIs. It was a good diversion for the moments we could get away from the reality of war. For most of us, these good times were punctuated with long periods of frozen, stark terror, experienced miles above the Earth.

I think all of us understood that there would be those of us who one day would be missing from the group. It was on everyone's mind, and when we'd leave town to journey back to the airfield we would bid farewell to everyone as if it were our last trip to the village, and as if we may have enjoyed our last beer. There were always toasts to us and to our success in our bombing missions and, foremost, to our safe return.

When I first arrived at Podington, I remember the disturbing news of another tragedy that had occurred. A group of B-17s took off on a mission, but were recalled. The crews explained that shortly after take-off they had heard an explosion near the field. The plane that didn't return contained a number of crew members who were on their 24th or 25th mission, meaning they were eligible, or nearly so, for return to the States, to fly in safer skies. It was an unexplained tragic accident involving the loss of the entire crew. With the news of this disaster came the immediate realization of how cruel life can be in time of war. It was very distressing and a terrible way to start, but it was only the beginning of a time where to survive, we needed to adjust to the many misfortunes that we all would witness and experience in the perilous days ahead.

Every day I would hear of bombers returning due to equipment malfunction, which naturally would be discomforting. There were incidents of oxygen system failure, oil leaks, faulty door mechanics, and engine problems. There were so many things that could go wrong, causing the imminent return of the frustrated crew before they could even make it to their target. I couldn't help but wonder about the condition of the planes that I was destined to fly in. One needed confidence in the equipment, particularly the machine that would transport you to and from your dangerous missions. Having seen and studied the workings of this sturdy aircraft, I tried to maintain the faith that I had in whatever Flying Fortress that would become my home in the sky for hours at a time. I did not need to trouble my mind with malfunction worries…but I did anyway.

Our bicycles would take us on many successful missions to town. I remember when I bought my bike, I wondered who had owned it before me. It seemed to me that the riders of these bicycles would change quite frequently. I couldn't help but speculate how many trips to town that the previous owner was able to make and, perhaps, the owner before him, and the owner before him. Would I get my money's worth with the miles that I would put on these wheels, or would my riding days come abruptly to an end in the more-than-possible circumstance that I did not return from a mission? Who would next purchase this bicycle? How many times would it have to be reregistered and the tags changed, and how long would it be ridden by the same person? The life cycle of a bicycle ridden by the GIs in England would be a very interesting story in its own right, in that the ownership would more than likely change several times, gathering scores of stories about different crews and missions flown.

We would not see any flight action in the month of December. Although we weren't involved yet, I kept up to date on the ongoing missions, the targets, their significance and, ultimately, the overall successes. I was working on my mental preparation for what was in store. The First of December marked the fiftieth mission of the 92nd Bomb Group and I would track the ten missions flown during the month on airfields, marshalling yards, port areas, chemical plants and industrial areas in Germany and France. I was getting the feel for the areas that I would probably be involved in bombing. I studied the maps and absorbed as much from them as I could.

One of my fondest memories of my time in Podington was the Christmas party at the base. Under arrangements made by the chaplains and their assistants, we helped to transport displaced, handicapped, and local kids to the party. How excited they were to be doted on and given presents and refreshments! It did everyone's heart good to escape into the world of children on this special day, engulfed in the innocence and excitement of the young ones. One of the airmen dressed up like Santa, and what a splendid celebration and delight this was to share with the kids. Some of the guys, like our waist gunner John Alexander, had children at home, and this was therapeutic for them, as they were missing the joy of Christmas with their families. It helped to soften the loneliness that could intensify on this important American holiday.

New Year's Eve is another memorable event during my time in Podington. I would pay for the number of toasts that were made. There were just so many things to toast to. I could not ride my bicycle the next day due to my large head, but it was worth it. It was a joyous time, and who knew how many more "joyous" times that any of us would have? If all of the things that I toasted to came to pass, we would be one lucky group of airmen. I made it through 1943, and now, with 1944 upon me, things would be different, as our crew would soon begin our bombing missions.

We all got pretty excited when the Red Cross Club opened the second week of January with Thursday and Saturday night dances. I had been checking on the progress of the Club since I arrived, sometimes lending a hand in its construction, and I was anxious for it to be completed. What a great opportunity to meet some ladies! I was never one to dance much, but I could not pass up an opportunity when a good "grinder" was played. Many of the British girls would come out, and the ladies who worked at the Red Cross Club were easy on the eyes, too. We would see them on the base when they delivered refreshments in the "clubmobiles" to the work crews and to the combat crews after debriefing. Of course there was no sense getting attached to anyone, because my future was so uncertain. I did make some good friends in a short period of time, frequenting the club whenever it was possible. Keeping busy helped me overcome my homesickness that was so prevalent at that time. Even as I rested in the evenings, I was reviewing things in my mind, things about America, my family, and my home in Salamanca.

Knowing that some of my buddies had wives and children at home and seeing how homesick it made them made me feel that I was lucky to be single. And there was always a possibility that absence did not necessarily make the heart grow fonder, but rather lonelier, so some wives back home chose to love the ones they were with. That would result in "Dear John" letters being sent to their lonely men who counted on their sweethearts being there when they returned. What a negative effect these letters could have on a guy. News of this sort could cause great depression and perhaps a good binge. On the positive side though, most guys who had wives and girlfriends at home received mail from them frequently, as well as their parents and other family members, so they had the luxury of so much mail, which could make the other guys envious.

The arrival of the New Year brought many new challenges. I became even more focused on the crews and the missions, and on my friends who had begun their tour of duty before me. The drone of the B-17 engines is an unforgettable sound and, in all of my years since the war, certain noises can trigger the memory of those sounds, returning me to the days at Station 109 at Podington. By the time we actually began to fly missions, I had come to know the Boeing B-17 Flying Fortress inside and out.

The "Fort" was powered by four twin-row Wright Cyclone radial engines. The engines were exhaust-turbo-charged for high altitude performance. The plane had a wingspan of over 103 feet, was about sixty-eight feet long and stood nearly sixteen feet high. The ship's gross weight was 47,500 pounds. The crew positions were protected with quarter-inch armor plate. The plane could carry a "payload" of seven thousand pounds of bombs, and was armed with thirteen fifty caliber machine guns located in the nose and tail, and on the top, bottom and sides of the fuselage. The Fort's top speed was slightly less than three hundred miles per hour (she cruised at about 185) and she had a range of more than 3,000 miles. Her rate of climb was

2,260 feet per minute. We studied her so thoroughly that these statistics have stuck fast in my mind.

It was an engaging sight to watch the crews readying themselves and the bombers for the mission at hand, and then, after they all had assumed their place in the bomber, to watch the B-17s take off, one by one, every minute and, at times, *every 30 seconds*, to join the formation that was sometimes not even visible, circling in the sun somewhere above the cloud cover that sometimes hung over our base. This was an exhilarating and memorable view to behold, and it has replayed in my mind countless times. It would not be long before I would be on my own mission, manning my position and on my way to enemy territory – a terrifying, yet stirring thought.

It was an ominous feeling, anticipating and then watching the bombers return, one by one, being well aware of the number that had departed from the 92nd, and hoping that the same number would touch down. The B-17s with wounded aboard would throw flares on approach to alert ground crews that medical assistance was urgently needed. Then there were the occasions when crews did not return, and what a sinking feeling that was. We would all try to find out who didn't come back, and hear the eyewitness reports to figure out if there was a chance that the missing crew survived, whatever the cause of the tragedy.

I'll never forget the wounded and the missing, and how badly I felt for them. This is why you tried not to allow yourself to get too close to any of the men in the other crews. It was too hard on us when they didn't come back. Even though I can admit that it was frightening to me knowing that soon I would be facing the enemy, I still never thought that it would happen to me – that *I* wouldn't come back. It was normal to have this uneasiness, I suppose, but I always thought I'd return. With all of the tragedies that I had learned about already, so close at hand, I was working on hardening myself for the worst, should any of my crewmates be killed or injured in flight. I wanted to be able to handle the worst nightmare. I didn't want to let anyone down, including myself.

Our green crew was becoming ready and anxious to begin flying the bombing missions that we had been trained for. We wanted the day to happen, because the anticipation was becoming worse than the reality.

Our Crew
Back Row: Thomas Mikulka, Tail Gunner; John J. Alexander,
Jr., Right Waist Gunner; Milo Blakely, Left Waist Gunner;
Jay Joyce, Radio Operator; John Kyler, Ball Turret Gunner;
John Booth, Flt. Engineer/Top Turret Gunner;
Front Row: Emmett H. Bell, Bombardier; Donald H. Caylor,
Navigator; Robert B. Bangs, Co-Pilot; Lawrence H. Cook, Pilot.

Bombers joining formation
Courtesy of James Pedacchio

B-17 Over English Channel
Courtesy of James Pedacchio

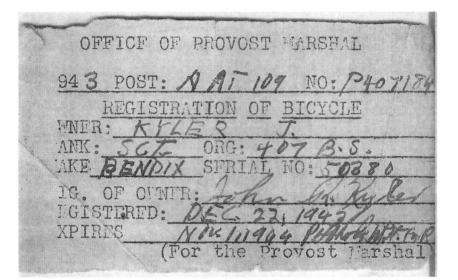

Bendix Bicycle Registration

9

Return to present…

PLANS TO FOLLOW IN MY TRACKS CONTINUE

One day in 2005, Candy learned about a tour group that next year would be visiting both the former Stalag Luft IV and Stalag Luft I POW camps, and she could not pass up the opportunity; these were two of the three camps where I had been held prisoner by the Germans. Candy had already toured the Stalag Luft I site near Barth, Germany, earlier in the year, and the next logical place, chronologically, would be to visit Stalag Luft VI, and *then* Stalag Luft IV, because that was the order in which I stayed in them. However, she felt that an organized tour of Stalag Luft IV, which involved a trip to Poland, was too good an opportunity to pass up, even though it would involve a revisit to Stalag Luft I. She resolved to take the two-site trip now, and cover the Stalag Luft VI site in a coming year. The double-stop guided trip also had the advantage of giving Sara a chance to see Stalag Luft I and for Candy to cover some ground she had missed on her first visit to Barth in 2005.

When Candy talked to Sara about her interest in this tour, Sara expressed a sincere desire to accompany her. This was an ambitious three-week endeavor, but it would cover many of the important areas where I had traveled during the war. Candy's plan was for them to first visit England and Belgium on their own to visit my old base at Podington and the crash site of my plane in Belgium, and then join the small tour group, head for Stalag Luft I, and on their last leg of the tour travel on to Stalag Luft IV, in Tychowo, Poland. It would be a perfect time for Sara to participate, as this excursion would cover an extensive piece of my history. It was not an easy task to undertake, but Candy felt that it was critical to her mission of reconstructing and reliving my war years, including the time I had spent in captivity. The details of the trip were finalized, and my wife and daughter would proceed with plans for their journey to discover my past.

10

Continuation of present.....

RETURN TO PODINGTON

I watched as Candy wrote in her journal at the airport and then again on the plane as she prepared herself for the days ahead. I also observed my Sara, knowing that a long air trip would not be easy for her at eighty-five, what with the connecting flights and the hours of waiting. I could see the struggles that the time change caused for the medications that she required. It was wise of my daughter to allow the both of them a couple days' rest upon their arrival in London.

Our arrival in London and the cab to a hotel was without incident. For convenience sake, Candy had picked a hotel in King's Cross, which was within walking distance of the train station, where we would depart for our trip to Bedford. At Bedford, Gerry and Audrey Darnell would be picking us up. Candy had learned about Gerry Darnell through her contact with my old outfit's veteran organization, the 92nd Bomb Group Memorial Association. The Association had understood her goals, and Newsletter Editor Irv Baum referred her to Gerry Darnell, an Englishman who resided near Bedford, which was very near Podington. I was happy for Candy's contact with willing guides who were familiar with my old air base.

It was difficult for me to be this kind of ephemeral spectator, having no control physically to help my wife and daughter in any way. I could only watch over them and use my strong will to keep them safe. Arriving on Monday, Candy called Gerry and arrangements were made to meet on Wednesday, September 20, 2006, two days hence.

Candy then tried calling an agency to schedule a brief local sightseeing tour, but it did not work out because Sara was exhausted from the trip, and jet-lagged to boot, and she needed to rest and get acclimated. In Candy's eyes, anyway, the important thing was the trip to Podington, and she mentioned that fact to her mother. Candy stayed focused on why she had brought them to England, and nothing else really mattered.

The two women were not what you would call typical tourists. They could just take it easy for a couple days. Candy did not want to tire her mother out doing things that weren't central to their "mission," and risk her being too tired to absorb the significance of the days ahead. It was so clear to me how much they both looked forward to their visit to the former airbase for my bombardment group – the place where I lived between missions – the base that I had left on February 4, 1944, never to return until…two days from now!

Who would have thought that over sixty years later my wife and daughter would want to visit there simply because it was a place that I had been? Better yet, who would have thought that I would be returning along with them? It was humbling to grasp the lengths that they were going to. Although I was not visible to them and could not speak to them, I'm certain they felt my presence.

When the day arrived, I was as excited as they were; the anticipation had been building in all of us. I was surprised at how anxious I was to return to the places that I had been during the war. Maybe it is because now no one could see any emotion that the memories would certainly trigger. Men's reluctance to show their emotions declines with age, but it never leaves them entirely.

In the morning, we would be catching the nine o'clock Thameslink from Kings Cross for a one-hour ride to Bedford. Overly eager to begin this day, Candy brought her mother to the station way too early, so they had to walk around for thirty minutes just to pass the time. It was a pleasant, sunny Fall morning, unseasonably warm, and a great day for a walk. They seemed to enjoy watching the people in the busy setting, who were on their way to work and rushing to catch a train or bus. The traffic was heavy. The two American women from Salamanca agreed they would hate to have to travel this way to work every morning.

Finally the time came to board the train. Candy and Sara settled into their seats and fell silent, deep in thought, lulled by the warm sun through the windows and the rhythmic sound of the wheels on the track. I was sure that they, like me, were realizing that in a matter of minutes we would see where my missions had begun – yet an area where I had lived for but a very short time.

I didn't expect that I would feel so energized to return. What would they think if they could see the thrilled look on my face? I wished that they could see the reaction of Dad, so they could know how grateful I was for their efforts. The thoughts and anticipation that overwhelmed me were totally unexpected, and we were not even there yet! I never thought that I would want to return to *any* place associated with *this* part of my life. I was wrong.

I read over Candy's shoulder as she wrote these words in her journal:

> *Here I am in another world at a different time than my father, and I am feeling like a different person – almost as if I am my father returning to relive his past. It is a strange yet familiar feeling for me these days.*

Little did she know that my thoughts paralleled hers. Her intense interest was making possible my return in an unusual, yet rewarding way for each of us. Her will, her imagination, was drawing me, Sergeant John Kyler, out of the past and into this railroad car with my wife and daughter. I realized at that moment, more than ever, that what she was doing was right for all three of us.

Gerry and Audrey Darnell arrived promptly, as did our train. Candy recognized Gerry immediately in his 8th Air Force cap and introduced herself and Sara to them. Gerry and Audrey looked to be quite pleased to welcome their guests. They were casually but neatly dressed; Gerry looked quite distinguished, with his full head of white hair. As we drove off in Darnell's tidy gray sedan to my old airfield, Gerry shared stories with us about his time as a young boy hanging out at the Red Cross Club where his brother had worked. Gerry said that when he had first seen my crew photo (Candy had previously sent it to him) he actually remembered me and a couple of other fellows in the picture. The more information that he gave and the more I studied him, now all grown up, the more I realized that, yes, I remembered him exactly.

Gerry remembered precisely what it had been like when I had been there. How pleased I was when he began to share these treasured memories with my girls. They listened intently as he recalled times past, and I was mesmerized, reliving each recollection along with him. It was all becoming so familiar to me.

Gerry had fond memories of playing the piano, snooker and table tennis and helping out at the Red Cross Club. According to him, the Christmas parties at the base were the highlight of the year, and I readily agreed to that with a nod unnoticed – though I had attended only one! The children were picked up in the base trucks and taken to the airfield where they would have their party, with entertainment, bags of sweets, fruit, chewing gum, and a present to take home. I remembered the uplifting reaction from the young ones, and how much it made me feel at home, back then, to see local children in our midst.

Gerry also recalled Saturday night dances, and how he got to know the Americans who attended regularly. He told us that James Cagney had visited the base and opened the airmen's bar, which came to be known as "Cagney's Cellar," and that Glen Miller also had played at the base. My love for Glen Miller music had stayed with me throughout my life. How fortunate that Sara and our daughter heard a first-hand account of events that had taken place during a significant period in my life as an American airman, told by Gerry as accurately as I could remember, given the brief period that I was at Podington. It was also of great interest to me to hear of events that transpired at the base after my final flight.

Gerry told my girls that the Town of Podington was much the same as it had been when I was there, and I agreed…silently, of course. So much of what he was saying matched my own recollections of the place! Candy commented that she could almost picture me riding my bike to or from town with other GIs on the same narrow wartime road that we had taken through the woodlands. Quite a few unexpected sensations swept over me as we drove down this same road that had seen my bicycle, my buddies, and me, on all our trips to and from town. The sights brought the sounds and events rushing back to me, and I knew that my wife and daughter were filled with these same feelings. I guessed they were imagining my life pretty much as I had lived it sixty years ago.

As we entered the town, we drove by a pub that Gerry said the GI's frequented, and I would have voiced agreement, if only I could. The girls were impressed that the pub was still there, with Candy saying that "Dad may very well have spent a little time in that building," and they both found humor in that, and it was true!

Then we came to a memorial. It surprised me to see it on the premises, complete with our record of missions. I felt pride in the 92nd Bomb Group, even though my career with it was short-lived. I was even more proud to have been a member of the 407th Bomb Squadron, and it brought tears to my eyes as I read the inscriptions on the monument. The inscription across the top reads, "We will always remember "Fame's Favored Few.""

Also inscribed are the words:

> *In memory of those brave airmen and support groups who gave their lives and who served during World War II for the liberation of Europe. The Group flew 308 missions, 274 from Podington Airfield.*

The memorial had been dedicated July 3, 1999. This memorial aroused in me quite an intense feeling. Candy had the same thought as she whispered to Sara, "I wonder if Dad knew he was remembered here?" It was uplifting to know that we were honored at this place, which today lacks any visible sign of what had occurred here so many years ago. Gerry took photos of Sara and Candy standing by the monument and, little did they know, I stood right beside them and smiled.

After the ladies took about fifty pictures of the memorial, we climbed back into the Darnell's car and continued along the approach road to the airfield, which is still there, and off to our left was a side-road that had once led to the station hospital. I remembered this so well, for I had once bicycled to the hospital to visit a friend. Along our way to the "new" re-purposed base, which had been converted into an automobile racetrack, the remains of small brick buildings were pointed out that looked like small houses. They were not the Quonset huts in which we had been housed, and I could not recall the exact use, but they did look familiar to me.

As we approached the airfield and drove the perimeter, I was filled with emotion as I looked upon a space that was a rather empty area now, but so distinctly recognizable to me. There remains the control tower, which has been converted to a residence. I was looking at this same structure, just as I had when I walked or rode by it sixty-two years ago, and Candy commented on how great it was to observe this old building, well aware of its importance to me when I served here so long ago. Viewing it now in its current use as a residence, I had flashbacks of what it had looked like when it had operated as our control tower. And I was pleased that this field was in England, for had it been in America, this old control tower would have been torn down and replaced with a convenience store or a split-level home years ago.

There were other buildings, once full of activity, that now appeared abandoned. Gerry pointed out the building where the Intelligence photographs would have been developed and printed. But at times I felt disoriented and uncertain. It is strange how time and memory can fool a person: I could barely pick out the spot that had contained the hut where I had slept with my crewmates, my friends. And there were many sleepless nights.

I finally did orient myself properly, looking at the former control tower and remembering the direction I once viewed it from. Digging into my memory, I could pick out the empty grounds where the mess hall once stood, which is where we went to be briefed before missions, and debriefed afterward, and also spotted the area where we picked up our supplies on the mornings of our missions.

We next drove by an old maintenance building that held my attention because I could envision our men walking in and out. The reactions of my wife and daughter to all of these sights were to me uncanny, for they could not possibly see what I saw, nor remember what I had once seen, yet they were clearly overcome by their surroundings – reverent almost. They were reacting to the place simply because I had been there, and it warmed my heart. I observed the faraway looks in the eyes of Candy and Sara, hoping that they were seeing much the same visions in their minds that I was reliving in mine. What historic tales those old buildings held!

Studying the scenery, I thought of being with my friends somewhere in this same area. I scanned the ground, appreciating the old memories of eating meals, talking, laughing, riding my bike, and going for mission briefings. I could see the young John Kyler preparing for flight and checking the armaments of the B-17 that was assigned for that day's mission. It was not the same time any more, but it was the same place, and all of these activities had once occurred. Together the three of us walked this area that is now an open field. We were walking where my comrades and I saw and heard events that Candy and Sara will never see with my eyes or hear from my lips, but I know that they could see and hear these things in their minds. It seemed to me that all these things were as vivid to them as if they had once been part of it.

The extreme anticipation and anxiety experienced when preparing for a flight, and the feeling of flying off in the B-17 that would be my home for the next several hours, loomed in my thoughts. My old feelings returned, those uncontrollable fears that would surface in flight, and also the questions – would she bring us all back unscathed? And, what tragedies was I about to witness? Yet I don't recall ever having these questions enter my mind as we busily prepared for flight and performed our assigned duties, but only later, when airborne and en route to our destination. As we stood in that field and stared into the open sky above, I could see that my family members were lost in similar thoughts.

My girls both remarked on their thoughts to the Darnells, imagining what it was like to have seen and heard all those bombers take off. It is understandable the love that anyone witnessing such a scene would feel for the B-17 and everything about this air base operation during World War II. Today, at this field in Podington, the sound of automobile engines pierce the air and the countryside at certain times of the year, as the main runway now serves as a racetrack. How times have changed!

It was obvious that Gerry cherished his memories of time spent in this region as we traveled it over sixty years later. Gerry said that the thrill that he felt in the 1940s stays with him still as he pointed out the location where as a young man he would stand to watch the bombers get ready for take off. I knew how he felt. He stated that he could remember the sound of the four engines of the B-17s in the early mornings as they taxied to their take-off point. He recalled the screeching of the brakes as the bombers reached the end of the runway and then the roar of the engines as full power was applied by the pilot for take-off. Fully loaded, the Forts would use the full length of the runway before becoming airborne. As they climbed out above the surrounding villages, one by one, the thundering bombers would gain altitude and begin to form up into groups and formations, getting ready for the mission at hand.

Take-off was always dangerous, particularly in bad weather when the visibility was poor, and of course accidents did occur. On one foggy Saturday morning at Podington a three-plane crash occurred, a mid-air collision over Irthlingborough (near the 305th BG base), and another mid-air collision at Thurleigh with the tragic loss of many young lives. Gerry somberly pointed out an area at the Podington airfield where a similar unfortunate incident had occurred after my time there.

After nearly sixty years, Gerry still remembered counting the planes as they flew out, as many groundlings did, including me on occasion, and then counting them back in. The empty spaces in the returning formations told the dreaded, yet inevitable and too-frequent story that some had not made it home. Battle damage to the aircraft was at times extensive, with holes in the fuselage and wings, and shot-out engines with propellers "feathered". There were also propellers that could not be feathered, and they were "wind milling," making it much more difficult to control the aircraft. And there was the all-too-familiar sight of flares being fired from the aircraft indicating there were wounded aboard. These ships would land first, be met by the ambulances, and the wounded were then rushed to the station hospital. Too often there were those who medical care could not help.

There were occasions when B-17s would land without undercarriage, where their landing gear had been shot out and the wheels could not be lowered, even manually, for a proper, safe landing. Those planes would be the last to descend after circling the airfield, using up fuel to reduce the risk of fire. My wife and daughter were totally immersed in the memories that Gerry was sharing, as was I. Audrey appeared to be very familiar with Gerry's recollections of days gone by and equally as interested.

Some of the targets of my 92nd Bomb Group included the shipyards in Kiel, the ball bearing plants at Schweinfurt, submarine installations at Wilhelmshaven, a tire factory at Hanover, airfields near Paris, an aircraft factory at Nantes, France, and a magnesium mine and reducing plant in Norway. Kiel, Wilhelmshaven and France are all familiar names to me in that they were also the targets on the missions that I had personally flown.

My last mission was to Frankfurt. It was on February 4, 1944, when I left Podington for the last time, never to return. My coveted bicycle was no doubt passed on to some other airman who would, hopefully, fare better than me. February 4 was a turning point for me and my crew – the day when we stopped fighting one type of war and began fighting another. Anyone who thinks that for an airman taken prisoner, his war is over, has never been captured and held in prison by an enemy government.

So many memories surfaced of the days I spent as a twenty year old, so motivated and ambitious, reviewing all of the preparations that were made for the role I would play on the bombers we would be assigned to, as well as the trips that were made to town. Every part of the road, every building, even the trees along the road and the vacant field stirred memories. The many faces returned to my reeling mind. The road into the former base, and the entire area that would have at one time been full of air crewmen and mechanics, was now quiet and vacant, as if Station 109 never existed; but I could testify that it did once exist, and for a short period of time I played a part in that existence.

Later that day, Candy wrote about this stop at Podington:

> This visit to Podington, as simple a stop as it may seem, is huge to me. My father arrived in England on November 15, 1943, according to his log book. England was to become his comfort zone – the place that he would desire to return after the long missions that were in store for him from Podington Airfield.

Candy found the information about my flight to my new home in England in a small log book that I had kept when I was training, and into which I merely wrote the places and dates of our route from the U.S. to our new home base. I had forgotten about that book and I can't believe that Sara found it, much less showed it to Candy. I wouldn't have thought it meant anything to anyone as it contained so little information. I agreed quietly with my daughter that, remarkably, this stop was huge for me. Although she was unable to hear me, I thanked her for bringing me to my old base.

PODINGTON CHURCH

We then left the old base and traveled to Podington Church, where in 1985 the church organ had been restored as a memorial tribute to the 92nd Bombardment Group. There is an inscription on the side of the organ, above a propeller blade from one of the B-17s from the base. The inscription reads:

In thanksgiving and in memory of Fames Favored Few
The 92nd Bombardment Group of the United
States 8th Air Force, 1943 to 1945.
In the cause of peace and freedom the group flew 308
missions, 274 from Podington Airfield.

This organ was restored by the 92nd Bombardment Group Memorial Corporation in the hope that the voice of this instrument will speak for them – the living and the dead – to the people of Podington every time it is played.

Dedicated by John, Lord Bishop of St. Albans, 18 May 1985.

There is also an American flag next to the organ. What a magnificent tribute to the oldest serving group in the U.S Air Force! This group, *my group*, flew 308 missions over enemy territory with the loss of many young lives. The sight of this memorial in this simple, beautiful church warmed my heart knowing that the members of my Bomb Group, living and dead, would never be forgotten in this, God's house. The admiration and appreciation of the people of the Village of Podington for the members of the 92nd Bomb Group was obvious. I sensed a strong connection, and it became apparent to me that my wife and daughter sensed it as well.

In Candy's words:

> *I appreciated the hospitality and generosity shown by a lovely couple on our tour of this wonderful village and realized that Podington was more than an air base. How gratifying it is that the voice and memory of our fathers is being carried on through the music of the organ, and in the permanent inscriptions at the church and the airfield. Once again a daughter's pride grows within me.*

Memorial at former Podington Airfield

Original Signpost across from Control Tower

Former Control Tower

Original Building at Airfield

Fames Favored Few Insignia

Podington Church

Inscription Inside Podington Church

Sara and Gerry Darnell-Memorial Inside Podington Church

11

THE MISSIONS BEGIN

The day came, finally. We were called up on the morning of 21 January, 1944 for a briefing at 0312. We were up by 2 a.m.! I recall that at breakfast we ate quickly, and I had to force myself to eat because I felt so nervous. I knew it was important to eat because who knew when I would again have the chance? And besides, breakfasts were great on mission days. I'd been told from the experience of others to have a good breakfast even if I felt queasy. I had a sick feeling from the combination of full-blown excitement coupled with rapidly stuffing myself with eggs and toast. I attended my first briefing. We were going to France! Our target that day would be LePlouy Ferme/Bellevue, and our bombing objective would be "V-weapons." At the end of the briefing we all synchronized our watches, because timing was critical – time of takeoff, time to join the formation – precise time was vital to the missions, and all of us had to be on the same time.

I remember having a flashback of the day I was forced to leave my mother and sisters to go live with my father. The vision of me hanging onto Mom and my repeated cry of, "please don't make me go," came to mind because this was a faintly similar situation. At odd moments in those first hours I still felt like a boy but, thinking positively, I would handle my fears like a man and do what I was there to do. I was committed to doing my job well for my mother, who I had clung to all those years, as well as for my sisters, my relatives and friends, and even those who I didn't know.

After briefing, we sergeants continued to the flight-line locker room to dress for the freezing temperatures. We picked up our flight rations, electrically heated flight suits, harnesses and parachutes, oxygen masks, and Mae West inflatable vests that would keep us afloat should we be forced down over water. As we donned our flight suits, we all cracked jokes to lighten up the situation, and I suppose it helped take off the edge.

We first put on a flannel suit that reminded me of pajamas, and to this we added booties and gloves made of felt. Over all this we wore an entire suit that was electrically heated, even at the wrists and ankles. We wore leather helmets with fleece lining to protect our ears and heads and accented our attire with a pair of goggles. Our cheeks were the only unprotected part of our body, but I didn't give any thought to this until much later. With airborne temperatures ranging in the wintertime from 40 to 80 degrees *below zero*, icicles would sometimes form on our oxygen masks, and it was a serious problem if an oxygen line became clogged with ice. After suiting up in all this stuff, we proceeded to the armament shop where we collected our forty-five caliber automatic pistols. Finally, we were transported by jeep to the airplane that would be ours for this first mission.

When all of my crewmates arrived at our aircraft, we went through the pre-flight checklists. The bomber had been pre-flighted once already, earlier in the morning, by our ground crew. We carefully checked our machine guns, ensuring that they were correctly mounted in their receivers and ready to go. It was my responsibility to check the armaments for the whole plane. I checked and double-checked the list of weaponry. Once our duties were completed, we exchanged nods and the wait began – one of the hardest things we did was waiting. Having been so intensely briefed and then having carefully dressed and pre-flighted the aircraft, our adrenaline was really pumping and we were ready to go. Yet we were left to sit in silence, waiting for the green flare – the sign that the mission was a "go." Some of us were sweating by this time, which we would come to regret later when our sweat froze solid under our flight suits. On that first mission we made so many mistakes that we would never make again!

Finally, I caught sight of the signal flare and realized that this was "it." My heart began racing as our pilots started the four engines on our aircraft one at a time, and the noise and vibration began adding to the exhilaration of the moment.

I recall a sheet instructing us on which plane we were to follow on the taxi-way. The radio checks began, the bail-out bell was tested, and soon we were taxiing to take our place in formation of the 40th Combat Wing of the First Bombardment Division. My crew members and I were sharing our first bombing mission! Each of us on that crew drew strength and courage from the other – upon boarding our assigned bomber we became a unit, each manning his position for the long ride to the target and the long ride back.

Up in the cockpit on the left sat our pilot, Lt. Larry Cook; on his right was Lt. Bob Bangs as co-pilot; standing slightly behind the pilots and scrutinizing the engine instruments was Flight Engineer/Top Turret Gunner Sgt. John Booth; beneath and forward of the cockpit were Bombardier Lt. Emmett Bell, and Navigator Lt. Donald Caylor, seated in the nose. Of course after we entered the plane, I would not see these five crew members until our return. Sgt. Tom Mikulka was in his tail gunner position. Sergeants Milo Blakely and John Alexander occupied the waist gun positions and Technical Sergeant Jay Joyce manned the radio.

Assisted by a waist gunner who helped make sure all my oxygen lines and electrical cables did not get tangled, I climbed into the ball turret once we were airborne.

We now began living the stories we would share with others upon our return just as, before today, we had listened to others recall their flights.

As we approached the area near the target, we received the disappointing news that we were being recalled to base due to cloud cover and bad visibility over the target. We were disappointed, yet there was a sense of relief as well. Our recall ensured that every B-17 from our airfield that morning would return, barring any mechanical failures. Thus we returned to base, landed, and reversed all of the procedures we had learned in order to stow our gear and return to normal dress. After nearly ten hours of close excitement and concentration, hundreds of gallons of fuel and many gallons of sweat, our first combat mission still lay ahead of us.

We had a few days off until we again received a call-up in the wee hours of the morning of January 30. Once again we completed all of the preparations for our flight, which were a good bit easier the second time around. That day we would be bombing Brunswick's Waggum Airport and, as had been done on the previous day's mission (that we had not been part of), we would be flying an "A" and "B" formation, unlike our first mission. The 407th Squadron —our squadron— would lead the "B" group. There was a heavy cloud cover over the target, so we were unsure of the bombing results at the time. We encountered enemy fighters during the mission, and it appeared to us that we destroyed or damaged many of them.

About ten minutes after bombing the target, one of our B-17s lost altitude, and in the pilot's attempt to regain his position in the formation his plane collided with the belly of another aircraft and exploded, tearing the left wing off of the higher bomber. As they both lost altitude, the higher bomber also exploded. As we flew home to England I continuously replayed the incident, astonished at what I had seen. Twenty men dead! It was a sobering reinforcement of just how dangerous our missions were. After landing, we sullenly attended the debriefing.

This was my first encounter with what had been certain death for those twenty crew members. Later that day I was relieved to learn that we would have a few days off, during which time I would try to regroup after what I had seen. The horrible collision, however, was not the only tragedy that day. I learned that evening that one of the friends I frequently accompanied to town had been killed instantly in an unfortunate bicycling accident. But I had to try to look past these misfortunes –– I had missions to fly. I had to look forward, not back. Some day we would return home and then we could grieve for our comrades. At this time, there was too much ahead of us that needed our undivided attention.

Our next mission was on February 3rd, a cold rainy morning. This time our target was the submarine base at Wilhelmshaven. It was another "A" and "B" flight with us in the "B" group, and take-off time was 0735 at one-minute intervals. The bombers rose to the assigned altitude and the formation came together smoothly. As we approached our target area there was extensive cloud cover, and we were signaled to drop our bombs from 30,000 feet. We picked up two fighter escort groups of P-47s at the Zuider Zee (over Holland) as well as P-51's in the target area. This was an excellent mission. At 30,000 feet the temperature was bone-chilling, and our heated flight suits were much appreciated. As we returned, and got close to home, a grinding noise was evident that was quite upsetting. However, our pilot Larry Cook brought us in smoothly and reported the noise to maintenance. I never learned what it was, but the important thing is that we made it back.

The Final Mission

As I approached my fourth mission on February 4, 1944, I was gaining some proficiency at making ready. The feelings of fear had left me and were replaced by impatience to get out there and win the war. Our crew's goal – and mine – was to survive twenty-five missions, after which we could all go home.

Called up early on this fateful Friday morning, we were briefed on our target, the railroad marshalling yards in Frankfurt, Germany. It was another "A" and "B" group effort, and the 92nd was flying in the high group in both flights. The only difference in this mission was that instead of flying a bomber from our Squadron, the 407th, we were assigned one from the 326th Squadron. But we had faith in any B-17 that was assigned, and getting a different ship was better then using the plane with the grating noise that we had flown the previous day.

Once again, we were off. This time we flew east, parallel to the German coast for a period of time until our turn to the south, into the heart of the Ruhr Valley, on our way to our target.

12

Return to present.........

B-17 FLIGHT

In her attempt to experience what it had been like for me as a young man of twenty taking my first flight in a B-17, Candy made arrangements for a ride in the B-17, *Fuddy Duddy*. She mentioned her plans to her mother, inspiring Sara's own desire to participate as well. Sara shared our daughter's wish to explore a part of my life that I had never talked about. They were both aware of my fondness of the B-17, recalling the programs and videos that I watched throughout the years about the "Flying Fortress," and the model of the bomber that I had built and displayed. They got very excited anticipating the ride, agreeing that it would be both a great adventure and a tribute to husband and father.

On the appointed day for the August flight they (we) were blessed with favorable weather for flying. The scheduled flight time was 9:30 a.m., and Candy and Sara departed well ahead of time on their drive to Prior Aviation in Buffalo. It was so important to Candy that they arrive early that they ended up waiting in the parking lot quite a while before they could register. I could see they didn't mind, because they spent the extra time admiring *Fuddy Duddy*, visible through the fence.

As flight time approached, a line formed at the gate and a noticeable excitement was building in the waiting crowd. When it was their turn,

Sara and Candy proceeded to the registration area, signed in, and received their souvenir boarding passes. As she registered, Sara proudly explained that her husband had been a B-17 ball turret gunner. It was the perfect environment for Sara and Candy to talk about me, attracting a great amount of interest from the waiting crowd. It made me feel pretty good to see the great interest shown about my job on the bomber.

There was time before departure to take pictures and more closely examine the waiting aircraft. The area of greatest interest for Candy and Sara naturally was the ball turret. Prior to take-off, the "crew members" were called together outside the plane to be briefed by Vinny, the Flight Engineer. As they climbed on board, he told Sara and Candy to sit in the "seats with cushions" in the back of the plane. He explained in the briefing how to fasten and tighten the seatbelts, and he proceeded to help my wife and daughter with that task. Vinny advised everyone that when they were in flight they needed to hang on to their belongings tightly in the area where the upper hatch was open, in the center of the plane. He also mentioned not to grab onto any of the "control cables" along the upper sides of the aircraft once they were given permission to walk around.

This was their first time actually *inside* of a B-17, and Candy and Sara studied the airplane's interior, amazed at the cramped quarters, especially given the length of the bombing missions that were flown in them. They agreed that the B-17 was not built for comfort, but rather for missions. I concurred with that!

We were beginning our journey into the past to cover another stage of my war experience, and I was overcome with thoughts and emotions even more complex and vivid than those I experienced in Podington. This was it! This had been my office, the space from which I had fought the war. Sitting on an old runway looking at dilapidated buildings was one thing, but this airplane brought the past and present together as no landscape could have. I was going back into my element and watching my wife and daughter as they experienced it for the first time.

The pilots were readying the ship for take-off. The firing of the first engine sent me back in time, awakening numerous memories of my bombing missions. I recalled the faces of my crewmates, the radio messages, the armament checks, and the unnerving wait for the signal to take off. The sound of the roaring engines and the sight of the exhaust smoke as they were fired up clearly were thrilling to my wife and daughter.

Their excitement was visibly building with the start of each one. I enjoyed watching how absorbed they were in every small detail as the ship was readied for flight.

It was wonderfully thrilling to be engulfed in my past! The view from the windows revealed the force of the engines, with clouds of blowing dirt and grass rolling behind us as we taxied out to our take-off position at the end of the runway. Candy and her mother made reference to how terrifying it must have felt to begin a bombing mission anticipating the anti-aircraft fire from the ground and a likely attack by enemy fighter planes. I think they could imagine how frightened I must have been as a young man to climb into the confined space of the ball turret. They felt as though that would be the most dangerous position on the plane. Had I been able, I would have told them that *every* position was dangerous.

The rattling of the cables and the thunderous noise of the engines as we taxied and then took off really energized my wife and daughter, and me as well. I think they both experienced goose bumps. The views out of the windows were breathtaking as we ascended, and the people and buildings grew smaller.

The light clouds in a beautiful blue sky served as a wonderful backdrop for the gleaming wings and propellers of the great ship. The silver wings and fuselage were almost blinding in the sun's brilliant light. I felt pride, just as my wife and daughter so clearly did, in flying in this magnificent bird, envisioning what a spectacle it must have been from the ground. This day brought to mind a mission day over sixty-two years ago when our crew had joined the formation to begin our flight to the target in skies much like these.

When the aircraft leveled off at what looked to me to be about 4,500 feet, the flight engineer announced that the "crew members" could now walk around the airplane to inspect the different combat stations. Sara was happy to stay in her seat, as it would have been too difficult for her to walk around in flight, but Candy was eager to see every position she had read about in preparation for this flight.

Of course I could not resist walking along with my daughter, and the first stations that she examined were the left and right waist gunner positions. I could still visualize Milo Blakely and John Alexander occupying this space. Candy looked out both sides of the plane, glancing back at her mother, who caught her eye and smiled. Sara was content to look out from her comfortable seat in the back of the plane. Looking into the aft section of the plane triggered my memory of the tail gunner on our crew, Tom Mikulka. Moving forward from the waist of the ship, Candy next checked out the radio operator's compartment. A picture of my friend Jay Joyce instantly popped into my mind.

It was amazing how clearly I could see the young faces of my crew family as Candy walked forward through the aircraft.

Standing just forward of the waist, Candy studied the ball turret, which on *Fuddy Duddy* was inaccessible. She squatted down on the deck to examine the turret more closely. Somehow, I knew that if she would have been allowed to climb into the turret that would have been the position she would have assumed on this ride. We continued to walk the catwalk to the cockpit area. More memories of our pilots, Larry Cook and Robert Bangs, flooded my mind as well as my recollection of John Booth, our top turret gunner. Although awakening memories of our missions might have been distressing to me, the recollection of these figures from my past had more of a calming nature. It was as if I could finally put to rest the unpleasant events that took place during my missions, and enjoy the fact that this bomber was a symbol of days gone by. For me, it was a touchstone to the thousands of crew members who flew in these ships and the many missions that they flew, and it was physical proof that our past would not be forgotten.

The climb down into the clear nose section of the Flying Fortress presented Candy with a million photo-ops, and she hurriedly snapped many pictures. This area of the aircraft brought me clear visions of Emmett Bell, our bombardier, and Donald Caylor, our navigator, who I had known well and liked, but sadness overcame me at the thought of Donald's ultimate fate, years ago.

Finished with the great views in the nose, we climbed back up into the cockpit and the pilot motioned out the window to show Candy that we were flying right over Niagara Falls! The view was spectacular from the cockpit window, and as we stared down, I was struck by the irony that I had entered the service in Niagara Falls, New York.

On our return to the back of the plane, the view from the waist gunner position remained awesome. Candy wanted to make sure that her mother was not missing the scenery below, and we saw that Sara had not missed the grand view of the Horseshoe Falls from her seat near the waist. Candy mentioned how appropriate it was that they were seeing Niagara Falls from a plane that I had acquired so much respect for over sixty years after my entry into the Army Air Corps from Fort Niagara. The two women shared a special and meaningful view from the window of the B-17.

Finally, and way too soon, Flight Engineer Vinny directed the passengers back to their seats to prepare for the end of this incredible flight. They fastened their seatbelts as the pilot began his descent back to earth. The mission would soon be over.

A heartwarming gesture was made as the flight came to an end. Vinny invited Sara to meet Pilot Dave and Co-Pilot Larry, and the three of them talked with her about my bomb group and position on the mighty B-17. She told them that I had been shot down and captured, becoming a prisoner of war. They treated her as royalty, making this day and this experience especially memorable and gratifying for all three of us. There was no doubt in anyone's mind that this flight – our flight – was meant to be. Candy and Sara agreed that I was smiling on them and, in Candy's words, was "as proud of his 'Queen' as she was of him." On the drive back they agreed that this had been the ride of a lifetime.

The amazing day and this short flight helped to rid me of the terrifying memories that were so deeply buried these many years, keeping me from flying again in my lifetime. Not only was I finally released from these bad memories but I was pleased to realize that a good memory of the U.S. Airman lives on.

Candy & Sara in front of the B-17 *Fuddy-Duddy*

View of Niagara Falls from the *Fuddy Duddy*

Sara under the nose of the *Fuddy Duddy*

13

THE BAILOUT

The bursts of black smoke that we encountered from the anti-aircraft guns were a frightening sight. On our previous missions, the flak from the installations had not been a problem. You could only hope that these bursts would not disable your aircraft or injure any of the others in your group. My clear view of the cluttered sky from the ball turret brought the realization of how unlikely it would be to evade disaster. It was simply impossible to avoid the dangerous areas – you were locked on your target, flying in tight formation, and the pilots were forbidden any defensive maneuvers. This was the heaviest artillery that we'd seen so far, and I was terrified as the ball turret took a glancing blow that I immediately radioed to the others. Thank God it wasn't full force but I became really excited — it had scared the hell out of me.

Flying at 25,000 feet, we successfully released our bombs over the target; however, as we turned toward England, the terror increased when I felt the plane lurch violently and saw the direct hit that our Fort took from another of those frightful flak bursts. I immediately radioed that our number two engine had been hit.

I began to sweat in the frigid air. One of my greatest fears when assuming the ball turret position had been the fact that I could not wear my parachute while in the turret, and that I wouldn't be able to get out quickly enough to put it on if the necessity arose. As I was thinking these thoughts again, the pilot called me out of the ball turret. I knew that the situation had to be serious for him to pull me from my position. I pulled on my 'chute and watched and waited in the freezing air.

Our aircraft lost speed and altitude, and with it the security of flying in formation. Our lone bomber became easy prey for the attacking German fighters who began spewing bullets at us. Everything was happening fast, and as anyone could imagine, the excitement was at its highest pitch.

Seeking the protection of cloud cover, we dropped to an elevation of about 17,000 feet. Our radio had been hit, eliminating our interphone communication. Far more seriously, our oxygen was shot out. My feelings of immortality disappeared. We were doomed if we stayed with the ship, as the fighters, about ten of them by my count, continued their attack. I remember locking eyes with one of the German pilots, frozen with terror that he would shoot me. He flew alongside us awhile and then veered off. He could have claimed my life, yet he didn't. We were no longer a threat due to the damage to our aircraft, and there were other, healthier planes for them to pursue.

With our bomber doomed and return to England hopeless, our only chance of survival was to parachute from our stricken plane. Suddenly, over the din of the remaining engines and all the air noise as we descended rapidly, I heard the Abandon Ship annunciator, triggered by the pilot. With the thought of jumping into thin air at 17,000 feet, feelings of hesitation and urgency surfaced. John Alexander, Milo Blakely, Jay Joyce and I wasted no time; we exited through the waist door. I don't even recall if any words were exchanged. It was a terrifying experience and I think we were all in shock. I uttered prayers quickly and excitedly as I jumped into the unknown.

My head was foggy. I was suffocating and became lightheaded from the thin air at the high altitude, and the force of the wind made it hard even to take a breath. I was frightened, but knew that if I was going to survive I needed to concentrate on a safe landing. I was getting dizzy from looking at the ground, but once trees and buildings became closer and more distinguishable I pulled the cord. I received a huge jolt as the 'chute opened, slowing my rapid descent and causing me to swing back and forth until I stabilized. As I drifted to the ground, my head was clear enough to pray that I and my crew members would survive.

My thoughts turned to controlling where to land – not that I was an expert at it! It was snowing heavily, yet I thought I noticed parachutes in the air as I drifted, but they were in the distance. I wanted to avoid getting caught in a tree, and knew that landing in enemy territory as I was, my chances were best in an isolated area. I thought hurriedly about what I needed to do when I landed. I needed to bury my parachute to hide any sign of my presence. I had my escape kit containing a map to help me find my way to friendly terrain. If I was lucky, the enemy was not watching my descent.

I couldn't help but think that if the enemy were tracking me, would I be killed even before I landed or would I be captured? I wondered if perhaps I was being observed by someone who would help me by hiding me from the Germans until the war was over. There was the possibility that I could be helped by kind people who would guide me back to England where I could continue flying my missions. If unseen, maybe I could find my way to friendly territory using my map. All of these possibilities flooded my mind in the moments before I landed.

I was entering a part of war that no training could prepare me for. It was up to me. I was facing the most defining period of my young life. I never felt more alone as I landed in a dangerous world.

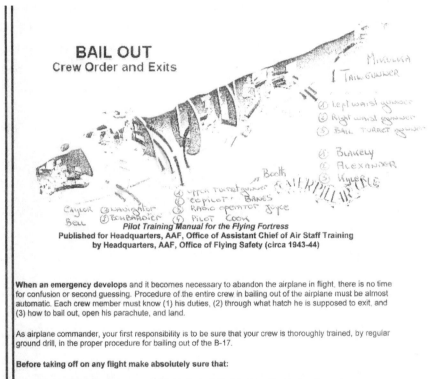

BAIL OUT
Crew Order and Exits

Pilot Training Manual for the Flying Fortress
**Published for Headquarters, AAF, Office of Assistant Chief of Air Staff Training
by Headquarters, AAF, Office of Flying Safety (circa 1943-44)**

When an emergency develops and it becomes necessary to abandon the airplane in flight, there is no time for confusion or second guessing. Procedure of the entire crew in bailing out of the airplane must be almost automatic. Each crew member must know (1) his duties, (2) through what hatch he is supposed to exit, and (3) how to bail out, open his parachute, and land.

As airplane commander, your first responsibility is to be sure that your crew is thoroughly trained, by regular ground drill, in the proper procedure for bailing out of the B-17.

Before taking off on any flight make absolutely sure that:

- An assigned parachute, properly fitted to the individual, is aboard the airplane for each person making the flight.
- The assigned parachute is convenient to the normal position in the airplane occupied by the person

Bailout Order
Courtesy of Guy Wendelen

14

Return to present…..

CANDY AND LINDSAY'S BAILOUT

Early in her pursuit of my wartime experiences Candy made up her mind that she would jump from an airplane. She realized, of course, that there would be no comparison to my one-time jump when bailing out of a crippled B-17 over enemy territory. But it would be her best attempt at feeling what I had felt. My bailout is an uncomfortable memory for me, but it happened so fast and I really hadn't time to think about it. I truly did not feel that this was a necessary step for her. However, she was dedicated to retracing and, to some degree, "reliving" my journey and, in her mind, this was a major segment. From my perspective, the bailout was only a marker, for it was the beginning of the most perilous time of my life.

Candy didn't know what she was in for. I remember her fear of heights as a child, and she wouldn't even ride a roller coaster because she hated that "falling feeling." I also recalled her talking about her anxiety whenever she flew in an airplane. But I guess she put her reservations out of her mind.

Her initial plan was to accomplish this mission on the anniversary of my jump, which would be February 4th. She made sure that this would be possible before she committed and was assured that, despite the weather that time of year, it could be done. I had no choice in the date that I jumped, but she did, so she set it.

When Candy called in advance to schedule her jump, as she had been instructed, she was told that the company did not operate in the winter due to inclement weather conditions. Because I had jumped in severe weather she decided she didn't have a problem with the climate. But the skydiving company did have a problem. That was a relief for me. She explained to them that she had been told it would be possible and stressed the importance of the date but that did not seem to matter. She had been told wrong, and that was it.

The jump could be rescheduled for a date after March. She asked for May 13th, which she knew was the date I had been flown from Barth in a B-17 after liberation. But on May 13th no flights were scheduled due to stormy weather. She then rescheduled for the following weekend, and again there was foul weather. Finally, Memorial Day weekend arrived. The weather was going to be perfect and when talking about it she would say what an appropriate weekend it would be to accomplish this goal in memory of me.

Candy's husband Brad had to work that Sunday, so he was not going to be able to accompany her. She asked her daughter, my granddaughter Lindsay, if she would like to go along for the ride. Not only did Lindsay want to ride along, she wanted to jump along with Candy! Candy called Skydive Pennsylvania in Grove City where the anticipated jump would take place and was told that it was no problem.

It was a two and one-half hour drive to the airport. As they took to the road for their destination, Candy shared her feelings with Lindsay, stating that she didn't feel excitement or fear. Candy was on a mission. She had no feelings other than the motivating force that brought her here–my jump on February 4, 1944. It was her best effort to parallel my exit from that crippled B-17 so long ago.

After they arrived, they walked into a large building where they signed in and were shown a video. They had to initial and sign a multitude of waivers. Even then it was obvious that Candy felt no anxiety or apprehension. People were buzzing in and out of the building, and the women watched as workers laid out the parachutes before folding them perfectly. The girls watched a safety video in the midst of this activity. The movie basically told them that nothing is perfect. Planes, equipment and people are not infallible so, in other words, anything could happen. People break bones and people die skydiving.

Then they proceeded to give instructions on the correct way to jump. The jumps would not be "solo," as that required classroom work, study and practice. Candy and Lindsay were therefore going to jump in "tandem," strapped tightly to their "jumpmaster" who would be behind them as they jumped as a unit from the plane. The video and those who worked there reiterated that the main thing to remember was to make sure that they would bend their legs back, up and around, to kick their jumpmaster in the butt. They didn't really have to kick him, but that was the correct position – arched back with legs back and up, knees bent and heels near their partner's butt. They both thought that seemed pretty simple.

They were signed up as Group 9 and would have a two-hour wait. It was a clear, sunny, warm day. They returned to the car and shared a cinnamon roll that they bought on the way there. Candy had her camera, and while they were waiting they took pictures of each other with the landing field in the background. Little did they know that I posed with each of them. They moved on to an area with picnic tables where they sat and watched the skydivers jump and land. Even then, Candy said she wasn't scared. Lindsay just thought everything was "awesome" (to this generation, everything was awesome), and was thrilled to have the opportunity to do it. I was proud of these confident women.

Group 8 was called, and the girls went inside to put on their gear. They were assisted in climbing into their blue "jump" suits. They then selected their helmets and goggles.

During the preparation, Candy was asked what the occasion was and she explained her purpose. She was there for one reason only and all of the waivers they signed didn't faze her. She was going to accomplish what she had set out to do during what she deemed to be a most appropriate time, Memorial Day weekend.

They slipped their arms into harnesses with attached fasteners that would be hooked to their "tandem master" when it came time to jump. There were also straps that they stepped into. All of these straps were cinched up tightly. An altimeter was put on their fingers so they could tell the altitude. They were going to jump out of the plane when it read 13,500 feet. When the finishing touches were made, their number was called and off they went across the field to meet the plane with their jump partners, and I walked out there with them. There was the four of them, two solo jumpers, and 2 video people, and it was really crammed inside a small white plane decorated with colored polka dots. I sat in the midst of all of them. No one seemed to mind.

We taxied and took off into the clear blue sky. I looked out the window as we climbed and could see my daughter and granddaughter doing the same. It was too noisy for them to talk, but Candy asked some last minute questions because she wanted to make sure she did things right. This was an important and meaningful jump to her and I was the reason for it. I was more nervous than the two of them put together. When the altimeter said 8,000 feet, one of the men opened the door and jumped out. The wind was blowing, and I think that Candy's heart had to be racing, yet there was no sign of fear that I could make out through those goggles. She had mentioned at the outset that this planned jump was in contrast to jumping out of a flak and bullet-riddled B-17 over German-occupied Belgium, only hazily similar, and critical for her to accomplish in my honor.

At those times in my life when the memories of our last mission would surface, I would wonder how I did it and how I survived mentally and physically. It was a terrifying time that I tried to forget. The recollection is quite vivid, yet I don't feel sick or anxious thinking about it, but rather I felt liberation from those feelings that had haunted me until now.

Dan, who was Candy's jumpmaster, said that when they reached 13,500 feet they would move over to the open door and put their right feet out of the plane; then rocking back and forth, count "one, two, three," and on the count of "three," simply fall out of the airplane. I watched Candy closely at this point, and simply jumped with her and steadied myself with a hand on her shoulder.

In their jumps, the girls and their partners fell free for approximately a mile, with the wind so strong that Candy, my hand on her shoulder, had trouble catching her breath. Her face became white and although told not to look at the ground, she did, so I know that it was spinning below her because I could tell she was getting dizzy. She forgot the most important part of their instruction, and Dan had to hit her leg a little to remind her of what she had been told several times to do—that was bend her legs back like she was kicking her partner in the butt. I'm sure she was embarrassed to have to be reminded about the most important thing that she was told to remember. As cool as she had been acting in the jump room, her nerves obviously had been on edge.

Then, a photographer with a camera strapped on his head appeared in front of Candy, and it was comical when she tried to smile, which only made her cheeks vibrate from the air entering her mouth. She tried to bring her hand to her cheeks to stop the shaking, but that just added to the humor of the video that, later, only she would watch in the days to come. Lindsay looked more natural, was laughing, and seemed much more comfortable than her mother.

Dan checked his altimeter, and when they reached 8,000 feet he opened the parachute, and what a jolt that was! Yes, I remember the jolt, and I watched as they swung forward and back and then drifted slowly back to earth. The air was no longer rushing and both girls commented on how peaceful it was to be floating, viewing the scenery from above as if they were "masters of the universe." Of course I also remember peacefully floating to earth, but at the time I was so frightened of what I would be facing that I didn't ponder the beauty of the countryside below.

The jumpmasters practiced preparing for landing a couple of times while everyone was drifting closer to the ground. They pulled down on the parachute cords, which slowed them way down, and they and their partners had to put their legs straight out in front of them. That was, by far, Candy's best skydiving talent. While drifting to the earth, she quietly whispered the thoughts crossing her mind. She wondered about the fact that I had jumped "solo," and if I even would have had sufficient training to compensate for the fact that, unlike she and Lindsay, I had no jumpmaster to guide me in for a landing. Candy said she could only imagine the feelings that I had experienced. If she could have heard me, I would have told her that I had very little training and I had never practiced a real jump. My bailout was a jump for my life—my only chance of survival—and I wanted to live.

Both girls ended their descent with smooth landings. They put their legs straight ahead, just as they'd been taught to do, and smoothly slid across the grass, slowing their forward motion. They touched down, completing a successful jump. It would be, as mine was, the first and last according to Candy. This event concluded another episode for her in my story.

A day after that skydive, Candy found out that a lady at a different skydiving place, who had also been making her first jump, had slipped through her harness when the parachute opened, and fell to her death. I guess this was the reason for all those waivers.

Candy wrote a poem to describe her feelings–another similarity between the two of us. As a POW, I wrote a few poems to express my thoughts. I was always embarrassed about them and never showed anyone after I arrived home. I just put them away and moved on.

A TRIBUTE

Some people thought it crazy
My jump out of a plane.
But it was to honor my father
It was heartfelt, not insane.

I thought of all those heroes
Called from good times to strife.
Who flew to fight a war
And bailed out to save their life.

When I ended my free fall
I knew I'd still be free.
Not so for those brave airmen
Captured by the enemy.

I landed so softly
In a field of grass and clover,
Full of many friendly faces
No words, "For you the war is over."

My mission was successful,
My first jump and my last.
Another small attempt
To retrace my father's past.

Candy's jump with jumpmaster

Belgium

15

THE GARDEN

I touched down in a vegetable garden, nearly unscathed from my first and only experience bailing out of a B-17. My ankle was tender, as I had twisted it on landing, but I seemed to be intact. As I removed my parachute I focused on the farm houses I had spotted while falling, now only a short distance away. There were some trees and fields around me in which I could hide. I was pretty sure I had landed in Belgium, but did not know whether I might be in "friendly territory."

I looked around and saw a young boy, maybe fourteen years old, watching me. I was pretty sure he did not speak English, so I reached into my escape kit, took out a cigarette, and offered it to him as a sign of peace. He smiled widely, and was more than willing to accept the free smoke. I hoped he could help me.

I heard voices, and a short distance away I saw two ladies walking toward me, shouting words that I could not understand. I forced a smile and tried to ask if they could help me, explaining I was an American. Winded from what I had just experienced, I tried to act calm so as not to scare them. I needed their cooperation if I was going to escape the enemy.

At a distance from the ladies I saw another boy, this one on crutches, but he ventured no closer. I understood what was transpiring, though—from all indications and motions, the ladies were going into the house to help me. They came back out carrying clothing—they were getting me civilian clothes to disguise me from the Germans! I felt a glimmer of hope, but suddenly they began screaming, crying and wringing their hands. As I turned around in the direction they were looking, my heart sank as I spotted men in German uniforms sighting their weapons on me. I raised up my arms in submission, as it was evident that I could not escape. I glanced in the direction of the civilians, now standing together, who had tried to come to my rescue, and thanked them with my eyes so as not to call attention to their attempt at help.

My role as prisoner had begun. My job as a ball turret gunner had ended.

The Germans had observed our disabled bomber and like vultures followed my parachute to the ground. I wondered how the other crew members had fared. How I wished that I could have stayed in the garden—a spot that had first appeared so far removed from the war.

16

THE ARREST AND QUESTIONING IN BELGIUM

Of course I was scared to be in the hands of the enemy, and I wondered if I would live to see another day. These particular German guards did not seem abusive, and I was poked along at gunpoint, limping on my tender ankle. The soldiers motioned for me to climb into the back of a truck, and I clumsily obliged them.

The truck I found myself riding in was a coffin truck. I was sitting on a coffin, unsure of its contents, pondering the possibility that it contained the body of a crewmate picked up on the way to grabbing me. I wondered if these soldiers would enlist my services collecting deceased fellow airmen, and figured they would. I hadn't noticed any other straggling bombers in this area, but in the panic and focus on our own dilemma there may have been many shot down that day in the same vicinity. These soldiers had zeroed in on me quickly. I hadn't a chance to hide much less attempt to escape capture. At least my parachute had fallen into the possession of those who would have helped me had the "Jerries" not shown up.

I had no idea where I would be taken or what I would face. I knew that I would be questioned, but did not know if I would be tortured, nor how much of that I could take. I decided that all I would divulge was name, rank and serial number, no matter the cost. I tried to remember everything I had learned in training about being captured. It was something I hadn't spent much time studying. We had been trained so quickly, and this part of it had not been a priority. Nor does any airman really expect it to happen to him!

And this was never supposed to happen to me. How wrong I was, and how right the German soldier had been in his words telling me that, for me, the war was over. I was now waging a different kind of battle.

In Podington, we were always concerned about the crews that didn't return, and now our own crew was a "no-show," and when the B-17s were counted back in I knew that they would be talking about us. We were now a statistic. On this particular flight, we had flown an aircraft from a different squadron. At the time, I didn't think it would make any difference, as I was never superstitious, but the way things worked out I couldn't help wondering if flying the "outsider" plane had somehow mattered. But there was no sense thinking about it, because the situation could not be changed. I had more serious things to consider.

As the truck bounced down the road and I stared out at the trees and houses, I remember praying to God for strength and for the survival of my friends and crewmates. I hoped we would all live through this. Were my comrades hiding out there somewhere? If they were, I hoped they would escape captivity. I had survived the jump, but would I be able to survive as a prisoner?

My mind was flooded with thoughts. I was young and in a dangerous place, forced to become a man in a matter of hours. No one could protect me here but me; I was alone. Flashes of home entered my mind, and the possibility that I would never see it, or my loved ones, again. But these flashed by in an instant, because I had the real world to deal with.

We finally arrived at what appeared to be a German military installation, judging by the number of vehicles and personnel in uniform. I was ordered out of the truck. This was my first encounter with the word *Raus*. My ankle was now swollen, but I was sure that it would heal. I was a little dizzy, in a dreamlike state as if I were watching myself from afar. Vehicles were arriving in the distance and one by one, I was reunited with four of my crew members. We didn't acknowledge each other, for we didn't want the Germans to know that we were part of the same crew, although they probably knew this, having watched our descent. .

We spent two days in Belgium as we were cycled in and out of dark, dreary cells for questioning. We were served only a thin soup; we relieved ourselves in buckets. I don't remember the interrogation being intense at that time. One of the guards spoke perfect English. I maintained the requisite spiel of "Sergeant John R. Kyler, Serial Number 32830356," and it flowed from my mouth time after time.

On the second day of questioning I learned from the German interrogator that our navigator was injured and in a nearby hospital; apparently he had been wounded. I wondered about the seriousness of his condition, and if he had been shot while in the plane or after he bailed out. Had he been with the crew members not yet accounted for? Might this whole story be untrue? Was it some kind of ploy by the interrogator to make me feel comfortable and open up to him? I only listened…and didn't ask questions. This was disturbing news, and I tried not to show outwardly too much concern.

Those of us shot down would be listed as "Missing in Action," until reports were filed, and in my case, the status would then be updated to "Prisoner of War." The worst report and coding that could be assigned is "Killed in Action."

The five of us—the radio operator, right waist gunner, bombardier, co-pilot and me—were together now, maybe for only a short time, awaiting processing of our transfers to a transient camp before being assigned to permanent locations. We would soon be leaving Belgium. I think back to the look in the eyes of my comrades. We had no way of knowing where we would end up, and the uncertainty generated some anxiety in each of us.

af/isd

WAR DEPARTMENT

THE ADJUTANT GENERAL'S OFFICE

IN REPLY
REFER TO

WASHINGTON

AC 201 Kyler, John R.
(15 Feb 44) PC-N 048020

21 February 1944.

Mrs. Grace Kyler,
197 Elm Street,
Salamanca, New York.

Dear Mrs. Kyler:

This letter is to confirm my recent telegram in which you were regretfully informed that your son, Sergeant John R. Kyler, 32,830,356, Air Corps, has been reported missing in action over Germany since 4 February 1944.

I know that added distress is caused by failure to receive more information or details. Therefore, I wish to assure you that at any time additional information is received it will be transmitted to you without delay, and, if in the meantime no additional information is received, I will again communicate with you at the expiration of three months. Also, it is the policy of the Commanding General of the Army Air Forces upon receipt of the "Missing Air Crew Report" to convey to you any details that might be contained in that report.

The term "missing in action" is used only to indicate that the whereabouts or status of an individual is not immediately known. It is not intended to convey the impression that the case is closed. I wish to emphasize that every effort is exerted continuously to clear up the status of our personnel. Under war conditions this is a difficult task as you must readily realize. Experience has shown that many persons reported missing in action are subsequently reported as being prisoners of war. However, since we are entirely dependent upon governments with which we are at war to forward this information, the War Department is helpless to expedite these reports.

In order to relieve financial worry on the part of the dependents of military personnel being carried in a missing status, Congress enacted legislation which continues the pay, allowances and allotments of such persons until their status is definitely established.

Permit me to extend to you my heartfelt sympathy during this period of uncertainty.

Sincerely yours,

J. A. ULIO
Major General,

SGT. J. KYLER MISSING AFTER BOMBING FORAY

Salamanca Gunner Reported Missing After Air Action Over Germany—Brother Also is Sergeant

Mr. and Mrs. David Kyler, 197 Elm street, have been notified that their youngest son, Sgt. John Roland Kyler, has been reported missing in action Feb. 4 over Germany. They received the information from Washington military officials by telegraph. He had ben on bombing missions since Jan. 21.

Sgt. Kyler was inducted into the army air corps Feb. 3, 1943 and was stationed at Miami Beach, Fla.

Last August he received his wings and sergeant's rating at a gunnery technical school in Lareda, Tex. His average of ninety-five per cent was the highest in his flight.

Four months previous Sgt. Kyler was awarded a diploma upon completion of a course in aircraft, armorers and bombardment at a technical school in Denver, Colo.

After earning his wings he was transferred to Salt Lake City, Utah. He also attended gunnery schools in Nevada and Nebraska.

Went Overseas last November

In November of last year the sergeant was sent overseas and stationed in England. His mother said she recently received a letter from him which was written Feb. 1. He wrote her that he was well.

Before his induction Sgt. Kyler was employed at the Bell aircraft plant in Kenmore.

His older brother, Sgt. Morris D. Kyler, a mechanic in the U. S. army air corps, was slightly wounded July 11, 1943 on the North African front. He returned to active duty the following month.

17

Return to present…..

RETURN TO BELGIUM

It was September 21 when their taxi arrived at the hotel in King's Cross, almost an hour earlier than scheduled, but Sara and Candy were all ready and very anxious to get going anyway. Candy was worried about the luggage weight and getting it all checked in at Heathrow so she decided to leave heavier items behind. This worry, combined with the excitement she was feeling in anticipation of the next stop on the agenda, was beginning to show, and I could see it but couldn't really calm her with a soothing word. Frustrating!

It was still dark on the ride to the airport, and Candy continued to fuss. She and her mother had experienced great difficulty with their luggage on arrival, mostly because they were not traveling light at all. I watched, helpless, as my little wife was completely bogged down, yet she kept offering to help her daughter with the bags. The backpack Candy wore was weighted down with all of the books she had crammed into it to reduce the weight of her checked bags. She winced from shoulder pain as she jerked the pack higher on her shoulders.

When it was their turn to board, the gate agent nixed the backpacks because they were too large to carry on. Candy and Sara did some rearranging and ended up checking their backpacks. It was tough for me, watching their struggles without being able to do a thing.

After they made it through security, they stopped for a bite to eat until their flight came up on the monitor; at last they could sit comfortably for a while. After a tedious three hours we finally boarded the plane.

I saw Candy write in her notebook:

> *Dad flying out of Podington in a B-17; Mom and I flying out of Heathrow in an Airbus A319. It was a hassle at the airport, but nothing like dad's flights. All we had to do was check in, go through security and wait. Seemed a pain but it would be worse to get briefed, check the armaments and man the gun in the ball turret. This experience was trivial by comparison. Our missions are different yet very connected. Now airborne for Belgium, we were seeing the English Channel where the crews tested their guns on their way to the target. This was the body of water that was such a welcome sight to the returning crews as they knew they would soon be back home at their base after a long, challenging day.*

Candy was so right; their flight was much different than my flights had been, I felt honored that they were taking this flight because of me.

We soon landed in Brussels, Belgium. The ride had been smooth, their luggage arrived quickly, and their prearranged *Taxi Bleu* was waiting when we arrived. I was relieved for them, and it made up for the frustration at Heathrow.

The two brothers who had been working with Candy for months arranging this part of our trip, Messrs. Guy and Willy Wendelen, were due to meet the girls at the hotel at six p.m. We were going to make it with time to spare, and I could see that Candy and Sara – so tense at Heathrow – were feeling some relief.

An hour later, the ladies were relaxing in the Hotel Radisson Hasselt, which was fairly new, sleekly modern, and quite comfortable. Internet access was a bonus, and there was no charge for it. The computer was Candy's tool for contacting everyone at home who would be especially concerned about how Sara was handling the travel. When they checked in, the young lady at the desk, who spoke perfect English, furnished Candy with a phone-line adapter so she could plug in her computer. All was well!

The ladies got settled in their room, and Sara was tired, so Candy and I went down to the lobby to wait for the Wendelen Brothers to arrive. We weren't there long when we spotted two men approaching the hotel, and Candy instantly realized that these were the Wendelens, and she was very happy to finally meet them in person. In fact, so was I.

I noticed that the Belgian men were carrying two large bouquets of beautiful flowers and a box of Belgian chocolates. Candy and the men exchanged hugs, and she invited them up to meet Sara. The men followed us up, and after Candy roused Sara from her light nap, they gave my wife the same welcoming hugs. We were finally meeting the men who had been corresponding with Candy for many months, and I continued to marvel at how modern technology had made their communication so quick and convenient. Willy didn't speak English, so Guy did all of the talking, and he spoke English very well indeed.

It was a joyful meeting, but it was also bittersweet, for as we had learned shortly before our departure from the States, Guy and Willy's older brother, Raimond Wendelen, had died suddenly. And I knew that Raimond had been very much involved in the research and planning for our visit. Although at this time no one remarked upon the loss, I'm sure it was on everyone's mind. I said nothing – silence had become a specialty of mine.

The four of them talked with excitement about a day they'd been planning for over nine months. Guy outlined the route we would take in two days, on Saturday, September 23, 2006.

The whole thing sounded unreal to me. Candy showed the men all the written materials and research she had brought, but they agreed they would have time to get together to read the research materials after Saturday's main event was concluded.

In order to have more room for our discussions, the ladies were invited by the brothers for coffee downstairs, and we accompanied the men to the hotel's quite comfortable café. The plans that Guy explained seemed like a dream. Guy told us the Mayor of Beringen would be offering some sort of tribute at the festivities planned by the city, and Candy asked if she should say something. Guy didn't think that it would be necessary, but

I knew that Candy would feel the need to thank everyone. I considered that these two kind men had worked hard on preparations for this visit by two strange American women, and I was humbled that all these plans were being made in my memory.

At last the group was all talked out, and it was growing late. The excitement was building for all, and it was agreed that Guy would collect the ladies at the Hotel at 9:30 a.m., two days hence.

I also knew that Ejvind and Bjoerg Jensen would be arriving tomorrow, on Friday the 22nd, and Candy would update them on the Saturday plans. Their friends, Nils and Bente Baaring, would be driving from the town of Mons in Belgium to pick them up and they would all then follow Candy and Sara, along with the Wendelen Brothers, to the town hall in the village of Beringen, a distance of only about twelve miles from our hotel in Hasselt. Candy could not wait to see Ejvind and Bjoerg Jensen again, and several times now she told her mother how excited that she was about connecting with them.

Candy expected that her mother would just love the Jensens. Candy had met them only the year before, during a visit to the sixtieth anniversary of the liberation of Stalag Luft I, one of my former POW camps – the one in Barth, Germany. (That trip to Barth had been one of her first steps in her journey to retrace my wartime path.)

This man, Ejvind Jensen, was an amazing and special person to Candy, and they had become close friends. Ejvind had explained to Candy that during the war he had helped two American airmen evade capture in Denmark. That caught Candy's attention!

After their meeting in Barth, they had continued their relationship via e-mail. Ejvind, a Dane who lived in nearby Denmark, knew what Candy was trying to achieve, and was as resolute as she in efforts to find pieces to the "John Kyler puzzle." Through his friends, Nils and Bente, Ejvind had obtained contact information for a Belgian military officer, the source of which was a library in the Belgian town of Houthalen. Ejvind had sent a letter to the librarian there, inquiring about resources that may be available to identify the crash site of my old Flying Fortress. Through the librarian, the Wendelen brothers were then contacted, and that is how they came to be present here in Hasselt on this incredible day.

In the long process of corresponding, Candy had learned from Raimond Wendelen that during World War II and to the day he died, downed Allied airplanes in this area had been his avocation and passion. To my surprise, and just as I had in Podington, I was feeling the excitement building in anticipation of actually seeing the areas that we were about to cover – areas that were tied directly with my past.

I feel it worthwhile to give some background of the events that led up to this visit; therefore, we will leave the scene in Hasselt Belgium briefly to explain how we all got here.

BACKGROUND – PIECING TOGETHER THE BELGIUM STORY

In the Spring of 2005, my daughter Candy first set foot in Europe for the purpose of visiting Stalag Luft I, a once-large former German POW camp located about 120 miles north of Berlin, in the German state of Mecklenburg-Vorpommern on the Barther Bodden, a bay of the Baltic Sea. At that time she knew little more about her father's fate than the date of his crash; she did not even know where the airplane had gone down, nor much of what happened to John Kyler thereafter. But Candy's chance meeting in Barth with the Dane Ejvind Jensen was to open a doorway to a road that would yield the answers that Candy had been seeking since that visit in 2005.

On January 8, 2006, Candy received an important email from one Mr. Kellens, a librarian in Houthalen, a small town about 80 miles northeast of Brussels, Belgium. The email was prompted by a letter that Kellens had earlier received from Candy's friend Ejvind, who wrote to Kellens, asking for the names of people in Belgium who might have the knowledge and experience to help Candy determine, with some certainty, exactly where my B-17 had crashed that fateful day in February, 1944.

Librarian Kellens really came through for my daughter, when he passed along Candy's contact information to a resource that Candy would have herself invented if she had the power: Kellens had passed her questions on to three Belgian men – Raimond, Guy and Willy Wendelen. And the Wendelen brothers, who were to communicate with Candy through Guy, sent an astonishing (to Candy) email one day that was revolutionary for my daughter.

The following are excerpts from that first email, received in January 2006 from the three Wendelen Brothers:

...Don't be surprised. We are a group of amateur researchers from Belgium and your request has been forwarded to us...

First of all: a happy New Year! If you want so, we can surely help you with all your questions concerning your father, Sgt Kyler John R, turret gunner of B-17F-100-BO Flying Fortress 42-30423 code PY-P, 92 BG – 407 BS (Podington) Operation n° 208 Frankfurt, Germany. Missing aircrew report 2237.

Candy, we know you still have a lot of questions concerning this crash:

Who was the person who talked with your father?

The location of the crash?

Did the plane explode?

What happened to the other crew members?

Lt Caylor Donald...

and perhaps many other questions.

Are you also willing to come to Belgium and talk with those who remember this crash and to see where the plane crashed?

Dear Candy, we can help you!

We have already placed an article in two local papers to become more information. There is response, but as you know everything that people say have to be checked. There is one little difficulty: there were 4 crashes in the same area. At this moment we can say Candy: there are people who remember this crash, saw the plane and saw some crew members after the crash.

If you agree with our help we want to ask if perhaps you have a picture from your father and yourself or a picture from your father in uniform and the B-17 or the complete crew.

Looking forward to hear from you very soon,

As I read this email standing behind Candy at her computer, there was no doubting the thrill that passed through her as she read it, and she could not respond quickly enough. She promptly sent the Wendelens a picture of my crew.

This was the break that she had been waiting for! It was unbelievable to her that she was reading those words. I confess that I had been less than thrilled over all this research, perhaps because you cannot so easily change a habit of over sixty years – I had filed away my memories of those years for keeps, and I was reluctant–even frightened–to be getting all that stuff back in the open, so to speak. Maybe it was better to leave it all alone! But the B-17 ride, the Barth visit and now this email from the Belgian brothers changed my attitude about the whole thing, especially Candy's rapidly forming plan to accept the Wendelens' suggestion to Candy that she "come there" to talk with eyewitnesses from that fatal day!

At this point, I knew that it was meant to be, and that I was meant to be part of it with her and Sara, even though I could only be there in spirit. It was difficult for Candy to digest the reality that someone was so willing to help her to walk where I walked, and to visit the area where my Flying Fortress came to rest. To her, it seemed too good to be true. Even though they were words on a screen, they conveyed the same enthusiasm that she felt for this project that began almost as an unattainable, impossible goal. The Wendelens were so willing to help her, a stranger with little to offer in the endeavor. She had to tell them right away that yes, she would be more than agreeable to go to Belgium to meet with those who remembered anything about her father's B-17 and his crew members. Of course she would, and so would I. She didn't know it, but I was involved in this mission as much as she was.

In her search for my past, it seemed impossible to ever find anyone who could remember anything about me for the short period of time that I was in Belgium over sixty years ago. To my daughter, that was a crucial time in my experience, a chapter in my story which she felt the strong need to pursue. She wanted to visit Belgium from the moment she realized that it was where my plane had crashed, and also the area in which all of the crew members had landed. Candy at first thought that our bomber had crashed in Germany, but after a lengthy investigation, and with the help of others, she realized that it had, in fact, crashed near Koersel, Belgium, not Germany.

I think that Candy could not believe—I certainly could not—that someone who did not even know her would want to help her in what many would consider a difficult undertaking. Of course there were those who wondered why she felt she needed to go there at all, and what she hoped to find.

Within a short time of her first message from the Wendelens, Candy began receiving prepared *statements*, made by Belgian citizens who lived in the vicinity of the crash site. Candy could tell from these statements that the people making them were in some cases well-informed about the event, and that the happenings surrounding our crash had left a lasting impression. It was also impressive that at least one witness knew the name of one of our crew members:

> *Witness 1 : <u>saw</u> a crew member hiding his parachute in "de zwarte beek" (in English, 'a small river'), and was then captured by the Germans.*

> *Witness 2 : Mikulka was hiding in a small farm and the day after the crash. They [Mr. Boelanders] gave him a coal miner passport and put him on an escape Network.*

> *Witness 3 : nearby the wood and near a small farm landed one of the crew members (perhaps your father, about 1900 meters [about a mile] from Mikulka).*

> *Witness 4 : the local farmer wives are having words about the parachute.*

> *Witness 5 : I was seven years old. I don't know anything about the War but I heard my parents often tell stories concerning a paratrooper who landed here at the farm and was captured by the German. We had his parachute. The small farm doesn't exist any longer.*

This is what the most reliable persons told us until now.

> *The distance from 1 to 2: about 1300 meters; 2 to 3: about 1900 meters*

The distance from 1 to 3: about 3200 meters

Witness 1: saw the plane circling round several times, 7 or 8 airmen bailed out.

Witness 2: saw the plane circling round several times, saw the wreck pointing the nose towards Koersel at the side of Hemelbrug.

Witness 3: from phone-talk, doesn't want to say his name. About 18.00 – 19.00 in the evening: saw 6 or 7 American airmen at Koersel City with German guards heading to Leopoldsburg (a German army place), one Belgium collaborator. The civilian people yelled at the collaborator and applauded for the American prisoners.

Witness 4 : phone-talk : heard several times the airplane, was descending from direction Koersel and crashed; Saw one airman landing in the Bosstraat, was hanging in a tree and immediately captured by the German.

Heard from two talks that the monks from Heusden have given shelter to one airman. This is going to be further investigated."

As well as the remarkable witness interviews, Candy also received a report that appeared to be a form that was completed by the waist gunner of our crew, Milo Blakely. I became intrigued by the flow of information that was being collected and forwarded to my daughter. The memory of my bailout and landing was vivid to me and I was being drawn deeply into the paths of my crew members. I found myself engrossed in every detail of the Wendelen's findings. I recalled fearing for my own life on that day but I had also been gravely concerned about the others. And now I was reading an interview given by Blakely to Mr. Gaston Matthysone, chief of the "COMETE" Escape Line in Brussels. He listed the causes of the accident as "runaway prop., oxygen out, aircraft fuel off". His commanding officer was noted as "Colonel Reid." In his summarization of the circumstances encompassing the crash he writes "we had number two engine shot out over the target and also the oxygen, so had to come down to lower altitude, were attacked by 10 enemy aircraft on our way back. The pilot lowered the landing gear and everyone was bailing out. Our interphone system was also out of order."

Milo Blakely had written his recollection of the tragic event precisely as I remembered it. I believed that the number of German fighters that he remembered attacking us was accurate. I also thought how different it would have been for me had I landed near him and taken a similar route in the Escape Line. I would have gladly given my account of the crash to the Belgian Resistance hoping to make my way back to England.

The Belgian researchers found that Blakely stayed in a camp at Daverdisse-Porcheresse in the Ardennes and on June 16, 1944, he was at Schaarbeek, Brussels, where he was hidden by a Ms. Bienfait for three days until he was taken to NAMEN where he met Angele from the COMETE Escape Line and was sent on to the Marathon Camp near Belvaux, making his way safely back to England.

In the same message containing the report, it was noted that Thomas Mikulka, our tail gunner, was hidden in Brussels by Ms. Anne Brusselmans. The Wendelens were in possession of a picture and a report of his interrogation also taken by Mr. Matthysone.

In a separate update received from Candy's Belgian friends, it was mentioned that a visit was made to the cloister of Heusden and the monks stated that Father Bertilius, now deceased, had been active in an escape line but they had no further information. The researchers were referred to Fr. Bertilius's former friend, Mr. Inpanis, who confirmed that he, together with Fr. Bertilius and the brothers Claes, were involved in the Resistance. It was believed that Blakely received help from Bertilius when being placed in the escape line.

Another message from the Belgian researchers during the months leading up to the visit contained a witness report from Mr. Schepers who remembered hearing a plane flying over and seeing a man landing in a parachute in a tree near his home. He recalled 2 flight jackets and a pair of shoes hidden in the straw. The airman in the tree was our radio operator, Jay Joyce. After we were captured, I recall him telling me about his landing in a tree. As far as the jackets, Jay was alone when he landed so they must have belonged perhaps to two of our other crew members.

In this same message was an interesting interview from Mr. Theunis who lived about 1 kilometer from the crash site. He indicates that he didn't see the plane crash but remembers that the track from the B-17 was deep and as he approached the wreck the track was less deep indicating that the landing gear had broken off while crashing. He had been told that one of the wheels was lying in the field but was unaware of the exact location. At the time there was no one around the wreck.

Guy Wendelen located and sent my daughter a report that he found in a book from the army library of our B-17 crash in Koersel on February 4, 1944. It contained additional crash information to include map number and aircraft details. "Anti-aircraft" was the reason given for the crash and all of the crew members, positions and status was also included. It seemed so strange to read my name followed by "MIA" status. A puzzling detail of the report was the reference to our last mission as "Frankfurt Nickname Margriet". Neither the Wendelens nor my daughter knew the origination of this name that appeared to be relevant to our bomber. It was not the name of the mission and was another piece of the puzzle that they would try to solve. I knew that it was not the name of our plane and had no idea what generated the mention of it in this listing.

Another uncertainty that I had, the more I contemplated this report, is the reason for the crash. I am not so sure now that it was anti-aircraft fire that was the true reason for the downing of our aircraft. Thinking back... the fighter planes picked us up before we reached cloud cover and when I bailed out I remember jumping through the clouds. The German flak batteries were aiming by radar because of the blizzard conditions so they really wouldn't have been able to see us. Perhaps it wasn't them who made the initial strike on our bomber. I had never given in-depth thought of our plight before this, as I never looked at any reports until now. It didn't matter because basically it doesn't change the outcome.

The intrigue was building as more and more information surfaced. Candy's dream would soon be realized when she visited the area. I almost felt like I was 20 years old again as the awareness of my past experience in Belgium was heightened.

There was a question whether permission would have to be granted for Candy and her mother to enter the area if it was on military land. She had written to the Belgium Embassy in Washington, D.C., and contacted Bauduoin Litt. He was another person in the chain who was more than willing to assist in whatever way that he could. Candy sent him my Missing Air Crew Report – a report that I had never seen which now piqued my interest in the fates of all of those on board our ship on that fateful day. Why didn't I look these guys up when I had the chance – when we were all still young and things were fresh in our minds?

It turned out that Candy did not need permission to enter the area.

Jetty Cook is another person who went out of his way to assist my daughter, sharing his expertise in World War II aviation history and his first hand experience in Belgium, having been helped to freedom by the Belgian Resistance. He saw a letter that Candy had written in the 92nd Bomb Group Newsletter and took the time to contact her, assisting her immensely in her endeavor. Lt. Col. Cook (USAF, retired) meticulously went through my Missing Air Crew Report after Candy sent it to him. He provided her with priceless advice and information utilized in the planning of this trip.

One thing that she would learn throughout her venture is the fact that there are so many kind people willing to help a stranger. I would be forever grateful to them from afar.

Early in September Candy received an e-mail from Guy Wendelen to finalize the itinerary of her and her mother's days to be spent in Belgium. He regretted to inform her that his brother Raimond, had passed away. She was heartbroken, as she had lost a friend that she would never have the pleasure of meeting. Suddenly, the planned visit to Belgium seemed unimportant to her. She wrote and explained to Guy that she would understand if, under the circumstances, she and her mother would have to cancel their visit. He responded by saying that if they did not carry on as planned Raimond's efforts would be lost. As difficult as it might be for them, the Wendelen's gave of their time and took over the final details of our visit – a visit from individuals who they had never met before. Perhaps it was a good diversion for them, but they were still grieving for the great loss of their brother and it had to be very painful for them to persevere in his absence.

Little did any of them – Candy, Sara, Guy or Willy – know, but they were doing the right thing. Raimond was given the chance, as I was, to oversee the business he had left unfinished: the meeting of our families. Although both our presences would be undetected, together we could observe, proudly, that his wishes would be carried out exactly as he would have asked his brothers in preparing for my wife and daughter's (and my) upcoming visit. The families would be coming together in memory of John Kyler, a flyer from the war, and in memory of Raimond Wendelen, the man who studied and catalogued the exploits and fates of those flyers, so many years later.

Op zoek naar informatie over vliegtuigcrash

KOERSEL-STAL - Raymond Wendelen (63) uit Hechtel is op zoek naar de ware toedracht van een vliegtuigcrash met een B-17 boven Stal-Koersel in 1944. De dochter van een bemanningslid, Candy Brown uit New York, zit immers met heel wat vragen over het vliegtuigongeval en zij komt binnenkort naar ons land.

Raymond Wendelen is op zoek naar getuigen van de vliegtuigcrash uit '44.

Op 4 februari 1944 werd de Amerikaanse bommenwerper neergehaald door de Duitse luchtafweer. De bemanningsleden konden tijdig het vliegtuig verlaten. Gewoonlijk bevinden zich aan boord van een dergelijk toestel tien bemanningsleden. Eén zou op slag dood geweest zijn, een andere zou in het ziekenhuis gestorven zijn. Onder de bemanningsleden bevond zich ene John R. Kyler, de koepelschutter van de B-17. Hij landde op een boerenerf waar hij werd opgevangen door een mevrouw of juffrouw. Die zou hem iets te drinken halen, maar voor ze terug was, was John R. Kyler al opgepakt door de Duitsers.

De dochter van John R. Kyler, Candy Brown, zou graag een antwoord krijgen op heel wat vragen als ze naar ons land komt, meer dan zestig jaar na de feiten. Haar vader is ondertussen overleden. Raymond somt de vragen op: wie is de persoon die destijds John R. Kyler heeft opgevangen? Zijn er personen die zich de crash nog herinneren? Is het toestel ontploft? Wat is er met de wrakstukken van de B-17 gebeurd en met de andere bemanningsleden?

Wie informatie heeft of wil meewerken aan het ontvangst, kan terecht bij Raymond Wendelen: 011-73 26 69.

PVM

Newspaper articles soliciting witnesses to B-17 crash
4 February, 1944
Courtesy of Guy Wendelen

Vliegtuigcrash in WO II

BERINGEN – De broers Raymond, Willy en Guy Wendelen hangen een waas van geheimzinnigheid over hun speurwerk naar de crash van een B-17-bommenwerper. Die is op 4 februari 1944 in Stal neergehaald door de Duitsers.

► De broers Wendelen zoeken informatie over de crash van de B-17 in Stal.

De broers zoeken naar getuigen van deze crash of personen die er iets kunnen over vertellen. De zoektocht is in gang gezet door de vraag van de Amerikaanse Candy Brown wiens vader John R. Kyler een van de bemanningsleden was. Ook over hoe deze vraag bij de broers terechtkwam, doen ze vaag. "We kunnen enkel zeggen dat bibliothecaris Kellens van Houthalen ons vroeg opzoekwerk te doen", aldus de broers. "John R. Kyler was koepelschutter van de B-17. Hij werd na de crash opgevangen op een boerderij. Vrijwel onmiddellijk werd hij door de Duitsers opgepakt. Zijn dochter wil meer weten over deze gebeurtenissen. Haar vader is ondertussen wel overleden.

Als onze speurtocht wat oplevert, dan komt Candy Brown naar hier." We spreken in Stal af op een neutrale plaats want de broers willen absoluut niets loslaten over de plaats waar de bommenwerper neerstortte. Ze hebben daar hun redenen voor: "Wij willen niet door andere speurders voor de voeten gelopen worden." Veel laten ze niet los over wat ze tot nog toe aan gegevens hebben verzameld. "De B-17 vloog van Frankfurt terug naar Podington (GB) en werd boven Stal door het Duitse afweergeschut Flak neergehaald", vertellen ze. "Het vliegtuig is na contact met de grond nog 300 meter verder gegleden. Brokstukken zullen we wellicht niet meer vinden." De broers Wendelen willen ook nog kwijt dat de boerderij ondertussen is afgebroken. Info bij Raymond op 011 73 26 69. (MV)

Willy and Raimond Wendelen at Crash Site
Courtesy of Guy Wendelen

Caption: **Articles found at crash site**
Courtesy of Guy Wendelen

Now, back in Belgium – PART 2...

After the arrangements were discussed, and the girls said their goodbyes to Guy and Willy, they went back to their room, obviously, both feeling anxious about the next day. Candy and Sara both sent e-mails home letting people know that they were now in Belgium, that they had met with Guy and Willy, and that their plans had been confirmed. Those at home would want to know that they arrived safely and, particularly, that their mom was doing just fine.

Candy and Sara (and I) would have the next day, Friday, to relax and rest up while waiting for Candy's friends, Ejvind and Bjoerg. That was another unreal component of the trip to her – the fact that she was actually going to meet Ejvind again to thank him personally for the efforts that he put into her mission, and the fact, also, that he was going to be able to share in the results that had been developing since they had met in Barth. Candy told Sara that she would be happy just to *see* Ejvind and Bjoerg and to be able to give them big hugs. She felt so fortunate all the way around. Of course the bit Candy had been told about Ejvind's war days – helping downed Allied airmen – explained to me instantly the kind of man Ejvind was and why he was interested in the current expedition.

Friday arrived, and Candy and Sara walked around town checking out the area. In their walk, they noticed a grocery store that they would go back to later to pick up some things they might want to take with them Saturday because they probably would not have a chance to eat. It was important, especially for Sara, to eat when she took her medication so it was wise to think ahead. Candy didn't want her mom, or herself, to grow faint from not eating on time.

Meals had become an issue for Saturday because Candy wanted to pack so much stuff into that single day, and one "extra" in particular was creating a problem: Candy wanted to make a side-trip to visit a war museum in Leopoldsburg, a place which she felt was relevant to retracing my steps. In order to squeeze in the time to visit the museum, something had to give, and that "something" was going to be lunch time!

The two ladies ate a late lunch at the hotel and looked forward to the arrival of Ejvind and Bjoerg. They went to their room for a little while. They then enjoyed their dessert, which was the delightful Belgian chocolates that Guy and Willy gave them. They were rationing them to make them last.

After lunch, the ladies left the restaurant and stopped at the grocery store to buy crackers, apples, and water for the next day. They walked around town for awhile, then went back to the hotel, and it was getting pretty late when there was a knock on the door. Finally Candy's Danish friends had arrived! She was so happy to be able to hug them. She then surprised Ejvind with a New York State license plate to add to his collection. I was happy for her because it was apparent how much she wanted to repay Ejvind for the role he played in making her dream become reality. He was extremely pleased and gave her another big hug.

Candy was very pleased that her mother was finally able to meet these people that she had talked about so much. After meeting them, Sara decided that she was going to turn in for the night rather than join them for coffee. She was tired and wanted to retire for the night.

Everyone was supposed to be at the Beringen Town Hall at 10 a.m. the next day, and Ejvind called the Baaring's to advise them of the time so they could follow. After a pleasant conversation over coffee, Ejvind, Bjoerg, and Candy said "good night" and went to their rooms, looking forward to the big day tomorrow. Sara was already asleep, but it would be a miracle if Candy could fall asleep with her mind so excited with the promise of tomorrow. I think I knew the feeling.

SEPTEMBER 23RD

Sara and Candy woke very early the next morning and went to the dining room to find a large and wonderful variety of breakfast dishes. Ejvind and Bjoerg soon joined them for breakfast. All returned to their rooms and agreed to meet downstairs by 9:30 a.m.

I remained downstairs and saw Ejvind sitting in the lobby when Guy and Willy arrived on schedule. Soon Bjoerg joined the group. Candy and Sara followed shortly thereafter. Then Nils and Bente showed up, and they (we) were off. The arrival at the Beringen Town Hall aroused many emotions in all of us. I could see how overwhelming that it was for my two family members, and looking on, I felt proud that everyone was gathered in recognition of my crew. The Mayor, the townspeople, Raimond's daughters, and others who I know that Candy had looked forward to meeting, filled the Town Hall. Candy also met Dirk Decuypere, an aviation archeologist. She had been corresponding with Mr. Decuypere via e-mail regarding the visit.

The American and Belgian flags were flying. It was unbelievably uplifting to think that my daughter and wife and the Wendelens – were responsible for these people, this town, remembering who Candy termed "the heroic Allied airmen and the very gallant Belgian patriots," whose sacrifice for our freedom should never be forgotten." The Mayor spoke in Flemish and then in English. I heard my name spoken, and although I didn't feel worthy, it still warmed my heart and I knew it was right for me to be in attendance. It wasn't just about me – I was a representative of the thousands of men, like me, and that's what this was all about - remembering.

$$*\qquad*\qquad*\qquad*$$

Recollections of Richard Heyligen regarding the day the bomber landed in his village were read in Flemish by his daughter, Ann.

RICHARD HEYLIGEN'S STATEMENT – (ENGLISH TRANSLATION)

B-17 crash

"It was Friday, February 4, 1944, between 13:00 and 13:30 hours. After dinner, I walked back to school. I didn't have a bike. It was snowing and there were also bright intervals. I was twelve years old and in the sixth year's course. Our house was about 1 km from the centre. Then I heard the sound of airplanes coming easterly, they were returning from Germany.

I saw big bombers, silhouettes like flying fortresses . I had a small book from the Germans with the silhouettes of all the different airplanes that time, so I could easily identify them. I saw several formations.

My eldest sister, 34 years old and married, lived next to my school. We watched the planes and there was one bomber left behind and attacked by German fighters. We took shelter under the style of the front door, afraid of the bullets that could got lost. The plane descended in circles. It was a big airplane. We also saw parachutes. The airmen bailed out, accept two crew members (this

I heard afterwards). The plane made a forced landing on the pastures of de valley called "de Zwarte Beek"(the black stream). The lessons at school started at 13:30 hours and I went back to school. In the class there were only a few pupils present. The others went looking for the crashed airplane. In the afternoon they returned dropwise and I thought that the teacher was going to give them a blame but no, on the contrary, our teacher Mister Schoemans was very curious and asked the pupils to tell him everything about the crashed plane. They told they saw the plane lying in pieces, paratroopers picked up by the Germans and so on…

After school, about 16:00 hours, I went back home to tell everything to my parents. My mother told me that they came to get Jules because there was one parachutist hiding in the small forest at the "Bosstraat" and there wasn't anyone who could communicate with the airman. Louis, son of Jozef Vanschooren, knew our Jules had finished high school at Beringen and that he was able to speak a little bit English. So Louis came searching for Jules to help him. My brother immediately agreed. I told my mother, knowing Jules, he was going to bring the American to our home. Jules was called up for duty in 1940. When he was 17 years old he was reservist and remained for three months at France. He told me his experiences every evening at bedtime while we had to sleep, we shared the same bedroom. At home we were 8 children (7 at home). Jules didn't knew danger. My mother was afraid because everyone who helped the allied would be punished by the Germans .

At nightfall he came home together with the American. Both were benumbed, it has been snowing. The whole afternoon they have been hiding in the wood while the Germans were looking for the airmen. At the edge of the wood there was a pasture where the American has landed and immediately he ran into the wood to hide. Meanwhile, Jozef Vanschooren, a farmer, was trying to make disappear the parachute. His son, Louis, came looking for my brother Jules to help. So together they kept hiding till the evening while the Germans were looking for the airmen. After a while when all became quiet, Thomas Mikulka took off his overcoat to wear a civil coat for not attracting too much attention. At the farm they took a pitch-fork and dressed like farmers they came to our home. At home, Thomas took off his uniform to warm up while my mother was baking bacon and eggs to eat. We were farmers and we had enough food. Thomas wasn't very talkative and perhaps a little bit suspicious but he told us his name and he showed us a white handkerchief with the sketch of Belgium and environs. He pointed us a place at the French border and if he could get there, he knew how to get back to England. For us this was a difficult task to bring him there because the distance through the Ardennes up to France was about 200 km. Tommy went to sleep in the front room. It was forbidden to go out at evening and the problem was how to travel safely at night. This was possible if Thomas could get a miner's passport. Fortunately Thomas had 6 photos and we only had to make a passport. Our cousin, Albert Boelanders, was watchman at the coal mine and he could help us. So Jules went to Albert to ask for help. Meanwhile Louis Vanschooren came to visit Thomas to see if everything was all right but Thomas was sleeping and my father, who didn't want to have much visit, told Louis that someone had picked up Thomas and that he didn't knew where they were going to.

Our Jules told everything to Albert Boelanders and Albert told that he could help Thomas to get away with help from the resistance. In the morning Thomas received my dad's new shoes and left through the pastures, over the stream, to Stal (village) to our uncle's farm. We received his address: T.J. Mikulka, Bertsch 329 w, Lansford,. Pennsylvania.

Meanwhile members of the resistance arrived at Jef's farm to pick up Thomas and to bring him to Kwaadmechelen. There was a funeral in our neighbourhood and Jules had to bear the coffin and I should take the garland. Jules decided first to go Stal to see if everything was all right. So we were waiting and waiting... I was afraid there was something wrong. Finally he turned up and told us what had happened; they were sitting in the kitchen when suddenly two collaborators came knocking at the door. The young men in the kitchen took to flight to the barn while my aunt went outside to stop the collaborators. They came looking for potatoes and my aunt told them to go to another farmer and she pointed them to a neighbouring farm. They left while a man of the Resistance and myself were sitting by the stove. Then it was time to escort Tommy to Kwaadmechelen. He had to bike but he never had been biking before. He only made two falls. He remained 3 weeks at Kwaadmechelen because he didn't want to give the code word and without this code word England wasn't willing to pick him up because they thought he could be a German spy. Thomas was suspicious and thought he was in bad company but finally he admitted. Then they went to Brussels (surroundings of Brussels) where he took a plane back to England. We listened to the BBC (British Broadcasting Corporation) to receive some news from Tommy. It was forbidden to listen to the radio and the messages were encoded but then suddenly we heard; Mikulka arrived.

We were happy to hear this news but now the problems started for us: someone in our neighbourhood saw that Jozef Vanschooren had been hiding a parachute and told this to a few collaborators and very soon the Germans appeared. They picked up Jozef to bring him to the German Headquarter at Leopoldsburg where he was interrogated and even beaten. But Jozef didn't tell them anything and he maintained he knew nothing. We were very afraid that Jozef told everything and that it could be our turn to be questioned. I was 12 years old and my father was afraid I would easily speak and my brother Jules surely would be arrested. So my brother and I had to go into hiding at Hasselt to my godmother, Rosa Aerts, Prinsenstraat 14. The woman who had spread the rumour about the parachute has been confronted with Jozef Vanschooren and she withdrew her accusation and Jozef was released. Afterwards there still were stories told about the airman and the parachute and when a pupil at school on the playground asked if we had been hiding an airman at home we had to deny everything. But the Germans were resolute and in June, Jozef Vanschooren was arrested again. Our Jules and I had to go into hiding again. This time we went to Ukkel near Brussels, Chaussée d'Alsemberg 658, to the Kirchoff family, acquaintances. Of course it was forbidden to come outside and only at night could we get some fresh air at the inner court. We stayed there for a week until Jozef was released. We were very thankful that Jozef was a real patriot and resolute. We received a telegram that our mother was cured and this was the code that everything was all right.

At school I was reported ill and there were examinations just before the vacation but still I managed to obtain 70/100 although I didn't do all the tests. Meanwhile we hid Tommy's clothes and not too close from our home. When all became quiet, we kept the uniform close to our house and in summer when the beans were full-grown I suspended the uniform between the beans to give it some fresh air and so that nobody could see it. We gladly wanted to keep the uniform until the liberation. I removed the badges and my father told me to burn them. Mikulka was wearing an undershirt, drawers and on it a kaki shirt and trousers. On it a blue wooly suit with electric wires with plugs on the legs, arms and belly and on it an overall. He also had high shoes of pressed wool with wires and on it boots with thick fur on the inside. We all kept these clothes till the liberation. The first liberators offered money for the uniform but we kept is as souvenir. Later on, the uniform was several times used on stage. We were extremely happy when finally liberation was a fact; we sustained many pangs of death between February and September and now we were free. My brother enlisted in the army (volunteer). There wasn't a regular army and he was incorporated to the English army. He served under Montgomery. He received a book with all the missions from the allied and I copied:

4th February

4939 ton of bombs dropped on Frankfurt, Germany-over 350 heavy bombers of the 8th A. F.

My brother Georges also joined the army (volunteer). The Belgium army was yet organized and he got his training in Ireland because the war wasn't officially over yet. My brother Jules wrote several times to Mikulka but he didn't receive an answer."

/signed/

Richard Heyligen

*   *   *   *

It was an amazing recollection followed by Guy's explanation of how he and his brothers became involved in Candy's mission to retrace my past. She and her mother were given gifts, which I knew they surely would treasure (Candy a Beringen Bear and Sara chocolate bears and a special bottle of liquor from Beringen with glasses displayed on a round mirror).

Candy gave a brief thank-you for such a warm welcome, and then read a statement that was written by her friend, Jetty Cook, which expressed his sentiments concerning the Belgian people; and, Candy thought, were most appropriate to convey to those present. It read:

I want to express my deep and everlasting appreciation to the many very brave Belgian patriots who risked so much to assist me and other airmen to evade capture and to safely return to our families. I, and thousands of other Allied airmen, owe the Belgian people a great debt of gratitude for their bravery and kindness. But, they shall always remain very dear in our hearts.

Candy and Sara were experiencing first hand, in different times and under very different circumstances, exactly why Jetty felt the way that he did about these special people.

It was especially touching when Raimond's daughters, Olga and Vera, presented a beautiful plaque that their father had made for Candy and Sara. It was a very emotional day for the two sisters. Their father's presence was greatly missed. My daughter and wife could relate to their sorrow. Both of their fathers should have been present, and they would have been happy to know that we were, indeed, present in spirit to witness this wonderful touching occasion. Their love of their fathers – Raimond and me – was the reasons that they were there. The plaque that Raimond crafted had my picture in the middle of a circular piece that was found at the crash site, and he had written the names of the crew members, the serial number and the place and date of the crash. It really was beautiful and I told him so and thanked him for paying such a wonderful tribute to my crew members and myself. I appreciated it and the girls loved it and commented how they will cherish the masterpiece and the memorable day. I wish that they could have met Raimond. It was enjoyable to watch the development of the events with him. He had worked so hard for this day, and I was happy that he could witness how grateful and astounded that my wife and daughter were by everything that was occurring. We were both proud of our families and delighted that they were united in such a heartfelt way.

There were also pieces of my B-17, their authenticity having been previously verified by part number, that were given to Candy and Sara. Raimond proudly recalled the day he and his brothers, Guy and Willy, recovered these precious keepsakes. I was astounded that there were actually remnants of my plane.

After the heartwarming affair at the Town Hall, they were graciously transported to the crash site by drivers in World War II jeeps provided by the Hell on Wheels Association. They were driven as close to the area as possible, as the ground became swampy and muddy. They jumped out of the jeeps and Willy had brought some big rubber boots which Candy slipped on, replacing the sandals that she had worn. They came up to her knees and served the purpose, but they did look a little comical. She wanted to be able to go where she needed to go and not worry about mud and water. They walked in a line and Guy pointed out the "Black Creek" when they got to that area. Raimond knew this area well and you could tell that he wished that he was with everyone, physically. The Black Creek was mentioned in the reports of the crash. Guy explained the direction that the plane came from with the landing gear lowered. There had been grooves in the ground at one time, and it was told that one of the wheels had come off in the field. I saw the final resting place of our broken bomber, and it was quite a sensation to think back about the happenings of that fateful day.

I could visualize the occurrence as Guy's explanation continued, and imagine how snowy and frigid it was on that day in February. Candy and Sara walked in the area where our B-17 had come through. Candy was happy to think that she could tell my pilot, Larry Cook, who she believes is the sole surviving crew member, that she walked where his B-17 had come to its resting place 62 years ago before being dismantled by the Germans. She talked about the possibility that some of my gear could have been strewn out of the plane into this very place. She and Sara agreed that they felt a closeness to me just by being there – a closeness to me when I was a young man in another time.

We moved on to the next stop in the path of Tom Mikulka, the tail gunner of our crew. Richard Heyligen had explained in his statement the critical role that his brother, Jules, played in Mikulka's road to freedom. He was now showing everyone the meadow in which Thomas landed, where the airman and Jules hid in the woods until dark, the field that they walked across and the Heyligen house, which he stayed in overnight. They all entered the home, which is now occupied by Jules and Richard's sister. She welcomed them, and Richard told of "Tommy" being in the very room that they were sitting. The table was not the same but it was the same place. They were led into the bedroom and it was astounding to see the original bed that Mikulka had slept in on his first night in Belgium – his first night as an Evader and I believe it possibly to also be young Jules' first night as a Helper. It was very special to have the Heyligen family contributing so much to this incredible journey. Candy made the statement that it was hard to explain, but even though she did not know Thomas Mikulka, she felt as though he was family.

I told Raimond, as we oversaw our loved ones combining to share the history of my bomber and crewmates that I wondered what happened to Tommy Mikulka and the others who I never saw again. I wished that he could have come along with us. This was so exciting for me to see where he had traveled after he bailed out. He was a good man and I enjoyed his company whenever we were together. Raimond and I were drawn there by our families. I was grateful to him and his brothers for helping my daughter and her mother be there too. I told him how impressed I was with the plaque, to think he would create such a masterpiece for people who he did not know.

Our next stop would be to the area where the radio operator, Jay Joyce, landed in a tree. The witness recalled that my buddy, Jay, had given him gum and cigarettes. He pointed to the place he remembered seeing him land, and gave his account of what he remembered of that day in February, 1944. Candy had been in touch with Jay's wife, Bea. She had been told by her husband that he, in his parachute, had landed in a tree. The Germans saw him descending and were there immediately to free him from the tree. He was liberated yet restrained. That was the beginning of his experience as a prisoner of war. Candy suspected that he and I may have seen each other when taken to Leopoldsburg, as there was not a large distance between landing sites, and she reasoned that, more than likely, we would have been picked up by the Germans at approximately the same time. She was exactly right in her assumption. I remember it well – the group of us coming together and being surrounded by civilians, as well as our guards, before we were locked up.

We moved on to the region that would arouse many deep memories. What a feeling that came over me, and I explained to Raimond how the memories of this significant place and the day that I landed there are still etched in my mind. I could recall standing there as a 20-year-old boy. I listened as the events of that day were explained by two different witnesses. The first expressed his memory of my landing in a garden. He saw me from a distance, as he had a broken leg. He was a young teenager and the ladies who lived in the house (gone now) went in to get me civilian clothes. It was upsetting to them when they returned to see the Germans arriving to lay claim. They screamed and cried. I remember this vividly and knew exactly where I stood at the time.

Candy commented how this witness account matched the story that I had told my sister, Helen, the day I returned from the war. The witness mentioned landing in a garden and the ladies crying and being extremely upset when the Germans arrived on the scene. The second witness showed the area in which he remembered seeing me land. It had been a garden then and he was the first one to see me. There was a large tree there, which was a landmark. He mentioned that I had given him a cigarette and, as stated previously, the Germans quickly zeroed in on me and took me away at gunpoint. I couldn't help but stare at these two men who I had been listening to, thinking of the day that they saw that young airman fall into the garden. My wife and daughter were gazing at someone that I looked at as a young boy, over 62 years ago.

What an extraordinary feeling; and, even though it was decades ago, I could visualize these two boys. The boy, now man, that I gave the cigarette to, became familiar, as I stared. It is a day that I will never forget, all those years ago, perpetuating this memorable day for all involved. I could show Raimond exactly where I landed and my ladies were walking through that area. He was so pleased to know because he had studied these grounds so completely when preparing this tour of the area. Sara and Candy were walking my route, and it was so apparent that they felt my presence every step of the way. They were seeing through different eyes, in a different time – the same people, in the same place.

The next and last stop on the agenda was the museum at Leopoldsburg. The building was a German hospital during the war and would most certainly have been the hospital that our navigator, Donald Caylor, would have passed away in. I did learn that later in the war. Donald was wounded when our plane was hit and died shortly after, apparently from the wounds inflicted as he operated from his navigator position. As we entered the building and looked down the hallway, I thought of Donald being brought in, and how sad it was for him to die alone. If only I could have been there for him. I was overcome with desolation. It had to be heartbreaking for his family to learn of his death, and torture to think of his loneliness so far away. I understand, through Candy's investigation, that his body was eventually repatriated to his hometown of Horton, Kansas. Mrs. Caylor, Donald's mother, visited Larry Cook, our pilot, after the war to see if he could tell her anything about her son, but he had no knowledge of what had transpired after he bailed out, as Don had not been with him. I had no idea at the time either. She was looking for answers, certainly, to try to find closure. That could easily have been my mother trying to find answers regarding me.

The area at Leopoldsburg would have been the place in Belgium that I spent two days after being captured. Driving by the familiar area sustained my thoughts. It was the beginning of my time as a prisoner of war. It started with my landing in the garden and continued to that very location – the reasons that Candy felt they needed to be there. It is why it was so important for them to walk and view the different significant areas in Belgium. There was a gracious guide who explained interesting facts about the history of the area and the building. Candy was pleased with her decision that they should forego lunch to make sure that they had time to stop in Leopoldsburg. It made this tour of key areas involved in my travels in Belgium complete.

The day ended with refreshments at Raimond's house, and the meeting of his lovely wife, Louise, and talk of the events of the day. The hospitality shown by this family was touching, when realizing what a void that they were suffering in the loss of their husband, father, and brother. I wished that I could tell them that Raimond and I were both reviewing the day with them, and how proud that we were of them in carrying on for us. It was obvious to our daughters, Candy, Olga, and Vera, that there were many similarities in their fathers. Raimond's collection of artifacts was indicative of his passion for World War II aircraft and memorabilia, displaying a propeller as a lawn ornament in his yard, as well as many other objects that he had collected. My wife and daughter were glad to see Raimond's vast collection and to hear about him. I could tell that it made Raimond feel proud to see how delighted everyone was with his treasures. I think that our presence was felt, and Candy commented to Raimond's family that he had to be very satisfied and proud with the outcome of the unforgettable day.

Returning to the hotel, everyone was very tired. The day was over, and what a huge letdown it was, that was unexpected to the ladies. The day was everything that Candy dreamed it would be and more, and it was inevitable that it would end and she mentioned this. She told her mother that she didn't like how she was feeling, but she thought that it was normal. She had looked forward to this day for so long, and the only way it could have been better, she felt, is if Raimond and her dad were there. Little did they realize that we were spectators of the entire day's events.

Guy advised the girls that he would come over Sunday to discuss the proceedings of the previous day and answer any questions that they had. They had that to look forward to. It would be good for them to rehash everything. Candy made a notebook of my memorabilia that she wanted to give him, and she had a book and a Zippo lighter that she had gotten for him and Willy. It was the same book that she had given Ejvind. She also had a lighter for Ejvind that she would give him Sunday as well. It was evident that Ejvind was in his glory, riding in the WWII jeep and talking with everyone. How appropriate and gratifying for him and Bjoerg to be present for such a rewarding day. Bjoerg, Nils and Bente took such good care of my wife and she just loved them. Ejvind and Candy agreed that they shared their own story in the planning and culmination of their efforts.

Guy arrived, as planned, Sunday, with his notebook of maps and information that he had used in planning the previous astounding day. Candy ordered her first beer in Belgium, Jupiler, and it appeared to taste pretty good to her. Ejvind and Bjoerg also joined them. She gave Guy the notebook she put together for him and the copies of my Missing Air Crew Report and POW notebooks, as well as the engraved Zippo lighters for him and Willy. The book, *Belgium Rendezvous – 127*, was written by Yvonne Daley-Brusselmans and Tom Mikulka's picture is in it. She thought that Guy would like it. She had told the Heyligens about it and said she would order them one when she arrived home and send it to them.

It seemed that Guy and Candy felt the same sort of letdown. Here they had been e-mailing and planning for months. They put so much effort into this occasion, and now it was over. Candy was grateful for the papers that Guy gave her to add to her information. I was grateful to learn so much more about our B-17, and the routes that some of my comrades had taken in Belgium. Guy was going to leave, but assured the girls that he would be back Monday night to say goodbye. They were glad that they would get to see him one more time before leaving. Ejvind and Bjoerg were going to leave Monday morning to go to Mons. Candy was already starting to feel sad about that, too. She gave Ejvind the engraved Zippo lighter with the Air Force insignia. She thought it would be good to put with his collection of 8ᵗʰ Air Force memorabilia. Of course, Ejvind was delighted with the gift.

They went to the hotel and ordered lunch at the bar. This was their last day together. Bjoerg had discovered a museum close by when she went for a walk, so they all decided to go to the museum for their last day. Candy and Sara were thankful and happy for the great company they were in. Candy told them that she wished that she could hold onto these days they had spent together. They walked through the museum, went outside and took some pictures, and then made their way back to the hotel. Ejvind had stopped to tell a stranger who had noticed his 8ᵗʰ Air Force patch about the incredible meeting with my family, and how they had spent the previous day. It began to rain a little, and Candy remarked that this was appropriate given the way she was feeling. They were all exhausted, and rightly so, from the excitement, which could be draining both mentally and physically, but they would not have changed a moment of it. They said their good-nights and promised that they would see each other in the morning before they took off.

They had their breakfast the next morning and Ejvind was planning on leaving about 10 a.m. He and Bjoerg stopped by our room to say goodbye, and Ejvind wanted to take a couple of pictures of the girls with the beautiful plaque. They hugged and said their goodbyes. Candy waited a few minutes and then told her mother that she just had to go downstairs to see them off. Candy and I rushed downstairs and she bid them her last farewell, which greatly saddened her. Their parting gave me feelings of melancholy, as well.

On their last day in Belgium, Candy and Sara took one final afternoon walk around the area. The reality of them having to leave Belgium was gradually sinking in. They packed their bags; everything was in order. In the evening, they ate dinner in the hotel restaurant for their last meal, and then went to their room to wait for Guy to call. It was hard for me to see them so depressed, but I certainly understood.

I am so grateful to have been a part of a venture that was really about me. I see things about my life more clearly now because of these helpful Belgians and their efforts. I can understand completely my daughter and wife's fondness of the people who had come together for me. It was a pleasure to meet and travel with Raimond. At least I could personally thank him for my family and me, and he could feel the same pride in his own efforts.

The bouquets were still beautiful, so Sara and Candy decided to give them to Guy as a memorial to Raimond. He did call, as he said he would, and they went downstairs, flowers in arms. I noticed the smile of appreciation on Raimond's face as the two of us, spirits from the past, looked on.

It was going to be another difficult goodbye for them. Guy, smiling broadly, was right there to meet them when they stepped out of the elevator, and then, just around the corner stood Willy, Olga, Vera, Louise, and Richard Heyligen, who also came to bid them farewell. What a wonderful surprise. Olga and Vera gave Sara and Candy more chocolates, and Richard brought a newspaper article with their pictures as well as a picture of his brother Jules, and a copy of a page of his book that had a picture and article regarding Milo Blakely, the waist gunner on my crew. After a brief visit and one last toast, their time together came to an end. One by one, they hugged and said their goodbyes. We, Raimond and I, were in the midst of these emotions, and enjoying each of the last moments that we would be together. We exchanged our last hand shake. There's no way of knowing if our paths will cross again, but we were grateful to have shared an unforgettable time together.

Raimond and I bore witness to two families carrying on the memory of their loved ones; my wife and daughter retracing my experience, and the Wendelen family carrying on what Raimond had begun in helping this American family realize their dream. Although it was over 62 years later, it was evidence that the tradition of kind Belgians assisting complete strangers from a foreign country carries on still today. It was different, yet vaguely familiar. The encounter with the many people convening in Beringen, who provided my wife and daughter such a warm reception, was indeed shades of the past.

The girls returned to their room, both feeling subdued from the evening and their unforgettable visit to Belgium. Morning would come very soon and they would be departing for the next segment of their voyage: the flight from Brussels to Berlin.

They woke up at 4:30 a.m. Sara was really tired getting up so early and it had been hard for them to sleep after saying goodbye to their friends. But they arose, finished packing, and climbed aboard the taxi for Brussels.

Candy and Sara at Beringen Town Hall prior to reception
Courtesy of Ejvind Jensen

Mayor Mondelaers speaking inside Beringen Town Hall
Courtesy of Ejvind Jensen

Ann reading her father, Richard Heyligen's, recollection of the crash
Courtesy of Ejvind Jensen

The book "De doodstraf als risico" belonging to Richard Heyligen, on display in Town Hall – photos of Milo Blakely and Richard's brother, Jules Heyligen
Courtesy of Ejvind Jensen

*   *   *   *   *

On February 7 (date is not correct) B-17s flew over Limburg, target Frankfurt.

One of these became involved in an air battle and crashed near Stal-Koersel. It was snowing.

The occupants: Bangs, Kaylor, Bell, Booth, Joyce, Kyler, Alexander, Mikulka and Blakely saved themselves by bailing out and made their escape from the Germans.

Henri Claessens, employee in the coal-mine of Zolder, together with Peter Meyer and Reymen took care of gunner Sgt. Milo E. Blakely until February 8. Teacher Albert Wouters, helper of group Peer, informed Dr. Verschueren, who in his turn informed Thiery. Rendezvous place was a café opposite to the mine of Zolder. As identifying mark Wouters was wearing a handkerchief in the upper pocket of his coat. After interrogation on the spot Blakely was taken to Herk and after that to Diest. As farewell he wrote: "Thanks to all the people who helped me and others who needed help like me to reach England again, February 9, 1944.

The tail gunner, an American Czech, came down in a pine-wood in Koersel. His name was Tony John Mikulka. Someone who had seen him coming down, went for John Heyligen, who could speak English. With an axe, pretending being on his way for cutting wood, Heyligen went looking for the American. They stayed together in the small forest until dark, talking about the war and their professions. After that Heyligen accompanied him to his cousin Albert Boelanders in Stal, where he stayed overnight. Next day a retired policeman from Tenderloo, Louis Hermans, took him to Albert Vandamme in Kwaadmechelen, who accompanied him to Brussels. According to Heyligen Mikulka had arrived in England.

"De doodstraf als risico" ("Death penalty as a risk") Belgium publication written in Dutch J. Bussels 1981 (Pages of book in previous photo)

(Translation Courtesy of Piet Brouwer)

Plaque made by Raimond Wendelen

Crash Site

Home where Thomas Mikulka slept overnight
Courtesy of Ejvind Jensen

**Candy & Sara-sitting on the bed that Thomas
Mikulka slept in overnight**
Courtesy of Ejvind Jensen

Area where Jay Joyce landed

Area where I landed in a garden

Witnesses (I believe Mr. Ayers and Mr. Krumpen)
to my landing and Guy Wendelen, far right.

Candy and Sara in approximate area of my landing

Museum in Leopoldsburg (Former German Hospital)

The Wendelen Family – Louise, Vera, Olga, Guy & Willy

Bjoerg and Ejvind Jensen

18

In the Present – locating our radio operator's widow...

JAY JOYCE — MEETING HIS WIFE, BEA

Candy spent months trying to locate the members of my crew. Of all my crew, I was closest to Jay Joyce and was pleased when she found contact information for him through his niece. Unfortunately, Jay had passed away years ago. Candy obtained his wife's address in Dravosburg, Pennsylvania, and immediately wrote to Beulah "Bea" Joyce. Bea responded quickly with a note mentioning that she had a crew picture and that she would send a copy. Until this time, Candy had no pictures, and she told Bea how thrilled that she would be to put faces with the names of the crew members who she had practically memorized by this time.

Besides the crew picture, Bea thoughtfully sent a photo of me wearing an oxygen mask during training in the State of Washington. I could still recall Jay taking that picture of me. I also remember asking for the camera to take a picture of him. Bea told my daughter that Jay talked about "Kyler" quite often telling her that we were good friends during the time that we were together. I was glad she knew of our friendship. I can remember Jay talking about his wife, often writing her letters. I can recall his excitement when he heard from her, and how proudly he displayed her photograph.

Candy and Bea began conversing on the telephone, and a plan was made for Candy to visit Bea in Dravosburg. Candy was anxious to meet Jay's widow and to see Jay's memorabilia from the war. She reasoned that Jay's mementos would likely be relevant to my experience. Jay and Bea had married before Jay went into the service, so Bea had quite a bit of information. Jay also kept a notebook, like I had. Candy asked Sara if she'd like to go along to meet Bea, because she thought they had so much in common, and Sara was happy to join them. Sara was as involved as Candy in anything pertaining to my role in the U.S. Army Air Corps.

Jay and I had been good friends and experienced so much together. I wished that he could have been with me to witness the meeting of our families. He had been gone from this life too long, and it was not possible. There would have been so much catching up to do. I don't know why we didn't keep in touch after the war. There were many times that I thought about him, but I had moved on and put that time in my life behind me. I guess he did the same.

Candy, Sara and I finally drove to Bea's address in Dravosburg, and my girls greeted her with big hugs. Candy took her scanner and computer along, hoping to scan pages from Jay's notebooks. She felt that with us having been together through training, our missions, and then for our long period of captivity, nearly everything in Bea's collection would be pertinent to my experience. They sat down and looked at the many books, postcards, and letters that they all considered treasures. It brought back so many memories for me. In fact, I was probably in the same room as Jay when many of the letters were written.

Sara and Bea hit it off so well. As I watched them, I thought how nice it would have been for Sara and me to have spent time with Jay and Bea. Candy and Sara felt fortunate that they could finally meet this kind lady and scan some pages from Jay's notebook. Candy had no time to even read what she was scanning, but figured she could do that later.

Bea had a display set up to honor her husband's memory, and it contained important pictures and documents from World War II. Candy searched for my face in a picture of a group in training but I had not attended radio school, as Jay had, so she was not going to find me.

Candy gave Bea copies of some pictures Candy had taken of Mr. Deferm, the Belgian man who had actually watched as Jay's parachute got caught in a tree near the man's home. One of the pictures showed Deferm pointing to the tree, and the other showed the area where Jay had come down. She also gave Bea pictures she had taken of the crash site. It was evident that all this meant a great deal to Bea, and Sara enjoyed telling Bea about her Belgian experiences.

During lunch the ladies chattered excitedly about me and Jay and what they knew of our wartime experiences together in the same crew. The visit ended far too soon, but Candy and Sara needed to be back on the road before dark. They exchanged hugs as Candy and Sara thanked their precious friend for her hospitality. How connected the three of them were through their husbands and father. This brief meeting triggered many recollections that had been dormant for years in my mind. Jay's papers, books, letters and notebook stimulated memories from our training together all the way through to our liberation.

After arriving back home that evening, as late as it was, Candy quickly looked at the writings that she had scanned into her computer from Jay's book. She became thoroughly engrossed. She read slowly and judiciously aloud to her husband, Brad, and digested every single word. She told him that two years ago she probably would not even have realized what she was reading, but it all made sense to her now, having learned so much from so many sources. It became more difficult to read as she realized that much of what she was reading had been written by a boy who was very close to me, the boy who became her father. She continued to talk about the two of us, who so long ago had helped each other and the young men who surrounded us overcome the fears and hardships of being shot down and becoming POWs.

Jay Joyce in training in State of Washington
Courtesy of Bea Joyce

Me in training in State of Washington
Courtesy of Bea Joyce

Bea in front of husband, Jay's, memorial display

Nino, Bea and Sara

19

In the present – locating our pilot...

MEETING LAWRENCE COOK

I was amazed, after months of looking for both crew members and POWs who remembered me, that Candy located our pilot, Lawrence Cook. I could remember my first meeting with him in Washington State, and our training as a crew in Redmond, Oregon. We adapted well to our positions on the crew and I gained great confidence in him as our pilot. We were together in training, but his spare time was spent with his wife, Lois. She had traveled along with him and rented a room close by, and he'd stay with her during his time off.

I had a lot of names for our pilot. Originally (and always on duty), it was "Lieutenant," and officially sometimes it was "Pilot Cook," but now I tend to think of him as "Larry."

Candy and Sara were joined by one of my other daughters, Dawn, in their plan for a surprise visit with Larry. Candy made the arrangements with his daughters Laurel and Janis. They were all excited about this meeting, and they realized that Larry may be the only person who actually knew and remembered me as a young airman. He told Candy in the many phone conversations that they shared what he remembered about me. My memory of Larry is pretty good – we were only together briefly, but we did train, fly missions, and get shot down together. His recollection of me was that I was "special." He described me as "quiet and a decent human being." I wished that I could return the compliment and share with them my high opinion of him, but it was too late for that, and hoped that Candy would be able to convey the message for me.

I think that Candy was hoping Larry would share his memories with Sara and Dawn just as he had with her on the phone.

As my three girls sat on the plane en route to Yucca Valley, California, they talked about how amazing it was going to be to meet the man that I had met and worked with over sixty years ago. Candy recapped some of the information that Larry had told her during their phone calls, explaining that had it not been for Lawrence Cook, I would not have lived to become a husband and father. She explained how he had called me out of the ball turret so I could put on my parachute, and added how the most frightening moments of our lives were experienced together. She was looking forward to giving Lawrence a big hug, shaking his hand, and thanking him personally for saving my life so long ago.

The flight to Palm Springs was smooth; the women collected their luggage, rented a car, and were off to Yucca Valley. They found the Super 8 Motel where they were staying, and called Larry's daughter, Laurel. Arrangements were confirmed for the following day, Sunday, to meet Laurel and Larry in the motel parking lot, and they would lead the way to Larry's church.

After the phone call, they realized they hadn't eaten since lunch and it was ten o'clock. They were tired, but they were also hungry. Dawn and Candy drove to the nearby KFC and picked up dinner. They finally settled in for the night about 11 p.m.

The next morning, they got up and dressed early and anxiously made their way down to the parking lot for their first meeting with Cook. His daughters told him that someone was coming to visit, but he wasn't told who. Candy walked up to him and said hello and asked if he recognized her voice. She told him she talked to him on the telephone and he loudly exclaimed, "Candy!" She gave him the hug that she had been waiting to give. The fondness that they felt for each other was obvious.

Larry was now 88 years old, but I was no longer a young man either, and this was quite a meeting for me, arousing memories of our time together. I was pretty happy to be here, though I could only observe Larry.

Candy, Sara and Dawn followed Laurel and Larry to the church. As they seated themselves, Candy made sure that she sat next to her Larry. She held onto his arm for the entire time and they all sang the hymns together. During the service it was asked if there were any first time visitors to "Valley Community Church" and, if so, would they stand up. My wife and two daughters stood up and gave their names. At that moment, Larry proudly explained that their husband and father had been his B-17 ball turret gunner in World War II, and that they had come all the way from New York just to meet him. Larry was so happy to tell this to his congregation, and Candy proudly added that Larry was her hero. It was moving to see this gathering of family members – two families brought together because of the fathers' past experiences in WWII.

After the church service, they all went to breakfast before going to Larry's daughter, Janis's, house. Janis and Laurel had found a box of pictures, newspaper articles, and letters that were a treasure trove of their father's military life. As they looked through the memorabilia, Larry began talking about his training and the path leading up to his role as a B-17 pilot. He told about meeting me in Ephreta, Washington, and then training as a crew in Redmond, Oregon. Our crew picture was taken in Grand Island, Nebraska. As he talked he would say "it's all coming back to me." He went on and on about arriving in England, our missions, and his evasion for seven weeks until he was captured and also became a POW (for over a year), at Stalag Luft I. He spoke of the Bible verse, Philippians 4:11, that gave him strength – "Not that I speak in respect of want: for I have learned in whatsoever state I am therewith to be content" – and recalled the elation he felt upon liberation. I knew that he ended up in Barth, just as I had, because I saw him after liberation at Camp Lucky Strike, in France. That was the last time that I saw him, until today.

It was an emotional and rewarding day for everyone. I sensed that some of the tales were being told for the first time. Larry elaborated, as he had on the phone to Candy, on the guilt he carried for all these years because after liberation he learned that he was not the last crew member to exit the plane. The interphones were shot out, but he thought he remembered ringing the bailout bell, and he was devastated to think he may not have been the last to jump. Five jumped from the front of the plane, and five of us from the back, but he was the last out of the men he was with, believing those in the back had already jumped. He stated that he always second-guessed himself about whether he may have been able to bring the Fort back to England. It was a split-second decision to bail out, but based on the extent of damage it was the only choice, and it was made for the welfare of his crew.

Candy could relieve his mind about where the plane crashed, and also reiterated the fact that he had saved my life. Everyone present told him what a hero he was and how proud they were of him. He made the right decision and could be at peace with himself. It's too bad Larry and I didn't have contact after the war and talk about this. I could have eased his mind of any guilt feelings years ago. I thought highly of him as our pilot; and while a POW I wrote a poem entitled "A Good Pilot." He was the only pilot I had ever flown with, and I was glad that Candy could show him this poem as tribute to the fact that he had performed his job admirably under extreme duress. No one could be prepared for what we faced.

Larry had expended so much energy in his explanations and demonstrations of the past that he became physically drained, and required a short nap. I sure understood that! He had just relived two difficult years of his life.

The day ended with the gathering of the two families at a local Italian restaurant. There was a definite connection—a bond—between them. It was heart-warming to a father, as was evident in Larry's demeanor, and if it could be seen, mine as well. All of my girls said they wished I could have met with Larry and what a wonderful reunion it would have been. They concurred that this was the next best thing, and how fortunate they were to have spent this cherished time with Larry and his family.

This was another difficult goodbye for my family. Hugs were exchanged by everyone. They agreed that it had been a great learning experience, and Larry now spoke proudly that he was a B-17 pilot during World War II. This visit had, in his mind, removed any cloud on the legacy to his children and grandchildren and, at the same time, it helped my family learn more about my role in the war. Meeting Dad's old pilot was another mission accomplished, and this time three members of my family had participated.

Lawrence in training
Courtesy of his daughters, Janis & Laurel

Lawrence and daughters, Laurel and Janis

Candy, Lawrence, Sara and Dawn

20

In the present – information provided by Lawrence Cook and his Belgian "Helper," Marcel Van Lierde.

LARRY COOK AND JOHN BOOTH
HIDDEN IN BELGIUM

In conversations with Larry Cook, we had learned that after everyone bailed out, he and John Booth, the flight engineer, could see each other as they fell to Earth near Hasselt, and so they teamed up. There were civilians around who pointed them towards the woods. Larry and John gave some Belgians their parachutes (silk was valuable!) and took off to hide in the area suggested to them.

The downed airmen became very cold, and after dark, they sought out better conditions; they soon found a barn with a haystack where they spent the night. The next morning as they walked through town, they were hungry and spotted a garden where they picked turnips for nourishment. They decided to knock on a door in a town Larry believed was Lummen, hoping to find help and routing to friendly territory. Larry could speak a little French, so when the person answered the door he asked the way to Spain. The kind person returned with a sandwich and told them to go and hide in the woods. They did as instructed and again slept in the woods, this time under the cover of leaves.

Toward evening, a man and his eight year old daughter walked into the woods, picked them up and took them to the man's home. They were given a hot meal–their first since landing–and civilian clothes. The next day they were again instructed to hide, this time at a nearby canal, and to wait for someone to contact them. It was cold and miserable and they lay shivering in the bushes all day. At dusk, two men on bicycles, each guiding an empty bicycle rode to their spot near the canal. It became obvious that the bicycles were for Larry and John when they heard the two men singing the English World War I tune, *It's A Long Way To Tipperary*. The two airmen joined the Belgians and they rode on as a foursome.

Larry recalled that the four of them, "rode to the canal and peddled across the bridge". He remembers seeing two Germans on the bridge, but they paid no attention to the "civilians." They eventually arrived at a home in Hasselt, where they were again fed and given a bed for the night.

In the morning, the airmen were taken to the town's railroad station. They were careful to always stay fifty paces behind anyone they were following. The person leading them went through the station gate alone, talked to someone, and then returned. He then boarded the train with them to Brussels where they were taken to a Catholic church and introduced to a priest who gave them wine and visited with them. They then continued their journey aboard a streetcar, accompanied by a pretty girl about seventeen years old. The car transported them through town to the outskirts of Brussels, along with part of the family that they had stayed with for five weeks – the Van Lierde's. They were told that the coast was clear to make their way to the Pyrenees, and they stayed several different places on their way. Finally, they boarded a train to Antwerp, and when they got off of the train, just as they rounded the corner in the station, two men got out of a car with guns and took them away in different cars; obviously they had been expected! Larry Cook and John Booth were taken to separate POW camps and didn't see each other again until after the war.

To the present...

MARCEL VAN LIERDE

As had become her custom since her decision to retrace my war career, Candy obtained the contact information for Marcel Van Lierde from Larry Cook. She had learned that the two families – the Cook's and the Van Lierdes, had kept in touch for years after the war ended. Marcel is now the only surviving member of the four in his immediate family, and he and Larry's family still talk at least once a year. Although this may have been slightly outside of her focus, it was another story of interest to her and she continued to feel that any bit of information about any one of my crew members was relevant to me. The more that she learned, the more she wanted to know even though it was a curve off of the main puzzle she was assembling.

Both Candy and I were determined to learn about Marcel's memories of the pilot and top turret gunner from her father's ship. Part of it, I think, was Candy's captivation with the degree of danger that was involved in helping the Allied airmen. She wanted to meet such a courageous individual who had risked his life trying to deliver her father's crewmates to safety, and upon our return to New York she wrote to Marcel asking if he would mind sharing his memories of the weeks that Larry Cook and John Booth stayed with his family. It was of even greater interest to her to hear his recollections as an experienced Belgian "Helper" during such dangerous times. "Helpers" faced arrest and imprisonment and possibly worse at the hands of the Germans.

Marcel Van Lierde graciously accommodated Candy's inquiry. He responded thoughtfully, sharing his and his sister Angele's recollections of his family's life in Belgium during a most perilous time, stating in his correspondence that he is, "the last living from the four who shared dangerous days with Lawrence Cook and John Booth, in our flat Boulevard Emile Bockstael in Brussels."

In October, 1996, Marcel's sister, Angele, aware that she was terminally ill, with the help of her brother, had written out her memoirs for the benefit of her three grandchildren.

The following is an excerpt from Angele's memoirs, *Children Go, I Will Tell Thee*, Chapter 9, "Courting Danger"[1]:

> *While the occupation dragged on, the Allies were paving the way for the landing in Normandy, and part of that preparation was to bombard railways, bridges, aerodromes, factories, depots, both in Germany and in the occupied countries. Waves of planes roared overhead most nights, and there were daytime alarms as well. More and more planes were brought down, and often the crew managed to save themselves by parachutes. A very brave young Belgian girl, Andree De Jonghe, had created an Evasion Line which ran from Belgium through France and the Pyrenees to Spain, where British diplomats took over, sending the men back to Britain. This was later called the Comet Line...*

One of my schoolmates, Marcelle Deleu, and her family were involved in this line. I knew about it, and occasionally gave them a hand as a guide, but I had never mentioned it at home. One day Marcelle asked me to find a new "safe home" as the line was clogged up, some people having been arrested, and perhaps an agent provocateur had managed to fool the line's security examiners. So there was extra danger, as people cannot always resist torture. Marcelle's brother Jean was arrested soon after. He had been a gentle twenty year old musician studying the piano and the oboe at the Brussels Conservatoire. He died during the forced march out of Auschwitz in 1945.

> *I asked my parents at lunch time, and my father after a short time for reflection said: "Yes, we'll take men in. Perhaps if Willy (brother) is shot down, he will also find shelter". And so it was that we became part of the line as a safe house. The norm was that a man was brought by a guide, and picked up the next day, or at most within 48 hrs, by the same or another guide. There was hardly time to get acquainted, just first names, nationality*

---

1 The text and letters are reprinted verbatim here, with only minor punctuation changes.

which could be British, American, Polish, Canadian, Australian… Hardly time to say hello-good bye and they were off, to everyone's relief.

One evening we were having a party for George Daelemans, a scout friend (Penguin) who had successfully escaped from forced labour in Germany and made his way back home, and later went into hiding at his sister's in one of the lovely old houses on the Grand'place. We had organized a young people's welcome for him and the house was full. The pre-arranged ring of the doorbell announced a "parcel" as the airmen were called. There were two "parcels," both American ones. We hid them under my parents' bed till the end of the party, which we cut short under some pretext or other, hurrying all our guests away.

Two lanky, gangling Yanks emerged from under the bed, dressed in ill-fitting civilian clothes, jacket sleeves and trousers too short, and rough peasant shirts. They ended up staying with us several weeks, every minute of which was dynamite. It was in February and March 1944, in very cold weather. The men must have been utterly bewildered, and hungry on our small rations, but they never complained. They sorely missed cigarettes, and Marcel asked one of his friends to obtain tobacco as none of us smoked and foolishly told him why. Marcel had always been too talkative! This friend, Loufi Jacobs, did not endanger us, but should never have been told, I thought then. However, Loufi supplied the very necessary identity cards, tobacco which they missed badly, English books, a little food, and visited the men frequently.[2]

The men were John Booth from Philadelphia, and Lawrence Cook from Los Angeles who is still a dear and close friend, as is his wife Lois. Lawrence was good

---

2 Marcel explains: "Loufi Jacobs belonged to the same group of "resistance" as I did. My sister didn't know it in that time – Our leader was the Chief of Police of Laeken – (N40). I was still student in Chemistry at a high school but Loufi was working at the town hall and was stealing there the necessary papers. (When she wrote her memories for her grand-children my sister was already suffering from "holes" in her memory, and was writing living her past again)."

at chess, and played many games with my father. During a chess game one evening, Lawrence started to shiver, seemed to have trouble swallowing, and his neck glands were swollen. He had a raging temperature. It was decided to call in our family doctor, Dr. Dieu. My father received him on his own, in the kitchen, and asked him:

-"Doctor, you are a Reserve Officer of the Belgian Army, aren't you?"

-"Yes."

-"And a good patriot?"

-"Yes" (in a puzzled tone)

-"And you have signed the Hippocratic Oath?"

-"Yes, of course."

-"If I was to tell you that an Allied airman is very ill in Brussels, would you accept have a look at him?"

The doctor hesitated at first, then replied:

-"All right, but on one condition: you must never tell anyone, not even your wife and children, about this."

-"Fine, I'll bring him in."

To the doctor's stupefaction, my mother came in with Lawrence.

-"But Monsieur Van Lierde, this is madness! Here, right here, surely you know the risk involved! Even your children are in danger."

-"We know all that, doctor, please take a look at the patient."

A double quinsy was diagnosed. We had not as much as heard of penicillin yet. The Doctor prescribed the best available medicine, giving my mother instructions. The examination over, we thought poor John must be fed up waiting in the freezing bedroom, and we called him in. The doctor exclaimed ,"Who on earth is this?"

160

"Just another one" my father replied.

The doctor shook his head in disbelief.

Of course we could not prevent our friends and relations from visiting us, but we hid the men in a bedroom each time, did not confide in any of our callers, and tried to get rid of them as fast as we decently could because they were actually in as much danger as we were should the SS happen to call. One exception was made (in my absence): cousin Reg Hine, who after all was an 'Englishman', dropped in unexpectedly with his wife and little Lucy. They were introduced to our two "guests" who were glad to meet a fluent English speaker. It was drummed into Lucy that she now held a dangerous secret, and should she ever reveal it, the whole Van Lierde family and probably her own parents would be shot. She was about eleven I think. She told me later that the knowledge of what we were involved in weighed heavily on her, so she told her favorite doll!"

Marcel, also, graciously shared what he knew about where Lawrence Cook and John Booth landed after their bail out of our damaged bomber. He stated that they landed in Lummen, hid their parachutes and remained in a wooded area. At dawn a peasant passed who upon noticing them made signs indicating that they should remain hidden until he returned. He came back along with another man bringing civilian clothes. In the following days they went from place to place, never knowing where. They did, however, remember being in Hasselt where they were hidden in the workplace of an artist, a sculptor, who was quite well known. By order of the Wehrmacht, the artist was sculpting a large memorial in honor of the German soldiers. Marcel explains incredibly that Lawrence and John were hidden behind the sculpture and could see the German officers inspecting and commenting on the work.

In his correspondence, Marcel told Candy that there were days during the time that the two airmen were hidden at his home that the evadees looked out the window from behind the curtain at the passing German units in the street.

Marcel shared many of his memories of the weeks that Lawrence Cook and John Booth were hidden with his family. He recalled their arrival and how they were questioned separately by his father who asked them to tell their story to assure that their stories matched so he could be certain they were indeed who they claimed to be.

Marcel calls the supper they were served their first evening a "war supper" consisting of 150 grains of bread and herring in vinegar. He remembers them going to sleep in the same room as he and his sister Angele slept in. They talked with them a little but Marcel noticed that the men's English wasn't what they were accustomed to. They were used to BBC English and the American accent was very strange to them arousing suspicion. Marcel says they did not say "Yes" but Yah", the same sound as the Flemish or German "Jah."

Because of his concern, the next morning at breakfast while the airmen were still sleeping, Marcel explained his fears that their guests may be Germans, to his father. That evening Lawrence and John were questioned once again. It was critical to be cautious because the Comete escape line was often broken by German spies. Marcel's father determined the men to be legitimate.

Marcel has written that life went on despite the traditional food problem. He felt that the songs they learned quietly from "their Americans" were compensation for the hard winter they experienced. He has memories of Lawrence teaching them, "I've got Sixpence…," and, "Up we go into the wild blue yonder, up we go to the sun…," recalling the singing as a respite from the stress of the times.

Marcel's friend, Henri Jacobs, was in the same Rover-Scouts-Clan with him and was employed at the town hall. He asked Henri if he could provide them with false identity cards and he accommodated them by going to the house and taking pictures of the men. In a short period of time he brought the cards with names and numbers that corresponded with existing people. Marcel remembers the periods of laughter in the lessons they conducted teaching the correct pronunciation of the airmen's new names. He comments that they never could pronounce them correctly.

The long winter, November through March, brought severe sub-zero temperatures. The only fire that they used was a coal stove in the kitchen. To conserve the coal and with only one hour of gas allotted in the morning, they used a Norwegian Cooking Pot (Marmite Norvegienne).

Being spoiled by California sunshine, Marcel tells that Lawrence suffered the consequences of the hard winter when a sore throat developed from his being hidden in the cold room under his parents' bed. He developed quinsy and the doctor came, as Angele had written, and prescribed an old drastic remedy – a mixture of 2 liters of warm water with one pound of bicarbonate. Lawrence had to rinse his throat every 2 hours day and night. When Marcel's mother bought the large amount of bicarbonate, she had to go to different shops to avoid questions. She spent the whole day with Lawrence during his illness and, with the remedy, his fever was reduced promptly.

After five weeks Marcel's family asked the service to take the airmen. The longer they stayed, the riskier it was for all involved. Marcel was told by Lawrence in later years that after they left the Van Lierde's home they had to change places every day and when they reached Antwerp, two German officers came to them and said "flight-leftenant Cook and airgunner Booth, you are prisoners of war." They were arrested and questioned about their hiding places but could not answer as they never knew where they stayed because they changed so frequently.

Marcel and his family all did their duty for the "Resistance" (Underground) and their father had insisted that they not tell each other details of their participation. It wasn't until after the war that they learned of each other's involvement. Marcel claims he didn't know the half of what Angele had written in her memoirs even though they slept under the same roof.

*   *   *

Without ever having met Marcel or Angele, Candy felt she had learned about two of the most amazing people that she could ever hope to know. The document that Marcel wrote in his words is, "a living picture how life was in the beginning of the 20th century and in war times." Candy was delighted with Marcel's letters, and truly impressed by his sister's rather detailed depiction of the unimaginable hardships experienced in their lifetimes. I think that these two people are representative of the courage and sacrifice freely made by many in those days, taking on the most dangerous roles of the times during harsh conditions, in German-occupied Belgium.

Candy wrote back to Marcel to express her admiration and her gratitude. He was another person whom she was honored to become acquainted with.

Candy had thus learned detailed information of yet another distinguished group of heroes, and obtained a different perception of life in Belgium during the war. This insight into what it was like for those who helped the Allied airmen helped her, in turn, to see a bigger picture of life in that part of Europe during the war. Of course I had understood this and learned it so long ago; I had met people who would have helped me had the Germans not arrived so quickly. Candy had been honored to meet our pilot Larry, and now she knew one of the people who hid him for five weeks in a Belgium town. Candy expressed profuse thanks and gratitude to Marcel for all this information.

Learning all about the route that Larry and John had taken after their landing in Belgium was naturally of great interest to me, as I had never made a connection with Larry after the war to learn these things. Of course I learned after my own liberation from Stalag Luft I that they had survived as POWs, but had no knowledge of their days of evasion before their capture.

Lawrence's false identification card photo

Frankfurt

40 and 8 Box Car
Courtesy of B24.net – Greg Hatton

21

ARRIVAL IN FRANKFURT — DULAG LUFT

We were loaded into boxcars "forty and eight style," using the same cars in use since WWI, holding forty men or eight horses. It seemed a long and grim ride, lasting an eternity and ending at a huge train station in Frankfurt. We jumped down from the cars and marched through the station into the streets where we encountered angry, highly agitated civilians throwing stones and spitting at us. The guards loudly shouted commands, protecting us from people whose eyes were filled with hatred and who cursed us, referring to us as *terrorfliegers* (terror flyers). These individuals despised us for the damage the bombers had brought to their cities, homes, and families. Some of them were equipped with various objects for punishing us. Had it not been for the protection of the German guards, I am certain we would have been severely beaten by that mob. Many of the POWs were hit before the guards were able to control the unruly crowd. I barely avoided several attacks; my noticeable limp made me an easy target. I was miserable, hungry and cold. I was young and scared, and why not? My existence was now in a strange world controlled by the enemy and, at this point, the guards actually seemed less of a threat than the irate civilians. Only those who experienced this would know how frightening life was for me then, and this was just the beginning, of my POW experience!

We were marched with the jeering civilians now maintaining their distance on either side of us, but keeping up with us, as we approached our next mode of transportation. We were ordered into what I recall as tramcars, and at least now we were out of the reach of the angry natives. It was a sullen ride to the place where we would be "evaluated." We left for a town about 30 miles from Frankfurt, that I learned later was Oberursel. My mind was less on the travel and mostly on what would happen to me at the other end, for I surely realized that an interrogation of some sort was in my future. In a short while we would find out what the processing of a POW entailed at the Interrogation Center, called "Dulag Luft."

I would be lying if I said I was not scared to death of what I would face. I had felt fear every moment since our bomber was hit. I was embarrassed that I felt so frightened, and could not help but wonder if this meant I was a coward.

Dulag Luft
Courtesy of B24.net – Greg Hatton

Watchtower Dulag Luft
Courtesy of B24.net – Greg Hatton

22

Return to present…

RETURN TO FRANKFURT TRAIN STATION

My return to Frankfurt on April 26, 2005, was actually my first excursion with Candy on her journey to retrace my steps. Although our journey could have begun in any number of places, starting in Frankfurt made sense for a lot of reasons. Candy could not possibly realize it, for me it was a good place to ease myself into the purpose of her mission. I was fairly sure that many deep and painful memories would be dredged up throughout this endeavor, but it didn't make me feel bad, exactly, and to some degree I had a sense of relief at finally coming to terms with the ghosts of my wartime past.

We had started in Frankfurt as part of a tour group that was going to cover part of my past, although following my steps chronologically would have been almost prohibitively expensive. We had taken advantage of signing up with a group of people who, like me and Candy, had some personal connection to Frankfurt, and to the air war against Germany – followers or children of the Eighth Air Force. In this tour, we would first visit Dulag Luft, a German interrogation center for all captured airmen, regardless of country, and then the group would move on to Stalag Luft I, one of several POW camps I was to "inhabit" during my time as a POW.

We traveled to the busy Frankfurt train station together with other ex-POWs (and also some children of ex-POWs) participating in the trip. As we ventured into the structure, the deeper we walked into it, the more familiar it became to me. The recollections of sixty years ago, when I had been herded through this station, with many other POWs, came flooding back. As we reached the far end of the huge building, I could visualize the entire route the German guards had marched us. I even remembered the door that we were taken through, and recalled the civilians taunting, spitting and stoning us, as we walked from the station into the sunlight. To them, we were "terror flyers" who bombed their cities, and they wanted revenge. If the guards hadn't protected us, this meeting may have been the beginning, and the end, of my role as a POW.

Very early the next morning, Candy and I returned alone to the train station for one last look. She mentioned to the guide, Ellis Gibson ("Gib"), that she was taking a walk and would return for the trip to Oberursel, the actual site of the German interrogation center known as "Dulag Luft." I watched as Candy, unfazed by all the pedestrian traffic that already was filling the place, carried out a plan that she wrote about in her journal the previous evening. To ensure that she walked where I walked, she crisscrossed in front of the track area where the previous day the ex-POWs in our group had said they arrived. She commenced walking back and forth, back and forth, many times. She paced the length of the track to where the train entered the station, all the while snapping pictures in both directions. Oblivious to the stares of passers-by, she continued this routine until she had stepped everywhere I had (and some places where I hadn't!), and then moved on to the area in the station that the ex-POWs had said they were marched through on their way out of the building. For good measure, she took several more steps, back and forth, and around the area. More pictures were taken, and she had a look of satisfaction on her face when she was finished. I couldn't help but feel that my presence helped guide her on the right path throughout the building, and I too was pleased with her efforts.

Frankfurt Train Station

Rails on which POWs arrived at Frankfurt Station

23

THE INTERROGATION

I vaguely remember our arrival in Oberursel, walking up a road to a large area with buildings where we would be put into cells and held in solitary confinement. How forlorn one felt in a small room with nothing but a bed and a pan to serve as a toilet. There was a slot in the door through which they served me soup and bread twice a day. It was very cold, and I moved around in the small space as best I could to keep my circulation going. My throbbing ankle protested, but if I did not keep moving, not only was I going to freeze, but I was going to lose my mind. I would intermittently sit or lay on the bed. It was so hard to keep my mind busy and yet control my thoughts! I tried to remain positive in such an unpromising atmosphere.

I tried to think of things that make me happy. I pictured in my mind what everyone must be doing at home, but I didn't really know what day it was. It was so dark inside this tiny cell that one could lose track of time, which was something that meant very little anyway. I was hungry when I arrived, as I had been from the onset of this nightmare. I supposed that I was given the soup and bread about midday or late afternoon. Now, it could have been the middle of the night for all I knew.

I repeated to myself over and over in my mind my name, rank and serial number. Naturally, I knew these things as my own name, but, I wanted it to be so routine that when I faced my inquisitor it would come out of my mouth automatically, as if these were the only words that I knew. Maybe it was my way of brainwashing myself to only speak these words. I also commenced to saying every prayer that I had ever learned in my life and then adding my own intentions. This was the only way I could push back against my loneliness. It kept me from feeling abandoned. As I kept at it, the repetition of my name, rank and serial number meshed with my prayers. Sporadically, to occupy my mind, I thought of words to songs that I knew. I was writing letters in my mind. I was replaying our last mission and the days that led up to this dreaded situation.

There was no getting around it, I was going to be questioned, badgered, and maybe abused when they tried to extract information from me. I had no idea what their means would be and the anticipation and anxiety was almost unbearable. Those uncertainties inserted themselves, uncontrollably, into my thoughts, causing uneasiness. The mind is a funny thing. I could not avert the worries I harbored for my future, where my utter existence depended on those who, days before, tried to kill me and my crew members by disabling our Fort.

When I first arrived, my cell was very cold, but I can remember feeling increasingly warm until I was in extreme discomfort. Were they trying to asphyxiate me with this smothering temperature? This added to the tension that I was feeling. I went from one extreme to the other. The memory of the door opening and the "invitation" to my first session stays with me. I was startled from a prone position, lethargic from the heat, as the door opened.

I was taken to a room that was somewhat more comfortable than the cell I had been in, and I fidgeted nervously. The German officer, who was to be my interrogator, was sitting at a large desk that was cluttered with papers. He surprised me with perfect English, so perfect, that had I closed my eyes, I would have thought that this was one of my fellow airmen. In pleasant tones he began to tell me about myself and other members of my crew. He knew the missions we had flown, and who my commanding officer was. He knew we were assigned to the 92nd Bomb Group, and he described a number of details of our base in Podington. He had newspaper clippings that he laid out in front of me. He gave the impression that he sympathized with my plight. Noticing my limp, he commented on that as well. He mentioned that our navigator had died, and I'm sure he noticed that I flinched on hearing this. There is nothing that I could even say about this sad news. While waiting to be questioned I had imagined my captors to engage in a number of ploys, but this German seemed forthright, honest, and sympathetic.

When this stranger began to tell me details of my life at home, I was astounded. It seemed that there was nothing that I could tell him that he didn't already know anyway. In my mind, I knew that he was trying to bait me, but I also knew that I wouldn't bite. I was definitely tempted to discuss with him the topics that he brought up about our unit and our base–I felt a powerful need to talk with *someone* about what I had experienced in the last few days, but I knew that this friendly interrogator was not the right person with whom I should relieve this need.

If he approached inquisitively, I maintained what I planned ahead of time that my only response would be – "Sgt. John R. Kyler, Serial number 32830356." He handed me a "Red Cross Form" to fill out. There were more blanks that he wanted me to fill in, other than the three areas I was prepared to complete. As I got up to leave I forgot about my injured ankle, and grimaced from the pain. Because of my injury, I was taken to a hospital to be examined (the Hohemark Hospital). They found nothing broken, only a bad sprain. My ankle was taped, which made it more tolerable to walk on.

I always had a fear that the guards in charge of me could turn in a second. Their guns were ready. It is torture to feel every day that you may die. It is a helpless feeling to be in the hands of the enemy. I never, for one second, felt at ease, even with the feigned empathy of the interrogator when I first met with him.

In one of our meetings, I was told by the interrogator, again in perfect English, about the reports that the Germans compiled concerning the shooting down of our airplane. He read from a report by a flak battery installation, as well as excerpts of reports supposedly from the fighter pilots who were also claiming credit for the downing of our bomber. All these reports of course piqued my interest, and I knew well the other side of the story, but again, I offered nothing.

The questioning throughout my eight-day incarceration in Dulag Luft became somewhat routine. In order to stay strong during this time, I found more ways to exercise my brain and body in my confined space. First and foremost were my prayers, prayers that I composed on the spot, as well as the litany of prayers that I knew by heart. I also reviewed our last mission in my mind, and the whole sequence of events comprising it. I concentrated on my home town, Salamanca, New York, and on drawing a map in my mind of all of the streets that I could remember, and the stores on Main Street, and the folks that I had left behind. I pictured every member that I could of my family, including aunts, uncles and cousins. I had nothing to use for writing but my finger. Utilizing my right index finger, as if it were a pencil, I wrote my story, beginning on February 4th when our B-17 climbed out of Podington on our last mission. I thought back to the days that led up to my solitary confinement at Dulag Luft, wrote them out, and traced the words with my finger. As I worked to recall as much as possible of my experience, I began to realize how many perilous days I had lived through so far.

The guards and interrogators became increasingly distressed at my demeanor during the grilling sessions, but I was going to stand my ground. I had worked hard to strengthen my mind every day between questionings, and it really helped.

I do, however, have a positive memory of my final interrogation session at Dulag Luft. As I was leaving the room, I heard my interrogator say, "Young man!" When I turned around our eyes met and in a sincere tone he finished by stating, "I admire you." I just gave a grateful nod and was led back to my miserable quarters. The memory of those words stayed with me my entire life.

I did not suffer any physical abuse during the interrogations, but the sessions wreaked havoc on my nerves; there was certainly no guaranty that I wouldn't become a punching bag for my guards. It is hell to live each day being questioned, offering nothing, and wondering if your silence may provoke a violent reaction. That torment, in itself, is torture.

Finally, my time in the transient camps was up and I would move on, with others, to a place called Wetzlar, to be "processed in," with photographs and fingerprints to be taken. I was then assigned and transferred to my permanent camp. I was hoping that all this processing would also trigger paperwork that would reach my family, showing them that I was still alive.

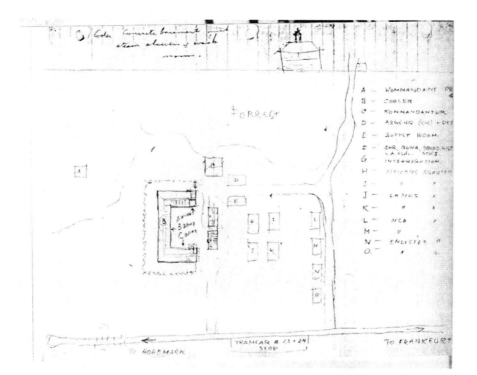

Map of Dulag Luft drawn by German Interrogator Scharff
Courtesy of B24.net – Greg Hatton

Kommandants
Courtesy of B24.net – Greg Hatton

Wetzlar
Courtesy of B24.net – Greg Hatton

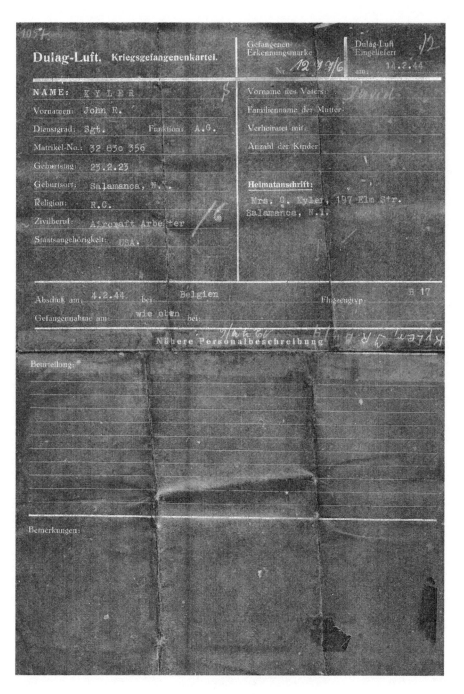

My Dulag Luft form

	Besondere Fähigkeiten:		Sprachkenntnisse:		Führung:

	Datum	Grund der Bestrafung		Strafmaß	Verbüßt, Datum
Strafen im Kr.-Gef.-Lager					

Schutzimpfungen während der Gefangenschaft gegen			Erkrankungen			
	Pocken	Ty.-Paraty., Ruhr, Cholera usw. – Sonstige Impfungen	Krankheit	Revier von / bis	Lazarett – Krankenhaus von / bis	
am	am	am				
Erfolg	gegen	gegen				
am	am	am				
Erfolg	gegen	gegen				
am	am	am				
Erfolg	gegen	gegen				
	am	am				
	gegen	gegen				

	Datum	Grund der Versetzung	Neues Kr.-Gef.-Lager		Datum	Grund der Versetzung	Neues Kr.-Gef.-Lager
Versetzungen	10. Feb. 1944		Sl. 4. 6. -	Versetzungen			
	26.1.45		Stpl Lg. 9. 1				

Figur:	schlank	Augen:	graubraun
Größe:	5,8	Nase:	lang gebogen
Schädelform:	lang	Bart:	ohne
Haare:	blond	Gebiß:	gut
Gewicht:	70 kg		
Gesichtsform:	länglich	Besondere Kennzeichen:	keine
Gesichtsfarbe:	gesund		

Rechter Zeigefinger

34830356

Front | Profil | Fingerabdruck

K/0257

Back of my Dulag Luft form

John Kyler Is Prisoner Of Germany

Mr. and Mrs. David Kyler, 197 Elm street, received a telegram from the War department Tuesday evening stating that their son, Sgt. John Roland Kyler, reported missing in action Feb. 4 over Germany, now is a German prisoner of war. It was through the Red Cross that this information was secured.

Sgt. Kyler, a gunner in the U. S. army air forces, had been on bombing missions over Europe since Jan. 21.

He was inducted Feb. 3, 1943 and trained at Miami Beach, Fla., Lareda, Tex., Denver, Colo., and Salt Lake City, Utah. He also attended gunnery schools in Nevada and Nebraska.

The Salamanca sergeant left for overseas last November and was stationed in England.

His brother, Sgt. Morris D. Kyler, a mechanic in the air corps, also is serving in the European theater of war.

—o—

24

Return to present....

DULAG LUFT

Departing at 9 a.m. on April 27, 2005, our drive to Oberursel, home of Dulag Luft, covered the thirty miles from Frankfurt in about an hour. The train station in Oberursel is still there, and Candy took pictures of it, inside and out, and the tracks in both directions, uncertain of the direction that I arrived from. It was difficult for me to remember, exactly, how I had arrived all those years ago. I did remember a very long walk, and I recall the Interrogation Camp being at the top of a hill. The flimsy structures that we were housed in for the days of interrogation were gone. The only recognizable structure still standing was a large vacant building that may have been a German administration building at the time. There was a cement pad, where the guide told us the Germans had played soccer, but I had no recollection of that, and I think I would remember seeing a bunch of enemy soldiers playing sports. The pad is now full of etchings of airmen, planes and a variety of images. There was a photo distributed of what the camp had looked like, and that illustration triggered my memory. We walked the entire area, and I could estimate, approximately, where the solitary confinement chamber that I spent days in was located. At the time of my stay it was well into winter, and I remember being so bitterly cold in the small barren room in which I was confined. Today, however, the weather was quite pleasant. That we now walked freely through these once heavily guarded grounds was very pleasing to me.

The property is now developed with condominiums, and there is an open, well-groomed section, much like a recreational area, where people appeared to be picnicking and playing games. It was a much better, and a more carefree atmosphere today than it was sixty years ago when we were shipped here, haggard and downtrodden, on our way to our permanent POW camp.

In the end, our visit to Oberursel was not that exciting. There are few traces today of the things that went on there in February, 1944 –– certainly no hint of my dreadful days of interrogation and incarceration on these grounds; the days that I would exhaustingly repeat my name, rank and serial number.

HOHEMARK

The next stop in pursuit of my history was at a site that had been utilized as a hospital for wounded prisoners during the war. Memories were aroused on my first glimpse as, at the time of my transfer to my new camp, I had a brief stay in this building due to my injured ankle. There was nothing broken, so after examination I was quickly passed on and cleared for the long trip to my first POW camp assignment. Of course back then, I didn't know that I would end up serving time in more than one POW camp.

There was no way to tell my daughter about my treatment at the German infirmary, and she assumed that I was never treated here. The injuries that I had incurred were unknown to her; my ankle was nothing that I ever mentioned to anyone. I never suffered any problems from the ankle injury later in life, and, until today, the memory had been lost.

We were allowed entry to the building with the gracious Administrator as our guide. He explained that this edifice was originally built as a mental hospital for the affluent until it became a facility to treat the Allied prisoners during the war. After the war, the Americans took it over and it was purchased by a Christian group operating as a mental hospital; it remains so today.

As part appreciation for the visit part public relations, I suppose, Candy and the others were given a memento, a small metal plaque with the raised image of this building bordered by trees, with the inscription,

"Klinik Hohe Mark." What a great feeling she would have had she realized I had been treated here! She wrote in her journal that evening, "Upon our return from Oberursel, if I were my father I'd say it brought back memories," and how accurate she was. Her last entry for that day was, "I've never heard that dad was there and probably never will hear." I'm sad that it is too late for me to tell her, and that she'll never know.

Tracks leading into Oberursel (Dulag Luft)

Dulag Luft today

Vacant building- Dulag Luft

Hohemark Hospital

25

TRANSPORT TO PRISONER OF WAR CAMP

After interrogation and processing, the Army Air Corps officers and non-commissioned officers were separated by the Germans, and would thereafter take different routes to different camps. A group of us "non-coms" were crowded into those unforgettable, horrid box cars for the trip to our permanent camp. None of us had any idea of the number of days we would spend in this confined, dark and bleak place, or what our destination would be.

My mind was overcome with grim anticipation of the future. How could anything that was lying ahead be good? Our freedom lost, we were fated to a life foreign to us in prison, in enemy territory. One couldn't help but speculate about our future treatment and, ultimately, whether we would survive the ordeal. So far we were fortunate—we were alive—but we all knew that our luck could run out at any time in our uncertain position. The not knowing was agonizing. We were now down to just three of our crew – Jay Joyce, John Alexander, and me. Our co-pilot and bombardier, Bob Bangs and Emmett Bell, who had traveled the route with us from Belgium through Dulag Luft, would now be sent to a different camp for officers. No one in our situation could know what to expect: our training really hadn't covered this eventuality. We were totally inexperienced in this new undesirable position.

As we clacked along the rails, we became hungry, thirsty and cold, but I knew that I had better get used to it. Our lives were now under the control of the German guards and their masters. We, however, had power over our ability to handle whatever we were to face. It was vital to remember that we still possessed a measure of control over our own destiny, and staying strong mentally and physically would help us maintain this capability.

One comfort I had was being in the boxcar with the two of my crew members. At that point, we probably had more in common with each other than any of us had ever had with anyone else in our young lives. We had experienced the most frightening and most crucial moments of our lives when we were forced to bail out of our crippled B-17 over Belgium into enemy territory. I think we all kept reliving the nightmare of our bomber being hit, the German fighters shooting at us, and our escape from the B-17. We sure had the time. We compared our stories about how and where we each had landed in Belgium, and what led up to our capture. I found it therapeutic to share our stories. We each described the last time that we had seen the others. We were concerned about the other five crew members that none of us had seen since our bail out. We couldn't help but wonder where they were, and if they had escaped, or if they even survived the jump. I expressed my concern about what I had been told by the German guard in Belgium about our navigator, Don Caylor, being injured. Jay and John had been told the same thing and they, too, reacted as I did, wanting to know everything about his condition, but not letting themselves be lured into a comfort zone with the guard. We all wondered about his condition and whether he was still alive. I feared what the guard had told me in Frankfurt may be the truth – that Don had died.

I now realize that sharing our thoughts and our fears enabled us to draw comfort from our common humanity. It was listening to the fears of others that helped me to realize I wasn't a coward as I had wondered about. How could anyone in our position not be afraid of what was in store for them in the immediate future? We had survived the most terrifying ordeal of our lives, but it was far from over.

As our time in the boxcars wore on, we began to feel like captive animals. The ride seemed like forever and I was losing all track of time. It was always dark in this miserable place, so I could not tell what time of day or night it was. My stomach was in knots and felt hollow, with pangs of hunger. My head ached. My sprained ankle seemed to be healing.

As the days went on, the early discomfort of the situation gave way to the beginnings of misery. We lost all modesty, having to relieve ourselves in a bucket passed around in the group that we were traveling with. Our spirits were flagging and the degradation of our treatment – being hauled like animals, was taking its toll. I didn't know how long I would be able to stand living like this and we were only days into a deplorable experience that could last months or even years.

Somehow, I knew I would never be at ease as this hopeless character that I was doomed to play. The car was so crowded we had to sleep standing up, if we could sleep at all. I wished so that we had made it back to England, back to freedom. When I closed my eyes I could imagine things at Podington. We were now among the unfortunate crews that we heard and read about with sadness. We were like so many crews before us who didn't return from their mission.

After seven days and nights of travel, on February 21, 1944 we arrived at a POW camp in a desolate area near the city of Heydekrug, East Prussia. It was called Stalag Luft VI.[3]

---

3 The town is presently known as Šilutė, in Lithuania.

*Stalag Luft VI
— Camp #1*

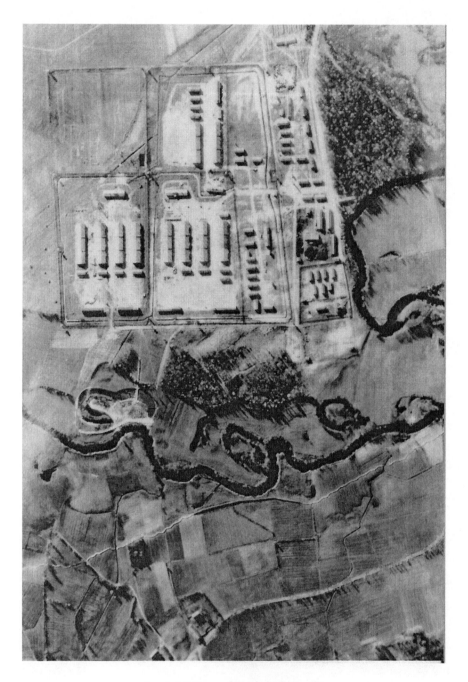

Aerial View of Stalag Luft VI
Courtesy of Joe O'Donnell

Barracks in Stalag Luft VI
Courtesy of Joe O'Donnell

26

FIRST HOME AS PRISONER OF WAR

The train slowed as it entered the station in Heydekrug, ending our long wearisome ride. We climbed down from the boxcars, closely watched by the guards, and unprotected from the biting winds. Under prodding from the guards, we began what was to be a two kilometer walk to our new home. It was difficult, after all the time we'd spent in such a cramped space, to put one foot in front of the other. Accustomed as we'd grown to the darkness of the boxcar, the brightness of the sun was blinding, almost painful. We had never gone this long without food and water, and it was unknown when and whether we would be fed. Looking about for the first time, I felt that the true test of captivity had just begun.

As I looked around in the bright sunlight I first felt exhilarated after the dark, filthy confines of the boxcar I'd spent a week in, but almost at once I didn't feel so good – I was now a prisoner, getting my first look at the land where my new prison was located.

We were marched from the train station along a cinder road through a remote, wooded area. It was an effort for me to walk with my still-tender ankle, but I hoped it would improve with a bit more exercise. I felt weakness from the days of starvation, minimal water, and confinement in the boxcars, and now I began feeling numb from the cold which, I think actually helped revive me a bit. Still the situation seemed unreal, as this ragged band of American prisoners trudged along under guard towards... what?

There was nothing that looked like home in this desolate area, so thick with trees. "We might be able to escape if we made a dash for the woods," I whispered to my fellow crewman, Jay. But we could both see the distance to the tree line and how close the guards were watching us, and I had to agree with him as he shook his head, "no." Still, I was determined to stay alert for an opportunity to escape, and every muscle in my body was tense.

As we approached the camp proper, I remember vividly my first view of a barbed wire fence surrounding the buildings that would become our new homes. The most foreboding sight was the strategically located wooden watchtowers manned with armed guards, partly obscured in the dazzling sunlight. We were being prodded ever faster towards our destination, and the pace was causing my ankle to complain with a growing throb. I sure did not feel like moving. However, if I didn't continue at the forced pace, I would surely draw harmful attention to myself. I gritted my teeth and trudged toward the gates with my comrades.

Entering Stalag Luft VI

I remember like it was yesterday, entering the complex through the gates and walking by two small stone buildings. A short distance behind these buildings were many structures that appeared to comprise a living area for the German guards judging by the number of uniformed, armed men standing about. Further down the road there were other men who were obviously long-time POWs observing us as we entered the camp. I would later find that these men were Brits with the Royal Air Force. They had been captives here for a long time, and they were about as adjusted as one could be to the dreary life of imprisonment. They sent understanding glances our way. We continued marching past these prisoners, to the quarters housing the American prisoners.

We finally arrived at a group of long, low wooden barracks and entered them clutching our meager belongings. We were hungry and thirsty and badly in need of a shower after days spent in utter filth and excrement. All of the things we had been accustomed to and considered necessities were now luxuries if, and when, we would be provided them.

There were some Americans in what was called Lager E, the American Compound. We exchanged words with these guys, asking and answering questions, and I realized that we were among the first Americans to arrive at Stalag Luft VI; these Americans had arrived only weeks ago. Together we would learn how to survive in conditions that were entirely new to us. Back in England we had learned how to *evade* capture and make it to a neutral country, but we had never really been taught how to exist as a POW in a prison camp.

21ˢᵗ Birthday in Heydekrug

My first night—it was cold and windy—was quite uncomfortable. I didn't have enough clothes, and we'd been given no blankets. I was hopeful that in time the Germans would provide some bedding materials—even the basic straw they gave us the next day was an improvement.

Two days after my arrival at Stalag Luft VI I turned twenty-one. At that point in time it had almost no meaning to me, and I didn't even realize I'd had a birthday until a day later. I hadn't yet accepted my new life—as prisoner—as a relatively permanent state of affairs. I look at all of it differently now and realize that I was lucky to be alive; so many were dead.

When I finally realized I was now a year older, I lay restless thinking about my family at home, who I thought were probably still wondering about my whereabouts, particularly on that special day. I killed some time in thought (a practice that was to become a frequent pastime) by recalling birthdays past, and all my relatives.

Camp Conditions

Stalag Luft VI was comprised of three compounds that I can still picture – American, British and a third compound that held a combination of British and Americans. Each compound contained ten brick barracks and a dozen wooden huts. The barracks were each designed to accommodate 552 men and the huts had a capacity of 54 prisoners, making a total camp capacity of about 6,200 men. We slept in double-decker bunks, and each room had tables, stools and lockers. The rooms were heated but the ventilation was poor because there were shutters on the windows that were kept closed at the insistence of the guards.

Centrally located for our use, there was a laundry and a theater with rooms for our studies. Here also was a separate barracks utilized as a chapel. In the same central area there were infirmary buildings, but they were not well-staffed.

There were three British chaplains in the camp who held services in the barracks chapel. Most of us attended these services. It was critical to maintain our faith. There was a request put in to the Camp Commandant for a Roman Catholic chaplain by those of us who were Catholics. We, nonetheless, were grateful for our British chaplains who assisted in combating our loneliness and encouraged us to turn to God to give us strength during our darkest hours. I think that some of the guys who had not been very religious started attending church services in the camp, but no one asked about it – religion was personal.

Getting Organized

We benefited a great deal from the trials and errors already experienced by the British, who had been inhabitants of Stalag Luft VI since June of 1943. They were now well established as resident POWs, and had made a life for themselves. We were grateful to them and the Canadians who, recalling their own first days in captivity, generously shared their food parcels with us until ours arrived.

As the Eighth Air Force losses mounted, the number of American POWs at the camp grew. There was the need to obtain the provisions required for us as POWs according to the Geneva Convention. We elected those who stood out as individuals most capable of seeing that the requirements would be met. I found as one of the early Americans assigned to the camp that I walked among the leaders, learning the ins and outs of the life of a prisoner of war.

It was by an overwhelming vote that Frank Paules became our elected "man of confidence," and Carter Lunsford became his assistant. These were men who I would come to know and respect as our leaders. Frank became well known among the German guards and it appeared that he developed a good working relationship with them – which of course worked in favor of the inmates. We were also especially lucky to have a man among us, Bill Krebs, who could speak fluent German. He effortlessly communicated our wants and needs to the guards so that we would be provided with our entitlements in the distribution of blankets and, eventually, our Red Cross food parcels. Sometimes they listened to him.

KEEPING FAITH IN THE FUTURE

I soon realized that if I were to maintain any semblance of a normal life I needed to keep busy, physically and mentally. I especially needed to resist the temptation of idleness, which would certainly lead to depression; we could see this as some of our fellow inmates became quiet and withdrawn. Losing hope would not help the situation, but make matters worse. I did my best to try to talk them out of it because I, too, was trying to avoid sinking into the same pit of blackness that they were experiencing. We were all in this together and understood this despair. We consoled one another when the need arose and learned to recognize those requiring attention. However, there were those few so deeply disturbed that they seemed beyond reach no matter how hard we tried to help them overcome their despondency. I was determined not to become one of them.

Permanent camp cleanup was a role I assumed to alleviate the boredom and gloom that was always around the corner. We didn't have to work, indeed, the Geneva Convention forbade our captors from putting us at labor, but I knew I needed structure in this place, and this job would help in that respect.

In our efforts to make the best of a bad situation, we roommates became like a family as we turned to each other for help and support. I was fortunate to be in the same room with my friend, Jay Joyce, and John Alexander was in the same barracks, so the three of us who had shared so much adventure frequently spent time together.

That was one thing that we had an abundance of – time. We tried to think of ways to utilize it, sharing our thoughts during the hours of confinement in our quarters during the freezing weather. We quickly befriended the roommates immediately around us. We were from diverse backgrounds – city and country, poor, middle-class and silver-spooners, but right now we had many common interests and similarities in our lives. It was a source of enjoyment and a great time-killer in our environment to share our backgrounds and our abilities, resulting in many positive results that benefitted us as a group.

I had become pretty close to Jay since our training, and we often shared stories of home. Jay had been married just three short weeks before he entered the Army Air Corps. His wife, Bea, went with him to Chicago when he went to radio school but he was forced to say goodbye when the schooling ended. He talked a lot about Bea and how much that he missed her. In a way I was jealous, but at the same time I could see that thoughts of his wife added to his homesickness, and his worries over her, and I would have felt that way too if I had a wife to worry about. On the other hand, Jay had someone to talk about and dream about and a real live person (and a woman to boot) to return to, and I could only dream of one day getting home and finding someone who would marry me. I was the only one of us three fellow crew members who wasn't married, and I didn't even have a sweetheart back home. That meant no letters from a girlfriend and no one to worry about whether I was even alive.

We couldn't change our present. We could only try to seek positive ways to get by each day, and that's what we did.

Beulah "Bea" Joyce
Courtesy of Bea Joyce

RED CROSS PARCELS

In time we received long overdue supplies from the American Red Cross. On delivery day, my most valuable possession became my Red Cross parcel allotment, which was supposed to be one per week. However, I vaguely remember that for the majority of my time in Stalag Luft VI our rations consisted of one-half a Red Cross parcel and one-half a Canadian parcel per week. I tried to make them last as long as possible. We would learn how valuable it was to save and hoard certain items, particularly cigarettes, to use for bartering, with each other and with our German guards.

To supplement our parcel, the Germans gave us a loaf of dark brown bread that had to be divided among our room mates, and it was difficult to keep the slices uniform. It was thought to be made of sawdust but, nevertheless, we all wanted our fair share, and the inmate assigned the duty of dividing the loaf received much attention and guidance. Any type of food that we received was a treasure and, when it had to be divided, there was always a peanut gallery.

It was amazing just how frequently food was on our minds. We would discuss all of our favorite dishes, and of course who made them. We would talk in depth about the preparations of different dishes, who we thought was best at preparing them, and where we had last eaten them. For a group of guys who knew little about cooking, the arguments about food preparation were amazing.

Although we always talked about our imaginary meals, the real food situation went from decent to fair to substandard to awful as more POWs arrived in camp.

The coveted Red Cross Parcel
Courtesy of B24.net – Greg Hatton

YMCA Supplies

We needed more nourishment than food and talk, and over time the inmates took up hobbies they never would have touched on the outside. It was a comical sight to see grown men sitting with their knitting needles and their crochet hooks fashioning scarves, hats, sweaters or vests – whatever they chose to tackle. I succeeded in obtaining my own yarn and hook, together with a set of instructions from which to learn a new craft. I had never crocheted in my life and it was not something that I pined to learn, but I thought it would help me keep my mind busy. And I was determined to create a finished product that would be useful to me in the camp. I thought that a nice vest would serve the dual purpose of passing time and giving warmth if I could only succeed at this strange art. The fact was that I had not been warm since I had been captured. The pieces of coal that we fed into the lone stove in the room were rationed just like everything else, and the supply was wholly inadequate.

Nothing was put to waste – we had so few "things" that a secondary use was found for everything, or the material was kept until a use could be found for it. Jay had whittled his own knitting needles to begin his attempt. There were some pretty talented fellows among us. I think that some of their wives and mothers would have been proud. There were many wise comments exchanged as we worked developing our skills in different areas. I was teased that I could make someone a pretty good wife some day as I worked on my vest. It wasn't so easy trying to hold the hook and the yarn. I started holding it too tightly and had difficulty fitting the hook in the loop, but eventually I got the hang of it and things went much smoother as I learned the right tension to apply when holding onto the yarn.

Musical instruments were provided to men inclined to use them. Their musical talent was welcomed by us all, and several musicians were especially welcome. A choir was formed, further enhancing the entertainment. Soothing music filled the air and for those moments, if we closed our eyes, our thoughts went out beyond the wire, and we were revived. Musical presentations were a source of entertainment as well as play productions on special occasions. There were men who before their imprisonment had never realized that they possessed such a talent in entertaining their fellow prisoners.

Reading was another great avocation, and there were about 6,000 much-fingered books available in the camp library. It was a relief to become immersed in the stories and it removed us from our prison without the need to use picks and shovels. We often shared our favorites with other prisoners and endlessly debated and reviewed them.

As time passed, there were even educational courses organized with POWs as instructors. The British had set up exceptional classes in numerous subjects, teaching skills that would prove valuable after the war. It was a remarkable academy, and an opportunity to keep one's mind from becoming stagnant.

My Finished Product (a <u>lined</u> crocheted vest)

The Treasured Notebooks

Ultimately, I obtained a Y.M.C.A. notebook and a pencil, and I immediately wrote my name on the front of it, as well as my POW number, "1277," and my new address – Stalag Luft VI. The notebook gave me another avenue by which to escape boredom. I was lucky to be given a second book when one of my roommates decided he didn't need his. I figured I would likely be a prisoner long enough that paper could be at a premium, so I was glad to acquire a second book. He gave me his pencil for a spare as well.

POEMS

To fill the hours, we often wrote poems in our notebooks, and many of us became pretty fair poets almost overnight. It was a way to express our inner feelings or make fun about nearly any subject. We would share our finished products with each other and sometimes the poems would be copied in one another's books. Jay wrote about our new home in Heydekrug. John wrote a poem about saying goodbye to his little boy. One of the poems that I wrote was about our pilot, and another about my position as ball turret gunner.

THAT LITTLE BOY OF OURS

by John J. Alexander

Ten tiny fingers, ten tiny toes
I remember them as I had to go
I bid him good bye, he didn't reply
But some day he will know.

He was so little and so sweet
Huddled in his crib sound asleep
As I left this room I didn't look back
There were tears in my eyes, that's a fact.

I crossed the ocean, but never lost sight
How precious he looked that very night
This war must end and when it is through
Hurry home to him is what I'll do.

Barbed Wire Hotel

by Jay Joyce

In Hydekrug, East Prussia,
There's a beautiful spot.
It's a barbed wire hotel
Where the meals are served real hot.

A seventh of a loaf of bread per day,
A bowl of German stew.
A tiny hunk of old horse meat,
A can of English brew.

All this comes free;
It doesn't cost a cent.
Your meals and sack –
Both go with the rent.

If you want to visit the hotel so neat
Try a mission over Germany
And let the flack beat.

There you'll meet Oberluft Volts
And you'll like him in spite of hell
For he's the manager of the barbed wire hotel.

A GOOD PILOT

by John R. Kyler

A pilot is a well-trained chauffeur
And is bossed by the entire crew.
But when it comes to pinches
(He'll tell you what to do!)

He keeps the plane in formation
Way up there in that blue
And when the fighters start coming in
He calls them off to you.

He sets up there so helpless
With no gun to fire back
But when it comes to courage
That's something he doesn't lack.

To him his crew's welfare
Is foremost in his mind
And when it comes to bailing out
You can bet he'll be last in line.

A GOOD PILOT

A pilot is a well trained chauffeur
And is bossed by the entire crew
But when it comes to pinches
(He'll tell you what to do.)

He keeps the plane in formation
Way up there in that blue
And when the fighters start coming in
He calls them off to you

He sets up there so helpless
With no gun to fire back
But when it comes to courage
That's something he doesn't lack.

(over)

SKETCHES

I invested much time making pencil sketches. One of them was of my home at 197 Elm Street, Salamanca, New York. I was always thinking about the house and the way it looked the day that I left, and I frequently thought of my last moments with Mom and my sisters. I wondered about my father, and my brother Morris. Morris, too, was serving his country, but we hadn't had contact in quite some time. There was no way of knowing if my family had received word of my capture. I could clearly visualize the inside of each room of my old home, and where each piece of furniture was. I painstakingly sketched a diagram of both inside and out. I thought of my sister Helen who lived next door with her husband Fred and young son Jim. Helen had been like a second mother to me, and I was certain she must be agonizing about my whereabouts as much as anyone. I longed for letters from home.

Dreams of my Home-197 Elm Street

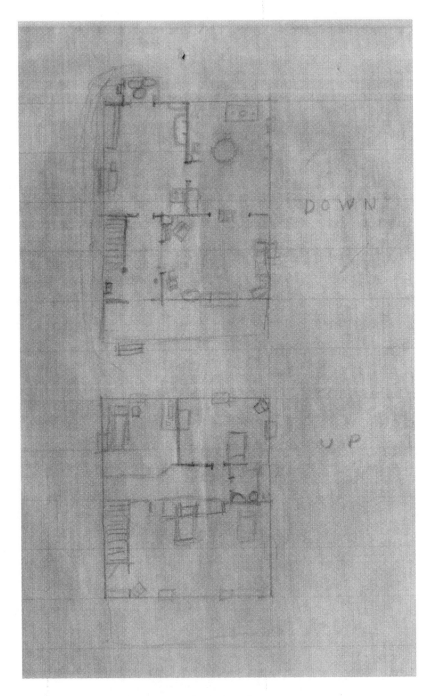

Diagram of inside of My Home

My Roommates

Throughout my days of incarceration in Stalag Luft VI, I would go about collecting the names and addresses of my roommates and other inmates with whom I was becoming close. I did this over a period of time and learned about each of the men that I wrote into my notebook. I documented whether they had flown in a B-24 or a B-17. We would exchange the stories of our missions and the details of the crash or the bailout, and the ultimate capture. Many of us who had seen fellow crew members shot or wounded by flak, or guys who never made it out of the ship had a story that could be painful to tell, but most found it healing to elaborate and recall the events that brought us together. We were all interested in learning about the days leading up to each other's arrival into camp.

As upsetting and terrifying as my own experience had been with my Podington crew, I felt lucky when I heard the stories that others told of injury and death far more horrible than what I had witnessed. There was always someone who had had it worse, or had seen worse, than you.

These conversations helped us understand why some were not handling their imprisonment well. They were still traumatized by the tragedies that had occurred as a direct result of our battle with the enemy, or with the sheer force of nature. Many were recovering from physical injuries as well as mental trauma. My ankle sprain was dwarfed next to the injuries of some of my new buddies.

Page from Notebook notating Camp Leader, Frank
Paules, and Assistant Camp Leader, Carter Lunsford

Food

Am I back to food again? I reiterate how often food was on my mind – so often that not only was it talked about frequently, but I would actually draw my favorite meals. Two of the beloved meals that I longed for were spaghetti and hamburgers and I remember carefully creating them on paper. These simple pencil sketches triggered memories of wonderful tastes that I sorely missed. The Red Cross parcel was such a treasure that many of us carefully inventoried it, listing the contents in our notebooks. Food was important, and you keep records of important things. I'm not too sure why we did this – perhaps we felt that by recording the contents they would last longer. And I would do everything I could to make my parcel last when I received it. One could not be frivolous, and it was wise to ration our wares. There were times, more than not, we had to share our parcels and did not each receive an entire box for ourselves. All in all, most of us were quite agreeable with sharing. It was during the lean times that I would read about what my parcel had once contained.

Calendar

Each day was another long day in captivity, but all of us maintained a certainty that we would one day win the war, and so it was also another day closer to freedom. So that I would never forget an important date, including my birthday, I drew a calendar in my notebook, and it was satisfying to cross each day off as it passed. This imprisonment would not last forever. I told myself – we all did –that one day we would all be free again. I marked the days that were significant differently than the routine days. These special dates were those I would never forget, and they would all be a link to an important day in my past.

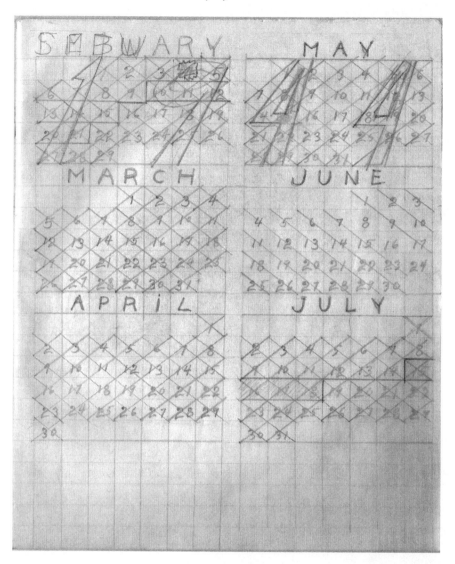

Counting the Days (notice 2/4 and 7/15-7/18/44)

TUNNELING

One of the great pastimes in camp for many was tunneling to escape. It was not something that I was involved in, for I always thought it was too risky. I would contribute my ideas, and help in any way that I could but I was not going to dig or take part in any escape attempt. Even if one could evade the guards, escape seemed highly improbable in such a remote area so far from any friendly border.

Our camp was on sandy ground, and that made chances of a successful escape even more unlikely because the tunnels were always caving in.[4] We all sacrificed the wooden slats from our bunks for the shoring effort. The tunnelers finally solved the problem of what to do with the dirt they were digging up every day to clear the tunnel. We had an area where we played basketball and the dirt would be gradually dumped and spread out on the court, eventually raising the grade level by quite a bit. I always thought that the guards were aware of what was going on but they didn't bother us because they shared my opinion of the unlikely prospect of escape, and they thought it helped to occupy our time. A failed escape had consequences beyond merely being discovered – you could be shot for trying to escape, and that was not a chance that I was willing to take.

I can recall that one of the plans was to tunnel under the latrine and under the fence on the other side of it. It had been progressing for weeks until a Russian POW walked over it, unknowing, and fell through into the tunnel making a horrible racket and nearly frightening him to death. The guards found it amusing, and all of the hard work had been in vain.

SPORTS

Although space was limited, with the equipment furnished by the YMCA we organized teams for softball, football and basketball; another great time-burner. There were some outstanding athletes among us. I was more of a spectator but I did participate sometimes to keep my strength up. There were also boxing matches featuring some real talented boxers. One of the fights I remember well, putting my money (cigarettes) on an American who also happened to be a roommate. You could wonder how anyone could stay in shape when the caloric intake was so limited, but he had been training for days and it paid off, because he won the match and I collected more bartering material.

Unbeknownst to the Germans, the sporting equipment was also a source of smuggled radio parts, which was our lifeline to the outside world.

---

4 The Luftwaffe typically located POW camps in areas with sandy soils to make tunneling difficult.

The fabrication of a hidden radio was another example of POW ingenuity. The information that we received by radio was passed from barracks to barracks by word of mouth and it kept us abreast of the war's progress. It also gave us a means of comparison to the unsettling German propaganda that our captors never tired of spreading.

CONFUSING THE GUARDS

Another form of amusement was bamboozling the guards during the roll call when there were men who were absent because they were working on escape plans. The number would always come out right because we would borrow men from another barracks and shift them into the lineup before the counting ended.

FALLEN COMRADES

It is difficult, after so many years, to remember the names of prisoners who died or were killed while in camp; and even though the recollections of these times fade, there are incidents that are burned indelibly into my memory and names that I shall never forget.

Tensions in the Camp had become elevated as a result of an event in March 1944 that would embarrass the Luftwaffe and greatly aggravate the Fuhrer. If there was ever any concern on the part of the Germans that they were in compliance with the Geneva Convention, that concern evaporated after this event. I'm referring to the mass POW escape that occurred from Stalag Luft III in 1944, during which about 75 prisoners (none American) had made good their escape from the camp. All but three were recaptured. The execution of fifty of the escapees was announced at Stalag VI, sending shock waves through all. Hitler was making an extreme example of these prisoners by this atrocious act. A failed attempt on his life in July of that year also infuriated him, camp security was heightened further, and it became apparent that any escape attempt was suicidal. Any confidence that we had that the war would soon end dissipated. The struggle of the prisoners to survive intensified, and nerves were more frazzled than ever. Both the guards and prisoners were on edge, and we felt that anything could happen. Our group of leaders consequently lost power as the Germans cracked down on us. One could sense a feeling of hopelessness. The guards who were considered fair were beginning to fear for their own safety.

A most tragic and upsetting memory that has lingered in my mind is the horrifying result of an escape attempt in April, 1944. The plan seemed brilliant and there was great optimism on the part of the few that knew of the plan that the escape would be successful. The idea for the escape sprung from a routine task that six prisoners completed every week, when they were allowed to leave the compound and walk over to the Red Cross supply building, called the Vorlager by the Germans. Each time the prisoners would dump empty food boxes behind the Red Cross supply house and then return with new supplies. The scheme involved hiding a seventh man—a slender ball turret gunner—in one of the large empty boxes. The guards were intentionally distracted when the prisoners arrived at the Red Cross building, and during this distraction one man, George Walker, hid himself between the boxes while the concealed gunner left his box and took Walker's place. There was nothing that appeared suspicious as six men took the boxes out and six returned. It was as simple as that. This same practice was executed for a second time successfully when Staff Sergeant Ed Jurist was replaced by the same ball turret gunner. This plot left two men, George and Ed, hidden in the Vorlager surrounded by empty boxes.

The plan was to cut their way out at nightfall. The Germans would never expect anyone to attempt an escape so close to their barracks. The weakness, however, in this well thought out idea was a German guard who should have walked the perimeter of the Camp but instead paced back and forth in front of the gate. The men crawled slowly, cutting the wire when the searchlight was shining away from them, but because the guard covered such a small territory, they hadn't the time they needed to cut through the wire, and he noticed them. Suddenly there were dogs and guards after them. George Walker, for some reason, stood up, and though his arms were up in the air in the universal sign of surrender he was shot dead on the spot.

I didn't witness his death but the word spread fast, and the atmosphere in the camp was one of gloom. Why when he was obviously surrendering would they be so trigger-happy? It was a despicable and reckless action.

There was a small burial plot at the edge of a grove of young birch trees where S/Sgt. George B. Walker was laid to rest. It was quite traumatic for all of us as we watched the funeral procession from a distance, attentive to the echo of "Taps" in the air. It was an empty feeling to think about his family at home, hopeful that he would return some day.

Once again, I was exposed to the harsh life as a POW when I was abruptly awakened on the morning of May 28th by loud German voices and the cold crack of a gunshot. I cautiously arose and moved towards the door, afraid of what I would find. My heart stopped when I realized that one of my comrades, Walter Nies, was lying outside the barracks in a pool of blood. What could he have possibly done to warrant his being shot? Just looking at his body, it was obvious that he had not been trying to escape. He had a towel around his neck and was lying along the path to the latrine. A feeling of nausea and anger both gripped me and the others who one by one became aware of this tragic and senseless murder. No matter how tough we tried to be, there were tears of sadness and tears of anger that such an outrageous and illegal act had taken place. We all prayed that our friend would survive and it appeared that he was still alive when he was taken away. On the following day, May 29th, Frank Paules, who had been with Walter, reported that Sergeant Nies had died. I was sickened by this loss; we all were.

On May 30th there was a funeral procession of over twenty of us and we gave our friend a military funeral. I felt very ill inside with overwhelming sorrow for Walter, realizing that his was another family that would never see their loved one again, and he was being buried far away from home with only his POW brothers in attendance.

As we pieced together the events of that night, it was clear that the German guards were to blame for this murder. They had failed to lock the door as they did every evening at ten o'clock. But that locked door was important to the prisoners, because after lights out it was impossible to know the exact time. Not knowing the time and taking the open door to mean that it was after curfew, three roommates made their way to the latrine.

According to one of the three, Mick Wagelie, in his account of the event, it became obvious that something was wrong because no one was around but the German guards. Mick tried to return to his barracks but it was too late. He saw his friend shot down for no good reason. The vicious dogs were running towards Mick so he ran to the latrine and tried to hold himself up to keep from being bitten. He was then arrested and put into solitary confinement for twenty-nine days. He explained what had happened to the guards–that the door was not locked! But it fell on deaf ears and to cover their mistake and justify their action, the Germans punished him as if he were trying to escape. We never saw the guard who was guilty of this murder in our camp again and we never knew where he had been transferred. Getting him out of our camp was a wise move by the management, and may have saved that guard's life.

Memories such as these revive deep feelings of anguish and heartache in me. That is exactly why I buried them in my mind, never to talk about them to those who had not been there. No one can ever understand how I felt except someone who shared the grief. I needed to forget these things or be torn apart by them inside, and that is why I kept silent in the years after the war. I never talked about these incidents and I never dwelled on them, but they were never forgotten either.

These two incidents brought a collective and oppressive gloom over the camp that we could not seem to shake. We needed to refocus on something positive and our leaders knew it. This is when sports became so important to keep us occupied and entertained and helped to raise our fallen spirits. Every diversion that was possible was exploited, and more invigorating activities could be increased as warmer weather arrived. And with the warmer weather came longer hours that we could remain outdoors.

I recall a third death, that of William Teaff, which was due to diphtheria. It was during the last days of our internment at Stalag Luft VI. We had to bury another of our fellow prisoners after he lost his battle with Nature.

The End of Time in Stalag Luft VI Was Near

We could hear the guns in the distance and it was apparent that the Russians were getting closer, and of course that gave us renewed hope. The word circulated among us that it was inevitable that the Germans soon would be evacuating the camp in the face of the advancing Russians. We didn't want them to know that we were cognizant of what was going on, so we behaved as normal, making plans for a Fourth of July celebration while at the same time preparing for the move to another unknown destination. We made backpacks out of our shirts and blankets to hold all that we could carry of our pitiful, yet precious, belongings. Once again our strong survival instincts kicked in as we began hoarding as many of our rations as possible without being too obvious about it. And, once again, we were disturbed by the uncertainty of what was in store for us.

One of the activities planned upon the arrival of the Fourth, what seemed to us to be an especially important commemoration, Independence Day, included a very potent concoction fermented by several dedicated prisoners into a strong alcoholic drink. Our Leader, Frank Paules, gave a well-prepared speech that many of us probably did not remember the next day due to their intoxicated state during the speech. Even with this diversion of the July 4th festivity, it was tough to keep one's mind off the impending evacuation and the unknown route we would take from here. It was another one of those times when I felt excitement as well as apprehension for the coming days, and I wasn't alone in these feelings.

27

Return to present...

RETURN TO HEYDEKRUG

Although Heydekrug, East Prussia, was my first permanent camp assignment, Candy was afraid this would be the one place she would not be able to find her way to. A return to Stalag Luft VI was not on any of the tour itineraries. But Candy was persistent, and she would not be satisfied with what she'd set out to accomplish until she tried every avenue she could think of to get to this important camp.

Candy decided she would only give up after every effort was exhausted. By finding and visiting the place, she felt she would have covered the territory necessary to achieve her aspiration of following my wartime path as closely as possible. I think she came to feel that if she did not set foot in each significant region of my war experience, my story could not be faithfully written. I know my daughter, and I believe she felt that to write my history she had to feel it by duplicating my route and following in my footsteps. There was no doubt in her mind that memories of my experience would come flooding back as she continued to remember for me, playing my role as I no longer could. She had applied this approach in every phase of her mission—with me by her side.

What had seemed an unreachable goal for my daughter became reality in a visit to Šilutė, (shuh'-loo-tay) Lithuania, "Heydekrug," when it was part of German East Prussia, and the former home of Stalag Luft VI. Her visit would be a side trip from a planned excursion in 2007, and the result of her contacts with the United States Embassy in Lithuania. The embassy people graciously provided a guide who had kindly volunteered for the job. We were to be accompanied on our trip by Chief David Ickes, United States Navy, along with historian Mr. Stasys Melinauskas, as well as Mr. Michael Karpusovas (a representative of the Commander of the Lithuanian Navy), and Ms. Roza Sikilliane, Curator of the museum adjacent to the former camp. Candy and I were about to receive a wonderful private tour of the area, a place I thought that I would never see again!

We were picked up by David Ickes from our hotel in Klaipeda as scheduled at 9 a.m. on a sunny and warm Monday morning. On our way to our destination we collected Michael Karpuzovas, who was to serve as translator for Stasys Melinauskas, the historian who we would meet at the site.

After a drive of about 20 miles from Klaipeda, we arrived at a small stone building that now serves as a museum, and it immediately brought back memories of my first view of this camp over sixty years ago. Roza, the museum curator, advised us, through our interpreter Michael, that Stasys was waiting for us at the cemetery. Together, we sauntered through the historic graveyard adjacent to the former camp, as Stasys gave the chronology of the various nationalities who had been prisoners of war in this area from 1939 to 1947. There are memorials placed throughout, representing the different groups interred as various governments came to power. There are commemorations for the Polish POWs and the German POW's in the vicinity to the east of where the American monument is located. Pine trees lend a serene setting for the rose-colored American monument etched with the names of my three fellow-American POW's.

As I listened to Stasys' words and Mike's interpretation of them, my eyes wandered throughout and beyond the memorials, and my visions of my fallen comrades and the services held for them came back to me as if it was 1944 again. It was extremely disturbing to me and it was obvious from the attentive and solemn look on Candy's face that she, too, was absorbing the past, recalling memories that she knew were mine.

Stasys continued to lead us on his tour of the area, calling attention to a Canadian memorial placed across the way in front of where we stood. This monument's design is identical to the American monument. The Russians who perished as prisoners of the Germans were also commemorated, and the Belgians and French who died here were remembered by a large inscribed cross. This cemetery contained many graves with no names... just mounds of grass-covered dirt. I noticed that some unmarked graves were nonetheless decorated with flowers indicating that the deceased buried there was identified and remembered. I know the pain that I felt as a POW and the fears I had lived with. When I think of the misery inflicted on these poor souls and what a lonely death they suffered I am sickened all over again. How horrible it was for the family never learning where the remains of their loved ones lie. These men had actualized my greatest fears.

I could not keep from thinking about the Americans whose loved ones had died in Stalag Luft VI. I wondered if they knew that somewhere in or near this cemetery lie the remains of their dear husband, father or son. I realized more deeply than ever how, although I never talked about them throughout my life, I had never forgotten them or their ultimate sacrifice. No one observed my tears, not then, not today.

As we continued from the wartime necropolis to the location of the American Compound where I had lived for a time, I could still recall the approximate area where the three fallen prisoners were originally buried. It is unclear if they had been disinterred and relocated, perhaps to the cemetery area just a short distance away. The American monument was not marking their resting place, just memorializing their deaths, with their remains buried somewhere on the grounds. It was relief to me knowing that they are remembered in this spot where their lives ended.

I was really surprised how clearly I could still remember the camp's appearance and my frequent walks around the compound sixty-three years ago. With the foundations that remain visible, it was easy for me to envision the layout. The first foundation that Stasys pointed out I knew immediately was that of the bath house, and I could remember a guard tower that had been nearby. So many recollections of days gone by were resurrected by just a glimpse of this simple foundation! As the others examined a diagram of the former camp, I wandered alone through what used to be the parade ground where we were called to twice a day to be counted. There was another foundation that I was certain was the cookhouse. I was walking the same ground that I had so long ago, and now my daughter was doing the same, viewing a place from my past life that were the remains of a camp I once knew. This area easily recognizable to me could of course only be shown to Candy through pictures, but even so, she was studying every inch of ground and taking in every view of the area that she could. I humbly realized what she was doing, for I had seen her do the same in the railway station in Frankfurt. She was studying the area to ensure that she saw what I saw and walked where I walked. She reasoned that there certainly were trees, grass, ground and sky that I walked under or through just as she was doing. She had written and mentioned to others before this visit that she knew that part of me was still here–the blood, sweat and tears that I shed from my arrival on Feb 21, 1944, to July 15, 1944, when the camp was evacuated. She is correct in thinking this way.

Before leaving the area, we returned to the small museum where Roza gave us a brief tour of the building, with Michael continuing to translate as the various displays were explained. This building may have been where the prisoners spent time as punishment in solitary confinement – the building was outside my compound, so I couldn't be sure. My mind returned to Mick Wagelie. He had unjustly spent twenty-nine days in solitary confinement, perhaps in this same building, simply because a German guard had left a door open. This is one of the many memories that remained in the forefront of my mind throughout this visit.

Stasys gave Candy some documents that contained a brief history of my camp and, to my great surprise, copies of pictures of the funeral procession of Walter Nies! It amazed me that pictures were taken of the sad event. She expressed her gratitude to him for his thoughtfulness.

Before ending our day, Candy proudly presented to Roza Sikilliane a notebook containing pictures and information concerning my history, and she seemed very pleased with it and said that it would be displayed in the museum. It was obvious how much this meant to my daughter knowing that her father and crew members were remembered in another area so important in my journey as a POW.

In our ride back to the hotel we drove near the railroad station where my walk to the camp began that winter day in February 1944 and ended on a hot sunny day in July as Stalag Luft VI was evacuated.

Candy sincerely expressed what an overwhelming and rewarding experience this had been for her and she extended her appreciation to all who made it possible. After the return to our hotel she wrote in her journal, "It is so rewarding to know now that I've followed dad's route through the region of his first camp, Stalag Luft VI. It is another area that I've paralleled in my father's path." She also added that "there is one more walk that I need to take – to a place that I am sure would look vaguely familiar to Dad." She put her pen down and donned her jacket for one final stroll in Lithuania.

Another important piece of the puzzle to her was a walk to the water, knowing that on July 15, 1944, I had been brought to the Port of Memel (now Klaipeda) after being evacuated from Stalag Luft VI. Through her own effort and perseverance she was staying in the same city that I, and hundreds of others, had once departed from for a treacherous voyage on the Baltic Sea. Crammed in the hold of an old coal boat, we sailed in misery to our next destination, Stalag Luft IV. Candy and I both gazed at the water one last time, realizing its importance in my historic journey through the war.

My stay at Stalag VI had been my first test of survival as a prisoner at the hands of the Germans. But it was not my last.

**American Monument in cemetery at the
former Stalag Luft VI Camp**

Michael Karpuzovas, David Ickes and
Stasys Melinauskas at Cemetery
(David graciously held "Rollie" (stuffed dog) for Candy in hopes
that one day Rollie will tell his tale of historic travels to children)

Remnants of a foundation in former Stalag Luft VI Camp

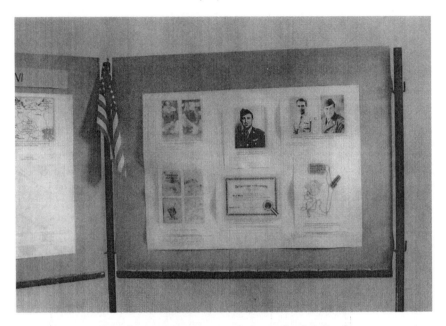

**Display in Museum at former Stalag Luft
VI Camp (photo of Walter Nies)**

Museum at former Stalag Luft VI Camp

28

Evacuation Of Stalag Luft VI

We could hear the guns in the distance and knew that the Russians were moving steadily closer, and it had become a question of evacuation or liberation. There were rumors that we were going to be moved farther west, away from the Russians, to another camp in Kiefheide, Pomerania, called Stalag Luft IV. We were told we would have a long hike ahead of us and we should pack a minimal amount of our clothes and possessions. This would mean packing a minimal amount of a minimal amount.

During our morning roll call, Frank Paules, our camp leader, announced that we would be leaving our "home" in Heydekrug...that afternoon! I guess that we should have felt happy and relieved to be vacating these premises, but on the flip-side we once again were faced with the question of, "where are we going now?" In peacetime, it might have been exciting, but in wartime, this was distressing. Also we had become adjusted to this way of life in this location and the uncertainty of what would be next was vexing. We all knew conditions could get much worse.

The final determination was that we were to make our exodus from Stalag Luft VI the following morning, July 15, 1944. In preparation, we carefully selected from our sparse possessions those that would be the most useful and important to take with us to our next assigned camp. We exchanged our opinions on what these essentials should be, hating to leave anything behind. It was almost a false sense of liberation knowing we would travel outside the barbed wire. The key word is "false."

After a distribution of one Red Cross parcel per prisoner, we abandoned our quarters in Stalag Luft VI, beginning our two kilometer walk to the railway station where once again we were herded into the "40 and 8" box cars; these dreadful cars that would actually cram in fifty-five men per car. We endured the four-hour ride standing and suffocating in the stifling heat, for it was the height of summer. Upon our arrival at the Port of Memel, we were turned over to a German captain whose hatred of American POWs was evident from his treatment of us. It was rumored that he had lost his entire family in a bombing raid, so he must have felt justified in his abusive behavior.

We were shoved, one man on top of the other, into the hold of an old freighter tied up at a dock in the harbor. Our packs had been taken from us upon boarding and were thrown forcefully down at us from above. We were supplied two buckets – one for water and the other for waste. Due to the dysentery that ran rampant among us from the filth in which we were immersed, both buckets soon became waste buckets.

For two days we suffered unbearable heat in the hold of this freighter on the Baltic Sea, in utterly deplorable conditions. We were caged like animals in the overcrowded dark, foul-smelling bilge of a broken-down boat. Food, ventilation and rest were non-existent on this God-forsaken "cruise." My living conditions had deteriorated dramatically and I realized bizarrely how by comparison Heydekrug had been almost luxurious.

Some of the British prisoners told us that we were traveling through waters that had been mined previously by their forces. Consequently, every noise we heard was unnerving. There was also a concern about Russian naval attacks. This two-day ride was nerve-wracking enough that one prisoner who could not handle the stress tried jumping overboard and was shot.

We were finally released from our stinking prison when we arrived at Swinemunde, and were relieved to be in the fresh air and on solid land at last. It was a relief that lasted only fleeting seconds until the Hitler Youth, young Nazi fanatics, took charge of us. These brown-shirted youths efficiently and brutally ordered us once again into the detestable freight cars, this time shackling our wrists and ankles together in twos. It was quite unnecessary, because we all were in a feeble state from the boat-ride, the heat, and lack of food or water. The accumulating filth on our bodies was also taking extreme toll, and lice-infestation and dysentery in this next segment of our transport was overpowering and exhausting us further.

Once again, the look in the eyes of those around me mirrored my terror and misery. The only positive was that we were all in this situation together and, as always, we supported each other – the stronger and healthier helped their weaker and less healthy comrades. There would be moments of strength and weakness for all involved and we took turns encouraging one another to hang on. But even slight camaraderie was difficult, chained together as we were. We were locked in these cars for another two days. Peeping out through the slats of our rolling prisons, we could see that much of our time was spent in marshalling yards and on sidings where we endured the threat of Allied planes on bombing runs. How much could one take? Our age was in our favor, but we were becoming progressively old beyond our years.

THE ROAD

Our situation became even worse when we reached Kiefheide Station on July 18, 1944. We were separated into groups, and forced at bayonet point to run four kilometers uphill to Stalag Luft IV. At the end of the line, men suffered in the heat waiting for their turn in what seemed like a suicide run. Many POW's who fell behind were bayoneted. The friend that I was shackled to was sick and weak and it was fortunate that I had seized every opportunity to exercise in order to stay as strong as possible. I did my best to help move him along so that we did not lag behind – it reminded me of a grim version of a three-legged race. To add to our problems, the Nazi youths set ferocious dogs on us that bit anyone who could not keep up. Most of us were forced to give up their belongings to lighten their load. Somehow, I managed to hang onto my bag. The rush of adrenaline combined with the will to escape the wounds that we saw inflicted on those falling behind helped us to reach the end of the road without serious injuries.

There were many acts of heroism that day. I witnessed an individual hanging onto his weaker partner and then bending to pick up another man that had fallen, assisting them both to the end of the road. One can assume these fellows would have lost their lives that day had they not been helped in their desperate state.

In retrospect we realized that the harsh treatment inflicted by the German guards was meant to incite us to attempt escape so that they would be justified in shooting us. I believe that Frank Paules, our elected "Man of Confidence," saved many lives that day by encouraging us to stay cool and keep together no matter what. Later, we learned there were Germans hidden in the woods with machine guns just waiting for the opportunity to shoot.

Reinhard Fahnert, German Guard
Courtesy of Joe O'Donnell

Walther Pickhard, German Guard
Courtesy of Joe O'Donnell

Stalag Luft IV
— Camp #2

Stalag Luft 4A
Courtesy of B24.net – Greg Hatton

Entering Stalag Luft IV
Courtesy of B24.net – Greg Hatton

29

MY SECOND HOME AS A POW

Over two thousand weary, lice-ridden POWs spent the evening where we came to rest out in the open after the strenuous run for our lives. Under different circumstances, in a different setting, the star-studded sky would have looked peaceful and beautiful on that warm summer evening. Gazing upward as I lay there, lost in the replay of what we had just been subjected to, I attempted, in my thoughts, to remove myself from this new unknown place. Many among us had suffered wounds and bites that required medical treatment, but for most that never occurred. I cannot be certain, but I believe that one of my fellow prisoners received so many severe bayonet wounds that he did not survive the horrendous ordeal.

We spent two days housed in tents in our new locality that we learned was called Gross Tychow, until we were assigned to our permanent barracks. It was chaotic claiming the possessions that had been seized by the guards who now took charge of making our lives as miserable as possible. Many treasured personal items were never returned to their rightful owners. I was fortunate to possess what I had arrived with, which wasn't much.

When a group of men is starved, exhausted, and inhumanely battered, mentally and physically, as we were, it leads to a subdued and disheartening atmosphere. Our morale had reached an all-time low. Any relief that we had felt upon our departure from Stalag Luft VI had evaporated. Our struggle to remain sane, as well as hopeful, became enormously challenging surrounded as we had been by such demoralizing sights, sounds and cruelty.

Camp Layout and Guidelines

The layout of our new camp, Stalag Luft IV, was different than our first in that there were four separate compounds, or lagers, that were arranged in a square. The camp was divided by a road with a gate leading into each unit. The familiar double barbed wire fence surrounded each compound as well as the entire camp. There was coiled barbed wire between the parallel fences to deter any escape attempts. As in Heydekrug, the guard towers, containing search lights and machine guns, were spaced at vantage points around the perimeter, and the grounds were patrolled by guards with dogs.

Each lager was laid out a little differently and some were still under construction. In my location, I recall that the buildings faced the parade ground where the roll call was taken each day, and that there were ten structures – five on a side. A kitchen, offices, sleeping rooms and a "Red Cross Room" used for miscellaneous activities, were all contained in one free-standing building. There were shallow fire pools in the completed lagers. Each room contained a bucket to contribute to a bucket brigade in case of a fire.

I recall that the quarters most familiar to me contained ten rooms leading from a central hallway that ran lengthwise. Each door contained a small window allowing very little light. There was one wash room with a concrete vat for heating water and one night latrine. Outside, on each side of the lager, there was a wash room that could accommodate approximately twenty POWs, and a latrine for about the same number of men. These facilities were grossly inadequate and seldom emptied. The rooms were designed to accommodate sixteen men in eight bunk beds double-decked. Upon our arrival, it became necessary to increase the room capacity, and the beds were tiered in threes and many times additional men slept on the floor, which was not much worse than the bunks. The beds consisted of a wood frame, six slats, and paper sacks filled with wood shavings for a mattress. The mattress would shrink, with wear, to the appearance and feel of a thin board. The rooms contained a small stove, a table and a few stools. Over time, when possible, the residents used their talents to construct additional furnishings, as needed.

We literally had no means of washing. Because there was only one coal-fired hot water heater of 100 liters in the camp of one thousand men, there were no showers. Fleas and lice were in profusion and no cleansing was done to alleviate the condition. We simply learned to live with lice.

Roll call, or *appell* as it was called by the Germans, was taken twice daily and at times in the middle of the night on the coldest nights. During regular formations we fell in by barracks around the edge of the parade ground in columns of five. If the total didn't balance, there were recounts and searches until they did. At the time of the count it was not unusual for a group of us to return to our room to discover that in our absence it had been ransacked by the guards. There were many items that came up missing, and this was a regular occurrence.

Lockup each night was in accordance with the season and the hours of daylight. In the summer, daylight hours would last until about nine at night, and in winter, the time would be as early as five o'clock. Doors were locked and the shutters were closed on all windows. Guards were ordered to shoot anyone on the lager grounds after curfew. During air raids, it was critical to be inside or it would be another excuse that the Germans would have for shooting a prisoner. And there were a few shootings even when it was obvious that it was a matter of confusion on behalf of the targeted prisoner.

Any groups gathered for any reason had to be approved by the lager officer and the presence of a German interpreter was required. It was forbidden to trade any articles with the guards, but in studying and discerning the approachable guards, there were many opportunities for bartering.

As in our previous camp, cigarettes were the medium of exchange. A system was formed of standardized prices and every item was worth a certain number of cigarettes. I expect that this was a normal practice in every POW camp, as there was no other currency available.

Frank Paules remained our "man of confidence," and room leaders were also chosen. The Germans were determined to maintain control, and paid little regard to our needs as expressed to them. Their behavior towards us continued to be abusive and they enforced control at all cost. Frank Paules would sometimes feel the wrath of the Germans in trying to assert authority as our leader. They usually refused to recognize him and ignored any requests. The conditions in Stalag Luft IV could be described as less than poor.

Appell in Lager A
Courtesy of Joe O'Donnell

MAIL

Each POW could write two letters and four postcards each month. There was no limit on incoming mail, however, for many, few letters were received and parcels were almost nonexistent. There was nothing that would raise our spirits more than receiving a letter from home. It was a waiting game, because it took months for us to receive a letter mailed from the States. I had written a letter to my mother and sisters at my first opportunity when interned in Stalag Luft VI, but it took very long to get to them, and even longer for their mail to get to me once they learned my address.

Some of the fellows around me received quite a bit of mail from their wives or girlfriends who I thought must have written and mailed them frequently. Most of the time it was good news, but there could also be some heartbreakers. That alone made me glad that I didn't have a woman at home spawning worries about whether or not she would wait for me for the unknown period of time that I would be away. When the only bright spot in your life is a letter from your girl –– and you receive a "Dear John" letter –– that could drive one to very deep depression.

There were occasions that a buddy might offer me a letter to read and it could be uplifting just to hear news from home, even though I didn't know anybody that was mentioned. I did not begin receiving letters for weeks after my arrival in Luft IV and those had been written months before. I would read them over and over almost memorizing them word for word. My letters were cherished possessions. Jay Joyce must have written to his mother about our friendship. We'd shared so many hardships together. To my great delight, I received a letter from her. It made me feel special that she would take the time to write me. I wrote to tell her how much I appreciated her thoughtfulness.

WRITE VERY CLEARLY WITHIN THE LINES. IN ORDER TO EXPEDITE
CENSORSHIP, LETTERS SHOULD BE TYPED OR PRINTED IN BLOCK CAPITALS.

Wayland, Kentucky.

July 18, 1944.

Dear Sgt. Kyler:

How are you this fine morning? hope you

having a"swell"time as my boy says.

We are all well, and working as usual.

That is about all we can do now, the

weather is too warm to go any place.

Am writing your mother today, hope she is

well. As it is getting late and time for

girls to come from work, I will have to

get busy and get them something to eat.

They are always wanting to hurry back to

work.

Will write again soon.

May God bless you,guide guard

and keep you is my prayer,

Your friend,

Mrs. Nora Joyce,

Box 1121,

Wayland, Kentucky.

IMPORTANT: FOR PRISONERS IN GERMAN HANDS, THE PRISONER OF WAR NUMBER SHOULD
BE CLEARLY INDICATED IF KNOWN. IT MUST N/T BE FONE?SED WITH THE ARMY SERIAL NUMBER.

W. D., P. M. G. Form No. 111
APR 1944

Letter from Nora Joyce, Jay's mother

RED CROSS PARCELS AND LACK OF THEM

The Red Cross parcels were opened in the German vorlager where cans were punched so they could not be hoarded, and articles were distributed piecemeal. The Germans also kept count of empty cans and sometimes food was withheld until a certain number of cans were returned. The camp leaders no longer had a part in the distribution of the Red Cross parcels as they had at our previous camp. Our relocation resulted in a great shortage of parcels. Thousands that were received before we were transferred were unaccounted for.

Food continued to be our obsession and the insufficient supply greatly affected our outlook. We were always hungry. We existed on a diet of thin barley or cabbage soup, a type of greens and boiled kohlrabies. At times we were provided a stew of dehydrated vegetables or turnips. Sometimes we were served a stringy meat thought to be horse meat. The Germans reported that due to Allied bombing transportation was a problem in delivering Red Cross parcels. It was doubtful that this was the case, but we were helpless to prove different.

We were issued a special Christmas box for the holiday with extra treats that were not normally included in our usual parcels. Despite a desire to quickly devour the goodies, I tried my best to make them last. But no sweets could eliminate the homesickness that I felt during this special season. Still, we felt some spirit even in that camp and Christmas carols were sung, and for the most part the mood was as festive as could possibly be considering the situation.

```
         XMAS PARCEL
Turkey
Plum Pudding              12 oz. can
Dates                     16 oz
Mixed Candy               14 oz. Box
      Nuts                12  "
Cherries                   7  "
Honey                      8 ¾" can
Jam                        8  "
Sausage                    6  "
Deviled ham                4  "
Cheese                     3  "
Butter (Preserved)         4  "
Tea                        3½"
Fruit bar  3               1½"   Box
Bullion cubes              4  "
Smokes                     1½"
Game                       3 Pks.
deck of cards              1
Gum                        1
wash cloth                 4
Pipe Tobacco (P.A)         1
Pipe                       1
```

Inventory of Christmas Parcel

STAYING SANE

In our previous camp we had learned that sports were a stimulating way to occupy our bodies and minds. Participation in boxing, football, basketball and softball either as a player or a spectator had been a healthy distraction from our situation. A supply of baseballs, bats and boxing gloves were available to continue these activities in our new surroundings, and good use was made of them.

Art work of several types (mostly sketches though) and poetry were among the activities that continued to fill the time. It was our escape from reality, and quite effective. I could get lost in my sketches, and there was plenty of time to concentrate and ponder every stroke of the pencil. There were no deadlines to meet in completing my work. Of course, there would have been nothing that I would have liked better than to have my sketching interrupted by my liberation.

I proceeded where I had left off in my notebook at Luft VI, continuing to draw the months in my calendar and crossing off the days. The list of names of my roommates grew as new acquaintances were added. The number of poems increased over time to go along with the sketches. Besides the valuable Red Cross parcels, my notebooks were my salvation.

The talented musicians, singers, and actors who had contributed so much to giving us a sense of normalcy by means of their great performances were all but silenced. Unfortunately there were no musical instruments here, hence no music-making to speak of. Those highly professional performances that provided enjoyment to all, including the German guards, became a thing of the past. Months after our arrival, however, the YMCA supplies made it possible for occasional stage productions.

It was the irrepressible creativity of man that made a real difference. Prisoners came up with ingenious ways of crafting something out of nothing. No scrap was wasted. We utilized everything, including cans and cartons. It was astounding how resourceful one could be if time was available to accomplish a goal. Together our innovative talents surfaced in the many useful inventions that were prevalent throughout the camp.

It is amazing how the loss of freedom and the hours of boredom prompt men to reach so deeply into their inner selves, bringing forth talents that they were unaware they possessed. These talents were evidenced in the production of great things that they never knew they were capable of producing. Prisoners scavenged every piece of durable material and turned it to a purpose. Cans of powdered milk ("Klim") were used for cooking pots, washing machine agitators, tallow holders for lighting, and kitchen utensils. Bars of soap were used to form molds that could receive the molten lead melted from the seams of the Klim cans, and thus all sorts of other implements could be fashioned. It was critical for all to seize every opportunity to keep their minds occupied lest they lose them, and creating tools and implements put all that energy and creativity to the benefit of all the prisoners.

As was the practice of many from first confinement, most of us walked the perimeter of our compound to stay conditioned. Our malnourishment made it very difficult to keep up our strength, but it was always best to try to get some form of physical exercise. And, as always, we drew upon the strength of each other. To stay mentally anchored was a chore, and you just couldn't do it alone. As we did early on as POWs, we took turns encouraging one another as trying as it could be at times when things were beyond rough. It was a comfort for me to share quarters in our new abode with the crewmates who were still with me here: Jay Joyce and John Alexander. We were accumulating unimaginable stories of survival together, having withstood and witnessed so many horrifying incidents. It was advantageous to discuss the various tragedies that we had observed as well as the feelings that they aroused. But this had to be done in moderation, we knew. Our time was perhaps better spent sharing memories of our home and our loved ones.

Camaraderie with our roommates was important to our survival in the prison milieu that we were in. I had developed many close relationships with those whom I shared quarters, and these proved beneficial to my well being. We existed with many different types of individuals among us. There were those who were meticulous, and conversely, those who were messy. There were those who were energetic or lazy; quiet or talkative; helpful or selfish; positive or negative; shy or bold. And a person could be any of these types at any given time.

Naturally with many of us together for so many hours, there were bound to be conflicts. Tempers could be short during stressful times, and there were moments when disputes would erupt like a flash flood. But to my surprise, collectively these were usually just as quickly resolved and there was definitely group pressure to resolve things and not fight.

For the most part, I think we respected our diversity. We adjusted and understood how to deal with each other once we recognized our strengths and weaknesses – also realizing that none of us was perfect. After spending so many days together and getting to know each other better, we could tease one another regarding the things that bothered us about each other and most of the time we could take it. There was nothing to gain by bickering. It was a waste of energy and our reduced caloric intake left us with no surplus energy. There was profit in working together. It took some of us longer than others to learn this lesson. When things were tough and it really counted, we were a unit.

There were religious services held in the camp, but hardly room for the chaplains to accommodate a group that grew to about ten thousand men. If it was not possible to attend a Sunday service, it didn't mean we didn't pray. I'm certain that the ten thousand prayers that were regularly sent heavenward mostly asked for "freedom," for if we were mercifully granted this precious gift, we would have everything that we could ever want.

*   *   *

A PRISONER'S PRAYER[5]

Oh! God my creator and protector,
I know that thou art near me,
And so I adore thee body and soul
and with complete submission to thy will.

Thou hast saved me from death
which has overtaken many of my companions
and hast permitted me to be a POW.
I will bear patiently and hopefully for thy love of thee and
all the difficulties of my state.

Bless me and all my companions here
Grant us to live in peace comforting and consoling
one another with paternal love and charity.

---

5   These poems were copied, with permission, from the notebook of Jay Joyce.

Bless my friends who are far away and my
family, and all I love, my country and my comrades
who are in arms. Give me peace and protect me
from melancholy and despair, and above all keep
me from offending thee. My God I thank thee for
all thy blessing.

I will try to serve thee as Jesus has taught us,
rejoicing in hope.

Amen[6]

SOLDIERS TEMPLE

There was no temple for our Lord
When we're banished to this place of soldiers exile,
Yet we saw within the barbs his lovely face

So we save up precious wood
Of crates from home and scraps of tin,
And build on the sands of solitude
A home where God may enter in.

GOD'S MINUTE

I have only just a minute
Only sixty seconds in it
Forced upon me can't refuse it,
Didn't seek it didn't choose it.
But its up to me to use it.
Give account if I loose it.
Just a tiny little minute
But eternity is in it.

---

6 This poem was read at a ceremony conducted in 2007 at Stalag Luft VI.

Entertainment Provided by the Guards

One of the most popular forms of amusement was playing escape games with the German guards. They came to believe that the name "Goon" stood for German officers or NCOs and of course we did not set them straight. You can imagine the fun for us in this deception. They would even call "Goons Up!" before entering the barracks.

The German Camp Commandant was obsessed with the fear that a mass escape, or for that matter any escape, would materialize. It would be a grievous offense to those in charge should there be a successful escape, and no German wanted to suffer the consequences. Since the "Great Escape" from Stalag Luft III the guards were extremely watchful and on edge. To some extent this great fear worked in favor of the inmates. A promise would be made not to attempt an escape if our captors would return the favor in some way. The Commandant was not aware that in July 1944 an Allied order was issued that escape attempts should no longer be made. Another deterrent to escape attempts was due to the directive by Hitler establishing circular areas of fifty-mile radius throughout Germany and occupied countries that any POW captured in these areas would be put to death. These territories overlapped each other, so there was no region that was friendly. It was great sport to make the guards believe that there was an escape plan when there wasn't, just to annoy them. They were kept busy with these antics and it was another means by which we POWs evaded the monotony of imprisonment, and gained satisfaction by harassing the guards.

RAF Warrant Officer Raymond Thomas Stephen

I shall never forget one of my British friends in particular. I became acquainted with Raymond Stephen in Stalag Luft VI. Upon arrival there, my group was starved and thirsty and he willingly shared his rations with us and as a veteran POW, gave encouraging words in our difficult period of adjustment. We had left Heydekrug together and endured the same hardships in the boat and train ride, and the treacherous "run up the road" to our new home. We had shared conversations about our lives before capture as well as our stories of the events leading up to our imprisonment. We were housed separately in our new location. I was in a barracks and he was billeted in what we called "dog huts" situated between barracks Nos. 2 and 3 in Lager B. There were ten men to a hut.

It was after lockdown on the evening of July 29, 1944, when a loud clap of thunder shook the ground and a lethal bolt of lightning entered the front of the hut in which my friend Ray Stephen was sleeping. The inmates were laying five in a row and the bolt passed over the first four, striking Raymond. He was killed instantly, serving as the ground.

To me, it just didn't seem fair. This tragic incident weighed heavily on my mind. All I could think of was what he had suffered and survived since his capture and what an injustice it was for him to die in this place and in this way – the injustice that he should die at all.

In my grief, I meticulously drew a sketch and composed a poem in memory of my fallen chum. This heartfelt gesture served in a small way to comfort me in the period of anguish that followed the loss. My unfortunate friend was not destined to leave the grounds alive, and was laid to rest miles away from home and family at Stalag Luft IV.

Fate

What Fate has man when close at hand
    Was Freedom, Liberty, and his Land
What Fate this Young Flyer,
    Who went out each day to die or no.
He lost his plane but not his life
    In prison camps for years he might
        For strife
What Fate had he who flew so high
    When peace so near but to die.

    Written in memory of
    W/o Raymond Stevens of The
        Royal Air Force
        Killed by Lightning

**Funeral Procession for POW Aubrey Teague,
killed in Stalag Luft IV before my arrival in the Camp**
Photo Courtesy of Joe O'Donnell

FINAL DAYS IN STALAG LUFT IV

I was grateful for every day that I woke up, because it was an indication that I had not given up. The situation was worsening and the anticipation of what the future held for us was growing intense. We tried to prepare for the severe winter conditions that arose but as usual, we were limited in our provisions. We had a roof over our head but that was the extent of it. The coal that we were allotted was nowhere near what we required to keep warm. The unavailability of adequate nourishment, always a problem, increased with the deteriorating weather conditions.

Rumors of an impending evacuation became widespread. We could all see that the guards were growing uneasy. The gunfire in the distance provided constant reinforcement of the fact that the Russians were advancing, and it was apparent that we were either going to be moved out or left behind to join the Russians. We all knew that the latter would not be the chosen option, but another forced move was also not very attractive.

30

Return to present...

RETURN TO STALAG LUFT IV

Our return to my former camp at Stalag Luft IV in Gross Tychow, now Tychowo, Poland, was made on October 1, 2006. Candy and Sara woke up early and went to breakfast in great anticipation of the day ahead of them. Their group was picked up at their hotel in Koszalin, Poland, and was taken by bus to the former Stalag Luft IV camp area in Tychowo.

Candy had compiled and brought along notebooks full of copies of my wartime information that she had left in Belgium, Barth, and also planned to leave in Poland, and she couldn't wait to show them around. Mr. Jupi Podlaszewski, who owns the School of English in Koszalin and was the organizer of the visit; and Maura and Amy, two young American teachers at the school, rode with us. My daughter proudly showed the girls some of the pages in the notebook and looked pleased at how interested they were in it.

We arrived at the camp area under sunny blue skies and were comfortable in the warm air. As we traveled down the narrow road approaching the former campsite, I felt anxious, because I had been this way before. My memories were not pleasant over the way we had arrived or exited over 60 years ago. But today's would be only a brief visit, unlike my previous six-month stay.

Just the view of the road brought back memories and looking ahead it was obvious that we were nearing my old home. My heart was heavy, yet I brightened a bit looking ahead at the uniformed persons and the many others that I could see in the crowd. My understanding of the reason for their presence today was moving to me. They were gathered in an area where a remarkable monument stood.

As we got off the bus, we walked through the crowd towards the memorial. I watched, feeling a bit left out, as my wife and daughter were embraced by members of the group caught up in the wave of emotion that the surroundings and the monument aroused. It was gratifying for me to witness this beautifully sculpted work of art and I, along with those present, took in every detail. The commemoration consisted of three separate monuments. The most outstanding middle section is the sculpture of the American Airman in the front section and etched in the left side is the replica of a prisoner of war on the "March" out of the camp. The right side contains the etching of the diagram of the layout of the camp. On either side of this grand memorial stand two large stones. The stone on the left contains a plaque with the following inscription:

May 1944-February 1945
Kriegsgefangenen Lager Luft IV
Kiefheide Bei Gross Tychow
/Podborsko/Where 10,000
American, Canadian, British
French, Belgian, Australian
Polish, Russian and Other
Airmen were kept Prisoners
Of War. On February the sixth,
1945, the camp was evacuated
By the "Death March" to
The Stalag XI B from where
Prisoners were liberated
On May the 2nd.

The stone on the right side contains the same message, inscribed in Polish.

The Mayor gave a speech that was smoothly translated by Jupi. His message was one of assurance that Stalag Luft IV and its history would not be forgotten. He proceeded to lay a wreath at the base of the monument and other officials followed suit. Amy and Maura, the young American teachers, read some "Dear John" letters that were received by husbands and boyfriends behind the barbed wire. There were many misconceptions about the life of a POW as indicated by other letters read. Memories surfaced of men I knew who had received such disheartening letters.

After studying the camp layout and regaining my bearings, I knew that we were in the area that was formerly Lager D. There was a potato cellar behind the memorial that I entered along with my wife and daughter. We then went across the road to what was Lager A, and investigated the fire pool that remains. All who were present had the luxury of listening to Walter, an ex-POW in our group, who had been interned in this area. He candidly shared his memories, stating that the purpose of the fire pools in the Camp was to put out any fires. Unfortunately, I could only be present as an observer, but it was as good as could be for my wife and daughter to be able to hear Walter's first-hand account. He had been held in Lager A, so he remembered this area well. There was a certain excitement when he looked around and told what he recalled during the time he spent there. He pointed in the direction of where he would have sacrificed over a year of his life. My girls were paying rapt attention to his every word.

While they were combing the grounds around the fire pool, I left them and made my way to the area where I had spent my six months in Stalag Luft IV. There are no buildings remaining. The years of mass overgrowth throughout the old camp hid the foundations, so it is not so easy to distinguish exact locations. My mere presence in this region, though, incited memories of sights, sounds and smells of a previous era known to me. My thoughts returned to those treacherous months spent in this territory. Surprisingly, the more I remembered, the less painful the memories became.

Returning to the group, I took pride in watching their interest in this chapter of my past. There was also an entertaining moment as I listened to my daughter proudly trying to explain that her father was in this camp to a group of small Polish children who did not understand English. After a series of her gestures it seemed that they finally understood the word "father," and made sense of what she was trying to express.

Before our departure, one last look was taken of this place that is so significant to my past, a significance now shared by my wife and daughter. The group gathered once again to board the bus to be taken to what was the Kiefheide (now Podborsko) railroad station. This is the station where I had arrived before being double-timed up the hill to Stalag Luft IV. Walter stated that nothing had changed, so Sara and Candy knew that they were looking at the same station that I had seen during one of the most dangerous ordeals I had experienced as a POW. The stirring memorial at the station commemorates the thousands of men who traveled through this place on their trek to Stalag Luft IV.

It was noticeable to me, as it had been in every stop, how absorbed that my family members were in these surroundings. It was important to Candy and her mother that they stood in or near the same spaces as I and my friends had. They were undoubtedly reliving my past, unaware that I was also with them. I believe that this memorial was as moving to them as it was to me.

We walked around the front of the station building and continued around to the back. I noticed Candy looking both up and down the tracks just as she had done at the station in Frankfurt. I am certain that she was imagining, just as I could visualize clearly, the doors sliding back on those old "40 & 8" boxcars, disgorging the weary men who had been crammed into them for so long. We were all in such a weakened state from thirst and starvation. This is the place that my march to Stalag Luft IV began – the run for my life at the mercy of the fanatical young German guards and their vicious dogs.

Candy asked Jupi to point out the infamous road that led to the camp and asked if it would be possible to go there. She had read and heard so much about our ordeal that she wanted to traverse the same distance that our group had been forced to cover–at bayonet's point–on July 18, 1944. She told her mother that if time permitted she would have wanted to walk the entire route or better yet, run it. Jupi told Candy it was not practical to accomplish that, but we did take time to stop at the road – the road where the so-called "Heydekrug Run" took place. Their short walk on this road became for them one of the highlights of their visit. Candy explained to her mother that I was chained to another person while running in front of ferocious barking dogs and the guards' bayonets. She added that I would have been suffering from malnutrition from the months of internment and the painful boat and boxcar ride that preceded "the run." She wondered about the belongings I had carried and whether I had made a backpack with my shirt. Ex-POW Walter had demonstrated how he and many others fashioned a backpack, and Candy said she thought perhaps that was how I managed to hang on to things.

This brief stop brought a flood of additional memories at every step. The partner to whom I was handcuffed was not healthy and very weak, but miraculously—together—we managed to survive. This road so full of yelling, barking dogs, gunshots, and raw human misery over sixty years ago now provided a peaceful walk in silent meditation for the moments we spent there on October 1, 2006.

Candy expressed her appreciation to Jupi for making this unplanned stop that meant to so much to her and Sara and, without their knowledge, to me also.

We continued to the Stalag Luft IV Museum to view the exhibition of many pictures and articles from the camp. This was another comforting assurance that the memory of our sacrifice is being preserved. Candy donated to the museum the notebook that she had compiled containing pictures and documents pertaining to me and my crew. It was vital to her that my crew, and the story that is so special to her, would be included with those remembered.

The hospitality that was shown to the group continued through the final stop at a picnic area where everyone was treated to a feast of Polish sausage, potatoes, salad and a beverage. With weather so conducive to picnicking, the day could not have ended more perfectly. Appreciation was extended and farewell hugs were exchanged as the group headed to the bus to return to their hotel.

That evening Candy wrote in her journal: "*Leaving these locations so significant to my father's journey is very different for me than it was for my father, of course, yet still very connected. My time spent here in memory of his time may serve somehow to be healing for both of us.*" She doesn't know how right she is.

RETURN VISIT TO STALAG LUFT IV

In her second visit to Poland, Candy was visibly more comfortable, feeling that she belonged. She was self-assured that this was her territory because it had been mine and she even said she felt at home here. As had been the case the previous year, the kind Polish folks provided a warm personal welcome for the visitors. Approaching the former camp area by bus, we could see vehicles and groups of people in the distance awaiting our arrival on this special day of remembrance. It was touching as I once again understood that the purpose of this gathering was to honor a group of individuals who are now called heroes. I could see the pride in my daughter's eyes as she understood that I was included among the men they were remembering. I doubt that the people in attendance had any idea how much their presence meant to a former POW.

In leaving the bus, the group joined the crowd gathered in the monument area. It was gratifying to study the beautiful sculpture again and to watch my daughter in quiet study, absorbing every angle as she had the previous year.

The tribute given at the monument was stirring as I observed young and old in uniform representing different groups including color guards, a women's auxiliary and the Home Army. There were rows of chairs set up for us ex-POWs and their families. My daughter stood and listened to what was being said, but I could see that she periodically looked back at the empty seats. Perhaps the empty "POW seats" were a symbol to her of my absence as well as her feeling of my presence. I was sitting in one of those seats and I think she felt it.

Each organization was recognized by the Honorable Mayor Elżbieta Wasiak as she graciously thanked them for their participation in this moving event that was arranged to recall the sacrifice and honor the memory of the prisoners who walked these grounds. The well-known author, Jane Pejsa, was also recognized as being in attendance with her husband. There were colorful flowers laid by local dignitaries, one by one, at the base of the monument. A band played several songs including the Polish and American National Anthems. There were excerpts from POW letters from home and poems read by Jupi and the two American girls who Candy had met during her first visit that teach at Jupi's school of English in Koszalin, Maura and Amy. Candy looked pleased that she had contributed to this comprehensive ceremony as they read one of the poems that she had given Jupi, written by my radio operator, Jay Joyce, entitled "A Prisoner's Prayer." She knew that Jay's widow, Bea Joyce, would be pleased when she heard that her late husband's poem was read as part of the observance. Three of the ex-POW's from the tour group told briefly about their experiences and expressed their appreciation for this wonderful memorial and reception. I thought about what I would have said had I been able to contribute. I certainly would have expressed my gratitude for our being remembered in this thoughtful ceremony. I could have told them the relief they have provided for me by their preservation of our past.

At the conclusion of the program Candy moved eagerly to the area adjacent to the monument displaying brick memorials. She had been involved in this project with her friend, ex-POW Joe O'Donnell, and she was anxious to see the display.

I am so grateful to Joe for the assistance that he has given my daughter in her mission. When she has had questions, she would ask Joe. He was also a former B-17 ball turret gunner and a prisoner of war in Stalag Luft IV. His published books were treasures to Candy in her researches into my past. She has referred to him as her "stand-in dad." The questions that she would have liked to ask me, she could ask him and his answer would be as close as she could get to what my answer would be. The granite bricks were beautiful, and a moving sight to me when I spotted a brick bearing my name. It was also moving to witness the response of those in the group as they viewed the inscription of their or their loved one's name.

After the brick viewing, Candy walked around the camp to again enter the potato cellars and walk to the fire pool. She picked up stones and brick pieces from a foundation. She was joined for a brief period of time by (I think) the same neighborhood children that she had met in the last visit. They seemed to have remembered her as well, and Candy again mentioned the word "father" and conveyed her connection to this area.

KIEFHEIDE 2007

After walking the grounds at the camp area, the group proceeded to the former Kiefheide Railway Station. I felt an unusual calmness overtake me when reading the inscription on the magnificent monument. The message reads:

10,000 American and Allied POWs
Walked (Along the Trail of Tears)
From Kiefheide (Podborsko)
Railway Station to Luft IV POW Camp
Between May, 1944 and February 1945

It also is written in Polish.

After viewing the monument, everyone went inside the railway building and Jupi and Zygmunt Wujek, the artist responsible for the monuments, gave a presentation regarding the prisoners who had passed through this station. They played a tape of music of that era set to "Stormy Weather," and it had added sound effects of the planes, steam engines, German guards yelling, and the sound of whips and barking dogs. It depicted so artfully what had occurred, as these chilling sounds gradually faded back into the music, returning us to reality. It was very moving because those were all the sounds that I remembered now so clearly. This abstract but highly realistic recording drew all who were present deeply into that time so long ago.

LAST RUN UP THE ROAD

When the ceremony at the railway station was completed, Gib, our guide, announced that our group would continue on to lunch. Candy immediately approached him to remind him that they needed to stop at the historic road along which the men had been marched to the camp. Gib then made another announcement, advising the group that we would make a brief stop. Thank goodness Gib agreed to the stop, else Candy would have had to come back afterward, because she was not going to leave this area until she had accomplished the run. The bus let out all who wanted, and those leaving were told that they would have ten minutes.

Candy took off running and figured that she would run for five minutes up the road and then turn around and run five minutes back, so to utilize every available minute. She looked at her watch and moved as fast as her legs would take her. Of course I ran with her – for me it was now nearly effortless. As we ran, this time I noticed the woods on either side of the road and realized that most of these trees had been witness to my run along this same route sixty-three years ago. The sounds from the whole experience echoed in my mind. The forest was silent this time, but I could still hear the Germans calling out the names of the cities that we had bombed. I could remember how I had sensed the machine guns pointed in my direction, and how I did everything in my power to try to stay calm, fully aware of the consequences of panicking or trying to escape. And somehow I knew that these memories of mine were the same thoughts that Candy was imagining as she made this run as a tribute to me.

When ten minutes was up, Candy stopped to pick up pieces of the road and also a pine cone, mentioning to members of the group that it may be from a tree that was there when I was.

Those who had walked or "ran" on the road returned to the bus and were taken to a nearby school and graciously treated to a wonderful lunch of chicken, potatoes, cabbage, shredded carrots and soup.

After lunch, the group proceeded to the hallway of the school where there was a display set up from the POW museum. A DVD was being played that Candy had brought to the museum during the previous year's visit. As she looked around at the different exhibits, the museum's curator came over to her and pointed to one of the displays. Candy was so pleased to see an arrangement of all of the things that she had brought last year pertaining to me and to my crew. Candy mentioned to her friend, Carolyn, how proud she was to see that my memorabilia had become part of a display, and how she enjoyed showing everyone her father's information. I was honored to see that my crew had been made part of the exhibit.

After a most rewarding day, Candy entered into her journal the following:

> *I don't know how special my father would feel these grounds are, but they are special to me, knowing he was there — where he spent months of his young life not knowing each day if it would be his last. His thoughts during that time seem to linger there as I imagine them.*

Jupi Podlaszewski and Zygmunt Wujek appeared the following morning to bid farewell to their American friends. They stood at attention saluting as we moved out of sight.

Monument at Stalag Luft IV

Jupi Podlaszewski, Amy and Maura at Ceremony

My name permanently etched in granite at Stalag Luft IV

Potato Cellar in Stalag Luft IV

Fire Pool in Stalag Luft IV

Foundation in Stalag Luft IV – possible latrine

The Group at Monument, Stalag Luft IV 2006

Monument at Kiefheide Railway Station

Walk on the Infamous Road where "Heydekrug Run" took place
Courtesy of Jupi Podlaszewski

Kiefheide Station 2006 – now Podborsko

Group at Jupi's English School of Koszalin 2006

The Move To Stalag Luft I – Camp #3

Stalag Luft I (St. Marien Church steeple in background)
Courtesy of B24.net – Greg Hatton (photo by A.J. Zywiczynski)

31

TRAIN RIDE TO BARTH

I was one of between two to three thousand inmates of Stalag Luft IV, approximately one-third of the camp population, who were marched out in polar weather for the two-mile trek to the Kiefheide train station on January 29, 1945, as we evacuated the camp. Many among the selected group were ill or injured, but prisoners who were fairly healthy were included in the draw. I considered myself among the fairly healthy prisoners. As we left camp, we felt badly for those left behind. I had no idea what the future held for either group. It seemed to me, though, that we were lucky to be leaving before the others.

Once again, those rail cars! God, we had had our fill of them, but in the cold any enclosure, even the stinking filthy boxcars, were better than being outside.

Rumors surfaced——the rumors were always plentiful among us—— that we might be left at some location that was in the path of the Russian advance, and that appeared to be the route we were traveling the first day. But that possibility disappeared when the next morning we moved slowly off in a different direction. And though we might avoid getting caught up in the battle surrounding the German retreat, there was always the threat of being bombed and strafed by Allied planes. I have a vivid memory of an American aircraft swooping low and flying the length of our train. Somehow recognizing that the train was transporting POWs, a second pass was made with the pilot waggling the wings to us. Our response was a resounding cheer from the ground.

As was always the case with large groups of humans subjected to crowded, filthy conditions, dysentery was widespread. A bucket served as the toilet and was continuously passed from one miserable individual to another. Because we never stopped, it was never emptied. Our journey became increasingly unbearable with the frigid, below-zero weather. The only protection that we had from the cold was the clothes on our back, a flimsy German blanket, and each other. Even in the freezing temperatures the suffocating odor from our filthy, lice-ridden bodies and the straw and human manure was nauseating.

The days spent in these cattle cars were days of abject hell. We were so thirsty, and there was very little water available. The guards would shove snow through a one-inch opening in the door – the same opening that we used to relieve ourselves. We chided the guards so they would throw snow balls at us that we hastily stuffed into our mouths to slake our thirst.

At one point, an air raid siren sounded and the Germans left us locked in the cars and fled to safety in the woods, while the Royal Air Force bombed the railway yard our train was occupying. As always since my bailout from our B-17 and subsequent induction into my life of incarceration, this was another day that I thought might be my last. In our exposure to danger in this uncertain life there were many different ways that one could die, and we were becoming experts. Eventually the raid ended and, untouched, our train pulled out of the yard and moved on towards...? Who knew? Today, few Americans realize what it's like to not know where you are going; to be utterly without any control over your future.

Another precarious situation was when we had to be protected from the civilians trying to break into the cars. The locals knew that soon this would become occupied territory and they were on the wrong team. They could not understand why POWs were being transported rather than Germans who needed to escape from the advancing Russian Army. Many Germans well knew how the Wehrmacht had treated the Russians over the previous three years, and realized that retribution was inevitable.

In my recollection of this seemingly endless ride through hell, we were only allowed to exit the cars once, at which time we all relieved ourselves and unlimbered sore, numb arms and legs. Our modesty had been lost long ago, simultaneously with our freedom.

On February 8, 1945, our train arrived in Barth, Germany, where we would next take up residence in Stalag Luft I, a POW camp for Allied officers, located on the shores of the Baltic Sea.

32

THE WALK TO STALAG LUFT I

After eleven grueling days of boxcar travel, we actually welcomed climbing down from the stinking cars into the bitter cold. I wondered if it was probable that the relocation to our new residence, Stalag Luft I, would be the end of the line for us or if it was that we would soon be moved yet again. We all "knew" that the end was near, but none of us could predict when or what that end might be, and neither could we forecast whether we would survive to once again be free. The ever-present thought that every day could be my last day remained a dark shadow on my conscious, as it had for over a year. We'd come so far under the most extreme mental and physical hardships, and it would be a grim irony not to live long enough to celebrate our freedom now that it was so close.

We were a sorry sight in our lice-infected and dysenteric state, and I think we all still felt some shame at our horrible appearance. These conditions had become a way of life for us, but we had not forgotten who we really were.

After clambering down from the boxcars we began yet another march. I remember walking through a town that was a quaint storybook village in a seaside setting. The road was narrow, and our column filled it for as far as I could see. We dragged on in our tiredness and discomfort, taking in our new surroundings. Wishing we were unrestrained, I fantasized about how it would feel to freely walk these roads. We were on a route to another chapter in our ambiguous life as POWs with the hopes that this stay would be our last in captivity. We were very relieved that we were not double-timed and bayoneted as we had been upon our arrival at Stalag Luft IV.

In recalling our pitiful looking group walking from the railroad station through town, the mental image of a very old brick church building with a towering steeple comes to mind. I remember it as a comforting sight even though we could only see the outside. The towering structure of the cathedral dominated the landscape for as far as the eye could see.

I have a memory of passing under a tower's archway as we marched through town. We continued past open fields and farmlands along a cobblestone road on our route to the camp. As we neared our destination, we passed a building that operated as an anti-aircraft artillery ("flak") school. The familiar sight of the double barbed wire fence and the manned guard towers were in close proximity to this military installation, no doubt intentionally located near a POW camp to protect it from becoming an Allied bombing target. We were nearing the camp that would become our next home away from home.

The Haunting Sight of the Fence and Tower
Courtesy of B24.net – Greg Hatton (A.J. Zywiczynski)

33

ARRIVAL IN CAMP NUMBER 3

By now I was becoming quite the expert on the design and layout of German POW camps. The appearance of Stalag Luft I was much the same as the other camps I had inhabited. The camp was located in a rather isolated pine woods area on a Baltic Peninsula well away from the town. The layout was like a backwards L with the West Compound on one side of the road and the three North Compounds on the opposite side. "North 1" would become my compound along with several of those I traveled with, including, thank God, Jay and John. I immediately noticed that the entire camp was very overcrowded, the rooms filled well over their capacity.

Upon entry we had to go through interrogation by a German intelligence officer giving the usual mantra of name, rank and serial number.

The arrival of the two thousand or more in our group caused the numbers in the rooms to grow to as many as twenty-four occupants rather than the sixteen men they had been designed to accommodate. As at the other camps, there were double-decker wooden beds with the gunny sack mattresses filled with wood shavings, and the usual two small cotton blankets and two sheets for bedding. Besides the beds, there was a small table, a bench, and stools in the room. The hallway contained two small double lockers for storage and the shelves appeared to be fabricated out of empty Red Cross cartons and bed boards. There was also a small stove in the room. There were two windows for ventilation that were covered at night by wooden shutters. Supplemental ventilation was provided by many cracks in the floor. Because the barracks sat up on stilts (to discourage tunneling) the cracks also were responsible for the rooms being extremely frigid. Heat was inadequate, as well, due to the scanty issuance of coal to fuel the fire.

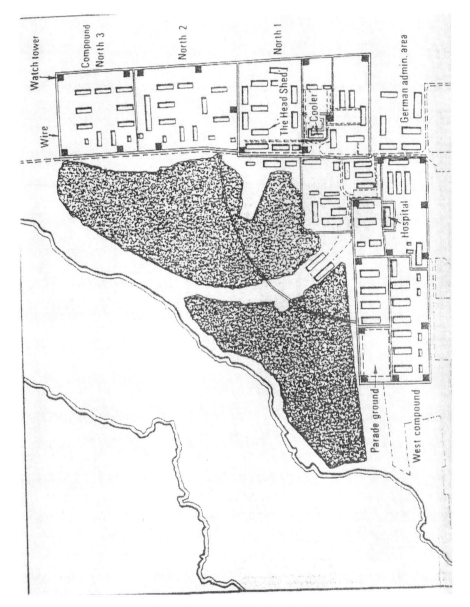

Camp Layout of Stalag Luft I
Courtesy of Dr. Martin Albrecht

Once again we had to adjust to new quarters with new guards and many more new faces among our roommates. Knowing that this was originally a camp for officers, and that we noncoms were outsiders, there were some concerns about our acceptance. We would soon learn that our rank was not a problem.

Roll call was in the morning and evening as in the other camps and here, too, we were exposed to the surprise *Appell* at the worst times – in the middle of the night at the lowest temperature, so as to make us more miserable than we already were.

Cigarettes were still an important medium of exchange in Stalag Luft I, with a similar system of a point price for all items that was expressed in cigarette value.

We had a large communal building that served as a mess hall and contained rooms used for theater and recreation.

Hygiene was difficult if not impossible to maintain when we were only permitted one hot shower every two weeks and a bucket for every room for sponge baths and, also, to do the laundry for as many as twenty-four men. Needless to say, our cleanliness left much to be desired. It seemed conditions deteriorated with every new camp that I was assigned to, which was understandable given the steady increase in occupants coupled with the deteriorating state of the German defense and economy.

The barracks were locked early every evening until sunrise and electricity was centrally powered and controlled by the Germans. While I was a resident, the availability of power was hit and miss.

ACTIVITIES

The ingenuity of the POWs was as evident in Stalag Luft I as it had been in the other camps with the crocheted and knitted jackets, hats and sweaters, and kitchen utensils formed out of Klim (powdered milk) cans, rebuilt stoves and many other examples of creativity and art. Out of necessity or simply out of want, amazing things were produced by determined and persistent fellows. The items could be very useful or just for show. Either way, creation of these things served to diminish boredom, which was just as important as the implements produced.

There was an organized band in Stalag Luft I, which was welcome entertainment for us coming from IV when there were minimal opportunities for a concert or an organized production.

There was a library, but with so many POW's in camp there were waiting lists for the books. A newspaper was printed (!) with news reports obtained from the hidden radios. The *POW WOW* was printed and distributed one per compound. The Germans were always astonished that we knew events before they had even heard them. One example of this was the death of President Roosevelt on April 12, 1945. In his memory, we all wore black armbands to roll call. When we were questioned by the Germans, they were amazed that we knew this. They realized that we had to have radios, but could never find them.

My notebooks and in fact everyone's personal writing materials continued to be an important pastime as the poems, sketches, and other creations kept us busy. I continued to add to my list of roommates and to keep track of each day I'd spent as a POW, which now numbered well over a year.

Having arrived in Barth during the coldest time of the year, sports did not begin until the Spring. In April, I recall some very entertaining boxing matches. Our camp leader, Colonel "Hub" Zemke, a former ace fighter pilot, was a competent pugilist, ably representing North 1 Compound.

A highlight that stands out in my mind was a visit made to our camp by Max Schmeling, a famous German boxer of the period. It was a good will gesture late in the war when it was obvious that Germany was losing and the end was near. I can remember that he was walking around shaking hands but there were some POW's who refused the offer.

lered
ould
and
ional

r,

John
secre-
Assn.
igues
etire-
yes-

Max Schmeling Held in Hamburg

HAMBURG, May 18. — Max Schmeling, former world's heavyweight champion from Germany, has been arrested here by British MPs for Nazi activities, the Associated Press reported.

The big German was picked up in civilian clothes, the AP said.

'ehind the Plate

Brig. Gen. M. M. Beach, 53rd TCC Wing CO from Detroit, catches first ball in game between 434th Golden Eagles and 436th Group for Wing title — and a week's exhibition tour of the Riviera. Batter is S/Sgt. Dick Rhodes, of Plymouth, Ind. 434th won, 3-1 All Eagles' runs were counted on homers by Sgt. Al Negrete, Union City, N.J., and Cpl. Jim Richardson, Syracuse, N.Y.

TCC Photo

came to our
P.W. camp

AIR RAID

When we arrived in Stalag Luft I, we were warned by those who had been there awhile of an ongoing concern. During an air raid, all prisoners had to return to their barracks and remain inside until they were given the "all clear." This was the same rule in my previous camps. The problem in Luft I was that the air raid warnings were sometimes not heard due to the number of inhabitants and the noise that could be generated by the enormous group of men.[7] The camp regulations stated that any POW outside their building during the alert would be shot by the guards. We became well aware of the seriousness of this issue about a month after our arrival. An officer in the British Compound inattentively left his barracks during an air raid alert and a German guard fired upon him. He was taken to the dispensary for immediate surgery to repair his severe internal injuries, and this saved his life, although he remained hospitalized for the remainder of the war.

During the same air raid, a second prisoner, 2nd Lt. Wyman, who had been visiting friends before the alarm sounded, began his walk back to his barracks. When he realized there was no one around he quickly turned to go back to the building he had just exited, but it was too late. He was struck in the head with a bullet and fell to the ground in the doorway. The friends who he had just left pulled him inside frantically trying to attract the attention of a tower guard. Lt. Wyman died later that day in the hospital. We had hoped, feeling that the end of our captivity was near, that we would not have to endure any more tragedies such as this. It was enough to withstand the hunger, the deprivation, the filth, the cold, and the loneliness, and the unnecessary loss of one of our own caused widespread gloom among all of us.

The serious injury to one POW and the death of another increased the prisoners' hatred of the German guards. The "goon-baiting" that had occurred in all camps where I'd been prisoner increased after these two incidents. It was a form of relief to insult the guards who did not understand English. In their oblivion, threats were made by the POWs with a smile and a friendly tone. Great satisfaction was derived from this somewhat childish activity.

7　During its history, Stalag Luft I housed up to 8,939 Allied Airmen.

Food

The food rations were slim when we arrived in Stalag Luft I. In our first week we were issued one-half of a Number 10 Red Cross Food Parcel per week. The second week our allotment fell to one-quarter parcel. From that time to March 27, 1945, there were *no* Red Cross Parcels distributed. We received only scanty German provisions until March 28th when once again we were allotted one whole magnificent Red Cross parcel per week. There was no shortage from then on. A full Red Cross parcel was indeed a prisoner of war's dream at this point. Things were finally looking up!

The End Was Near

The increase in the food supply brought rejuvenation to all of us who for so long were so empty. A report that Hitler had ordered the *execution* of all POWs evaporated as it became more and more apparent that Germany was indeed losing the war and that surrender was imminent. It was not only evident to us, but to the German guards as well, who began adjusting their attitude and treatment of us. The camp morale was on the rise, and for the first time in many months our confidence returned, with a feeling that better news and better days would soon arrive. We sensed that this time our dream of freedom would become reality.

Hitler Wanted to Kill All PWs

The Swiss Radio confirmed yesterday reports that in the last days of the war Adolf Hitler ordered all Allied prisoners of war shot.

Heard by BBC in London, the radio quoted Dr. Burckhardt, president of the International Red Cross. He said that the Wehrmacht had refused to carry out the order and that in March he had met representatives of Heinrich Himmler and obtained permission for the Red Cross to enter PW camps and prevent any last-minute executions.

Last March, at the time of Dr. Burckhardt's visit to Germany, reports that Allied prisoners in Germany would be killed were widespread, but Himmler was blamed at that time. The reports never were officially recognized because of Allied concern over what might happen if Burckhardt's mission were a failure.

Dr. Burckhardt also said that Hitler always had wanted to renounce the international conventions relating to prisoners of war, and that toward the last days of his life, his temper steadily grew worse.

Hitler wanted all POWs Killed

34

LIBERATION

On April 30, 1945, a mere eighteen days after Roosevelt's death, there was excitement in the air from the rumors buzzing about the camp. German families with wagons, carts, bicycles and trucks piled full of household items and food gave credence to the rumors that the end was very near. The German guards left the camp *en masse* at eleven o'clock that evening. The explosions that we could hear in the near distance made it clear that the Germans were destroying their military installations in the path of the oncoming Russians. At long last, the end really was near! The enemy had fled.

The euphoria I felt upon waking the next morning, May 1ˢᵗ, to see American POW's patrolling the fences and manning the guard towers is a feeling that only a prisoner of war would understand. The loudspeakers that had been used for announcements and German propaganda were now airing radio programs from the British Broadcasting Corporation. Our future became even brighter when the Russians arrived at the gates of our camp at 10:25 p.m. that evening and then brighter still when the first Hit Parade radio program we had heard in months was interrupted at 11:00 p.m. with the news of Adolf Hitler's death. Shortly after this announcement the song, "Don't Fence Me In," echoed in the night air as a fitting end to the long-awaited for day of liberation.

On the morning of May 2, 1945, I arose to see, the American, British and Russian flags flying above the camp. It was a day of celebration, as well as chaos. We were rapidly and willingly caught up in the joyous celebration. I joined a number of *ex*-POWs and Russians on a trip into the Town of Barth. I could now walk freely through this village just as I had wished I could on the cold day in February when we were first marched through on our way to the camp.

During our travels about the area, our excitement turned to gloom with the grisly discovery of a German concentration camp near the airport that was only a few miles from the camp. The gruesome mass of skeletal figures of living, dead and dying individuals was a haunting scene, and served to put our own treatment at the hands of the Germans in bitter perspective. It is hard to comprehend how people could treat fellow human beings the way these poor souls had been treated…with a total disregard for their humanity. There was nothing that we could do for them and they appeared beyond any medical help short of a miracle.

With our mood shaken, we made our way back to camp. After such an upsetting sight, I realized even more just how lucky that I'd been. I was riding around celebrating my freedom when freedom for the unfortunate beings we had just seen came too late. How grateful I was as I reentered Stalag Luft I with the realization that soon I would leave this place for good, and as a free man.

Food was plentiful in our last days in Barth due to an abundance of Red Cross parcels and the slaughter of over forty cows.[8] Our only problems now were overeating and when, not if, our stay would end. We were all so anxious to get home. And then, General Eisenhower announced via radio that we should "stand by" for an impending air evacuation.

While we waited, the Russians provided entertainment to help break up the monotony of our remaining days. Then, on May 12, 1945, the first group of prisoners, comprised of British and wounded, was flown out of Barth in B-17s. I flew out with a group on May 13th, and that was to be my final ride in a B-17. The planes taxied in, collected thirty of us, and taxied out without even shutting off their engines. I will never forget the thrill of watching out the plane's window as Stalag Luft I disappeared in the distance and I caught my final glimpse of the beautiful church that I had stared at so often from behind barbed wire.

---

8 The Russians, without regard for the private property of the Germans, had simply herded them into our camp. At that point, we weren't too concerned about the Germans, or their property.

Ike Pledges Freed PWs He'll Get 'Em Home—and Soon, Too

By Charles F. Kiley
Stars and Stripes Staff Writer

ST. VALERY, France, May 23.— Gen. Eisenhower yesterday told more than 40,000 repatriated American prisoners of war that he was personally doing everything to get them home as soon as possible.

The Supreme Commander, speaking over a public-address system from atop a truck, said he had issued orders for America-bound ships carrying liberated PWs to be loaded to capacity, even to the extent of asking men to share individual beds and to sleep in shifts in order to fulfill their wishes of getting home soon "even if we have to swim."

The repatriates, captured from two months to two years ago, have been here awaiting shipment home. Some have been here only a few days, others three weeks.

Gen. Eisenhower spoke personally with more than 100 men during his visit and joined one group for lunch.

He reminded the men of the war still to be waged against Japan.

"There is a great deal of activity now in progress to take care of the war with Japan," he said, "and if we can't supply the shipping for you immediately it is only because we must also think of your fellow soldiers fighting in the Pacific.

"Speaking for everyone in America, I want to express our gratitude to you all in helping defeat Germany. You men carried the ball for us and we will not forget it."

"Speaking for everyone in America, I want to express our gratitude to you all in helping defeat Germany. You men carried the ball for us and we will not forget it."

Courtesy of Carolyn McGory (wife of Ex-POW Thomas McGory)

Page in Notebook documenting final days in Stalag Luft I

Barth Airport Control Tower
Courtesy of B24.net – Greg Hatton (A.J. Zywiczynski)

35

Return to present...

BARTH, GERMANY

Barth, Germany, was the first of my former camp areas that Candy traveled in her mission to retrace my journey as a POW. In May, 2005, she joined a tour group led by Ellis (Gib) Gibson, returning for the sixtieth anniversary of the liberation of Stalag Luft I. She knew relatively nothing about my experience in WWII at the time but felt that this was a perfect opportunity for her to visit the camp, especially as many of the people in the group were ex-POWs. She hoped by chance that she would find someone who remembered me and could tell her about me as a young POW. She had stored up so many questions to ask! I thought it unlikely that an old comrade would be on the trip – there had been nine thousand men there! But it was this hope that was a driving force in her mission.

It was a difficult trip for her, stirring up a mixture of so many feelings. It had been less than a year since my sudden death. There were many times that she would feel weepy, but she would find that the other children of POWs who she traveled with had their weak moments as well. She spent as much time as possible listening to the stories shared freely by the former prisoners. None of the men, however, had been my roommates. This excursion provided her with many valuable contacts who were quite willing to assist her in learning about the life of a POW. Also, her meeting with German historians, Helga Radau and Dr. Martin Albrecht, provided her with extensive insight into the history of this camp. They have spent years of dedicated research preserving the memory of Stalag Luft I, and they graciously answered all the questions that Candy thought to ask of them.

It was evident that Helga and Martin had extended their hospitality to, and shared their extensive knowledge with, many visiting ex-POWs and their relatives by guiding them through the area. An informative Documentation Center had been established, with pictures and articles displaying the history of Stalag Luft I, the concentration camp that existed in Barth, as well as the military installations in the area. During the visit to the exhibition, Helga took Candy aside to try to find which compound I had been held in. She produced a history book listing the prisoners' names and their compounds, and I was listed under "Heydekrug Sergeants," with no location indicated. It was a disappointment to my daughter as when she went to the camp she wanted to focus on the area where I was held. There was also a video playing in the museum of the air evacuation of the POWs and, upon viewing it, Candy was excited to see a man that she thought to be me. It was so long ago but when the film was replayed several times for Candy to study the clip even through my eyes the man in question did appear to be me.

When the group left the exhibit center and continued on to visit the camp area, there were many tears among the ex-POWs and relatives who were present. They were pleased to see the camp monument and a display at the site with pictures of the past. The former prisoners were honored to see that they were remembered in the area in which they had sacrificed so many months of their lives. I knew how they felt.

Candy walked off by herself after she explained to the others that she had to cover the entire area because she was uncertain of my compound. She walked through the West, North 1, North 2 and North 3 sections until she was satisfied that she had walked where I had. Reuniting with the others, she stated that she felt secure in believing that she had walked where I had over sixty years ago. She commented on the church steeple and how deeply stirring the image was to her, knowing that I would have gazed at it from behind barbed wire. I had of course accompanied her as she walked around, but I stayed in the area that was most familiar to me until she had walked over all of it. The grounds once so overcrowded and full of activity were now quiet and empty, with no trace whatsoever of the "town" of nine thousand men who had occupied this site.

After the tour group left the camp, a stop was made at the Barth railway station. The station looked just as I remembered it all those years ago when I began my walk to Stalag I, my third prison-home since my capture. There was talk between Candy and some of the others that they wished that they could take the walk that their dads' had, from the railway station to the camp. However, there was not time left to accomplish this – it would have been a very long walk.

The tour group continued by bus from the camp area to the airport. My presence there brought back the elation that we all felt as we waited to board the B-17s that would fly us out of Barth. It was strange but it looked like the entire group was almost remembering and feeling the same joyful feelings as they looked at and walked on the runway.

When our group left Barth the next morning, Helga came to bid us farewell. Candy would say goodbye to people who she decided she would keep in touch with in the months to come. She had so much more territory that she felt she needed to cover. She exchanged addresses and e-mails with Helga, Martin and Ejvind Jensen. Ejvind was a Danish fellow who came to Barth in memory of two members of a crew whose bomber had crashed near his home town. He had quite a story that Candy hoped he would tell her in full one day. They only conversed briefly during the time spent in Barth. It was important to her to maintain communication with these kind people who were so willing to help her piece together the puzzle of my past.

This trip had been Candy's first step on her journey to retrace my entire wartime route. But she had arrived in Barth with so few of the facts that were pieces of the puzzle. She said that she felt insignificant knowing so little about my experience compared to the others she had met. She wasn't sure that she belonged in the group, but by the time she left Barth, she had no doubts that she belonged there. *She* belonged because *I* was there. She was determined to continue to add on to what she had learned from others on this brief visit. This tour was the foundation of her total commitment and it had provided her with many contacts and resources from which to continue to build my story. Most importantly, she would gain the confidence that she required to continue on in my steps. This was just the beginning of her journey in pursuit of my own journey of sixty years ago.

"POW Kids": Nancy Thayer Haggerty, Vicki Morgan, Jim Morrin, Mellisa Ledlow, Ruth Lawrence, Candy Kyler Brown (May 2005)

Former POWs in Barth 2005
Bud Bodie, Joe Reus, John Tayloe, Bob Bueker, Don Menard

SECOND VISIT TO BARTH, SEPTEMBER 2006

This second visit to Barth was part of the three-week trip Candy and Sara took together during September-October 2006. They were first in Podington, England and flew from London, to Brussels, Belgium, and from Brussels to Berlin, taking a bus the 170 miles to Barth.

They joined the tour group of eight others in Berlin for a day's tour of the City. The following day, they began the early morning bus ride to Barth arriving to enjoy lunch in Zingst, a small coastal town just north of Barth. It was a beautiful day and after lunch the three of us took a walk with Joe and Shirley, one of the nice couples in their group. Sara walked on the pier with them as Candy walked through the sand to the water to put her feet in the Baltic Sea.

As the bus arrived to collect us, Sara and Candy both mentioned that it felt like a dream that they were there together. They said that the deep blue sky, the warmth of the sun, and the atmosphere were all indications of my presence. Sara repeated several times to our daughter throughout their time in England and Belgium and now Germany that she wondered if I could see them. The weather had been gorgeous everywhere they had been so far. They agreed that this was a sign I had interceded on their behalf and that they were being watched over. Bad weather could have restricted Sara from going to the areas she wanted to see. I was convinced that my presence was felt.

Candy was happy to be reunited with two friends that she had met the previous year in Barth, Vicki Morgan and John Tayloe. John had worked in the cookhouse as a prisoner in Stalag Luft I and had many enlightening stories to tell, and Vicki's father had been interned in this camp. She too had experiences of her late father's to share with us.

The tour group stayed in the Hotel Speicher Barth, and my girls had great difficulty getting their heavy luggage up the steep stairs that led to their rooms. It took two men to handle some of them. The weight of the luggage had been an ongoing problem on this trip.

Candy was anxious to meet Helga Radau again and to introduce Helga to her mother. They had kept in touch since Candy's visit to Barth in 2005. On the first evening of Candy's second visit, the group attended a meeting in the Mayor's office. The ex-POWs who were on the tour were interviewed after the meeting and then everyone returned to the hotel for dinner. Candy was pleased to have Martin Albrecht join them after dinner, and she was in her element elaborating on the astounding places that she and her mother had visited before their arrival in Germany. She updated him on her progress in researching my story since her last visit to Barth. She had come so far since then, and was quite pleased to tell him about the things she'd done and places she'd been paralleling my route. Confidence was no longer a problem for her presence as it had been the previous year. I enjoyed watching her speak enthusiastically about everything. She and her mother were both still energized from the incredible visits they had experienced in England and Belgium just days before.

The next day began at a morning conference, when the group met with Helga. I saw that Helga was very kind and attentive to Sara, especially during the time that Candy was interviewed along with two of the ex-POWs. Candy had hoped that she was able to get her message across to the crowd, as it was difficult to talk smoothly having to use an interpreter. She elaborated as well as she could on her research and expressed her regret that she did not begin her inquiries until after my death. She ended with a statement that, "the reason we are happy is because of our freedom," and she continued, "our freedom is a result of their courage." She expressed the importance of keeping the memory of Stalag Luft I alive so that history does not repeat itself, and she praised the efforts of Helga and the Documentation Center Association in ensuring that Stalag Luft I would not be forgotten.

I know it wasn't easy for Candy, but I could not help but feel pleased at the way she talked about her commitment to writing my story. She explained how she was determined to accomplish this by talking to others who were there and walking where I walked. It was her way of remembering me who she said "represents the thousands of others who sacrificed months or years of their lives for the freedom that we now enjoy." She then presented Helga with a notebook of copies of pictures, articles, and documents pertaining to me and my fellow crew members. It contained the same information as the notebook that she had left in Belgium.

After the conference, a lunch was provided before they moved on to the Exhibition where they spent time examining the many interesting displays of the history of the area during World War II. It was nice watching the ex-POWs having the opportunity to talk and to indicate various features of the camp using the large replica of the layout of Stalag Luft I that stands in the museum.

The group then rode from the museum to the airport. My wife was a bit awestruck, having seen Candy's film of the POWs being evacuated from these grounds in an unending string of B-17s. Sara, too, had picked me out of the great number of men who were shown in the video. A bit overwhelmed, Sara again remarked that she couldn't believe she was actually here in Barth.

Having visited the previous year, Candy seemed much more comfortable and this time in better control of her emotions. This had become her territory as well as mine, and you could tell in her deportment how sure she was of herself. Candy's demeanor served as a comfort to Sara whose thoughts of me at times made her very emotional.

The group continued from the airport to the camp site. The ground was dry, and it was easy to maneuver through the fields. My wife traveled everywhere that our daughter did in this large area that once housed over nine thousand prisoners. Helga guided them to the remnants of a foundation in what was formerly the North 1 Compound area. It was difficult for me to figure out what building had stood there. It may have been the mess hall, but I couldn't be positive. I recalled that during the last days in camp the mess hall mysteriously burned. Sara and Candy stood for several moments taking in the surroundings, always turning in the direction of the Barth church steeple in the distance. They walked across the road to the camp memorial, the same road that we marched in and out of the camp on. They examined the plaque which read:

> *This Plaque is dedicated by the citizens of Barth and the Royal Air Force Ex-Prisoner of War Association on 28 September 1996 to commemorate all those held prisoner at Stalag Luft I. Sited here from July 1940 to May 1945: Members of the British Commonwealth and United States of America Air Forces and their allies from the occupied countries and the Soviet Union.*
>
> *"Nothing Has Been Forgotten."*

The group also studied the display containing pertinent information and photographs of what the camp area had once looked like.

The group then continued on to walk with Helga to the West Compound section of the camp, which was adjacent to the monument. It was a very interesting walk as she explained the layout of the camp mentioning the hospital and motioning toward the area across the way where the German Vorlager was located. She pointed out a fire pool and an entrance to the Flak School. I could picture everything and every area that Helga spoke of. As they walked along, the visitors picked up stones, pieces of the old road and broken pottery pieces and glass. Candy commented that these collections would be kept as a keepsake of the part of my life they were assembling. They returned for moments of reflection to the monument area, again gazing out across the field at the church steeple before they returned to the bus and headed for the railway station.

As they arrived at the Barth train station, largely untouched since 1945 (though well maintained), Candy explained to Sara that this was where I would have climbed down from a train of boxcars, starving, sick and exhausted with hundreds of other men when we were transported from Stalag Luft IV in an eleven-day journey from January 29 to February 8, 1945. Candy told Sara about the long and exhausting ride without food or water in freezing temperatures, and she explained that without any respite or refreshment we had then been marched through town to the camp. Candy told her mother that one day she would like to take that walk. Again, as had been the case in her first visit, there was not the time.

Later that evening, after an enjoyable dinner, Candy returned to their room and wrote in her journal:

> *There is something that draws me to this place and it is hard to explain it to anyone. I could see it if I had been there 62 years ago and came back but that is not the case. I am only me. I have felt this way every leg of this trip that was part of my father's route.*
>
> *This time spent in Barth was a very gratifying and significant facet of our expedition. Things are so much clearer to me now than after my first visit. I was confused then and it was important to me to know the route that*

> *the men took from the railroad station through town and*
> *to the Camp as well as their walk from the camp to the*
> *airport. I can picture it all so much better now and it is*
> *my dream to some day walk dad's route to camp. It all*
> *makes sense and I feel good about that. I have grown in*
> *my knowledge and understanding of this area and feel*
> *that I belong here as my father's daughter. When I visit*
> *I am returning in his place and remembering this lifetime*
> *for him and the thousands of men like him. Things have*
> *begun to look familiar to me as they most surely would to*
> *him. I was looking at places, though, almost as if I was*
> *seeing them through my father's eyes.*

If she only knew she was as close as she could be to seeing through my eyes.

The next day, Sara and Candy awoke early to take a short walk to absorb one last look at the water, the town and the church. There was a boat, *Roland,* that my wife wanted her picture taken in front of. She always called me by my middle name, Roland, and how surprised they were at the irony of a vessel with that name being docked in this harbor. They felt that it was another sign that I was among them. They walked slowly back to the hotel for their last breakfast in Barth.

Once again, farewell hugs were exchanged as the group said their good-byes and expressed their appreciation to their friends in Barth who had made the visit in this charming town so special. They waved to Helga through the bus window until she was out of sight.

ONE LAST LOOK AT STALAG LUFT I

Another tour was planned for the Fall of 2007 which included a brief stay in Barth. Candy felt she still needed to visit one more place significant to my role as a POW, and thought it to be the perfect opportunity to add Lithuania (Stalag Luft VI) to the itinerary. To return to Barth again would give her the last opportunity to take the longed-for trek from the railroad station, through the town, to Stalag Luft I. In her correspondence with Helga Radau, Helga agreed that they could take this walk during her planned visit there with the tour group. She was excited to think that her dream would finally become a reality.

Once again Candy returned to territory that was now quite familiar to her. She was reunited with her dear friend, Helga, when the group arrived for a special service in the beautiful Barth landmark, the St. Marien Church.[9] They exchanged greetings and hugs and entered the building with melodious tunes from the church organ filling the air. Helga told the group that it was being played for the American visitors. This church held a significant meaning for all of the POWs present who had viewed the St. Marien steeple from Stalag Luft I, perhaps a reminder to them that a supreme being was watching over them all. It was stirring to be inside this historic place that until now had only been viewed from the outside. An informative presentation was given on this extraordinary building that all of us who had spent time in Barth remembered.

The weather on this day was cold, rainy and windy – not favorable for a long walk. Candy had written in her journal that if the weather did not cooperate and the walk could not occur, she would try not to be disappointed but would just be happy to be in Barth again.

My daughter mentioned how her very presence in this Church turned her thoughts to me and she whispered a prayer for me reflecting on my days past in Barth. She knew that I walked near this structure on my way to Stalag Luft I on a cold, wintry day in February, 1945. The anticipation of her taking the same walk was building, and I could see her nervousness. After the church history was presented, Helga told her, "we will take our walk now."

As they began their venture arm in arm, they felt the whipping of the brisk wind and the pelting of the rain as they huddled under Helga's umbrella. Of course I needed no coat and no umbrella. The plan was to begin this journey at the railway station, as I had, so they walked there from the church. Candy was living her dream with Helga as her guide and me as an observer of this walk that was momentous to her and every bit as significant to me. Helga would no doubt make informative comments throughout their walk as they hurried along through the stormy weather. They passed the church, continuing to the infamous Barth gate – the "West" archway that I remember so well passing under. With the increased precipitation, they quickened their pace through town. I glanced back and saw Candy do the same to gaze at the prominent view of the tower in

---

9 The church was first constructed in the fifteenth century. The 80 meter tower was completed in 1450.

the background. Even today I feel a sense of serenity when I observe this landmark. Its outline against the sky viewed from our camp seemed to have provided a cloak of peacefulness over our captive bodies.

Moving along, you could catch yet a different angle that both the church and the gate provided from a distance away. It was another view that flashed into my mind from sixty-three years ago. Candy, too, was studying the scene, and I thought that Helga would grow impatient over these small pauses but she did not seem to mind.

Continuing to trace my route, they walked for a period of time on a blacktopped road. Helga mentioned that it was not the original road but still they were traveling through the same area that we covered as prisoners on our hike to our new home.

We finally drew near an old building that I recognized as the old anti-aircraft artillery (flak) school during the war. Helga pointed it out to Candy and they walked into a vacant, muddy area to capture a good look at it. I remembered it well, because a bomber airman whose seen action never forgets an experience with flak.

To me it was extraordinary to be following this road, realizing that they were walking on the original road leading to the camp that once existed on those now empty grounds; and I, too, was retracing my steps. It was the last stretch of what Candy commented was a remarkable journey as they finally reached the place where once stood my last camp as a POW – Stalag Luft I.

They spent some time at the memorial that marked the former entrance to the camp, which has become well known to us. Candy and I then together wandered off, concentrating on the West and North 1 Compound areas for the last time. If only I could somehow let her know that my time in Barth was spent in the North I Compound. I am happy knowing that it has been one of her main suppositions.

An entry in Candy's journal at the end of this day read…

> *What a gratifying sensation at the end of the long, talked about and dreamed about walk that we had shared. It had begun at the Railway Station at 4:06 PM and ended at the camp area at 4:52 PM. It could not have been a better 46 minutes for me regardless of the weather – a day I will never forget. Thanks to my special friend,*

*Helga, it was another one of my aspirations that I was
so fortunate to accomplish.*

So, a journey that had begun for Candy and me in 2004 finally reached
completion over three years later. Candy and I had both learned more
about things than we had ever dreamed possible. Both of us had changed,
but this change was more important for my daughter, who still had so
much of her life yet to live. Walking back from the camp I thought of all
these things, and wondered if this would indeed be the end of Candy's
journey.

It had become harder to say goodbye with each visit to Barth, and
Candy was pretty sure this would be the final one, but she and Helga
promised to always stay in touch.

More feelings and memories were resurrected in my return to Barth. I
was more at ease and pleased that I was able to be present during this visit,
and, for that matter, all of the visits. I was fortunate to be part of anything
my daughter did or any place that she traveled in revisiting my past even
if it meant returning to a place more than once. I could participate until
the route was finished. Each return was easier for her and for me and,
unknown to her, we were both making the best of the time that we were
able to spend in these regions.

Fire Pool – West Compound

Helga Radau on foundation North 1

Candy & Sara at Stalag Luft I; Church steeple in background

Sara standing on original road leading to former Flak School

Barth Train Station (beginning of Candy & Helga's trek)

Walk by St. Marien Church

Trek through town

View of Steeple across field on walk to the Camp

West Archway POWs were marched through

Flak School near Camp

Original road to Camp

The walk ended at Stalag Luft I Monument

Former POWs in Barth 2007
Milt Klarsfeld, Everett Statton, Norm Rosholt, John Tayloe, Bill
Moore, John Bryner, Verlyn McGraw, Richard Hanson, Gerald May

Barth Airport Control Tower

Runway at Barth Airfield

The Conclusion: What I Never Told You

May 1, 1945, was the date of our liberation from Stalag Luft I, but it has occurred to me, over sixty-four years later, that I was never truly liberated until now. With each stop and with every completed segment of my daughter's mission, I took increasing comfort. I found that watching my history unfold gave me a sense of relief from the many repressed memories that had remained bottled up during my lifetime. Each sojourn played an integral part in bringing closure to what was "unfinished business," for both of us. In these visits, Candy was remembering my past as if she had been there, and now they are her memories too. I think she came to know S/Sgt. Kyler as well as I remember him.

The visit to Lithuania in September, 2007, was a necessary component of Candy's mission and this successful episode of our journey was the finish of my allotted time on earth. Even though my presence was undetected, we shared the completion of her endeavor. I can now pass on to the afterlife feeling relieved of the memories that were buried inside me, and the skeletons that had remained cloistered throughout my life– feelings and things I had seen that I had never conveyed to anyone. I am not certain if I helped by being with her, but I know that it helped me face and relive once and for all the unspoken life that my daughter was in search of. I was one of thousands who traveled similar paths as prisoners of war. It will wit well with all of my comrades knowing that we are remembered – those who were able to share their painful memories, those like me who could not bring themselves to share them, and those who did not live to tell anything at all. Remembrance of me is also commemoration of them.

On May 4, 2004, my life had ended abruptly. My departure from life marked the beginning of my daughter's mission to uncover and revisit my wartime history – a time in my life that was put away but not forgotten. Candy remembered an occasion during my life when we were listening to the old music that I loved, and my comment when *Sentimental Journey* was playing that I wanted it played at my funeral. This remark was forgotten in the confusion and shock of planning my funeral, and my daughter was distraught when she realized it too late. In her journal, she wrote of her mission, calling it a "sentimental journey," as if trying to make up for failing to remember my request. Candy did not realize it but she has taken me on a most unforgettable sentimental journey in learning enough to tell a story that I had never told her.

Candy and Me

Appendix

LETTERS TO AND FROM HOME....

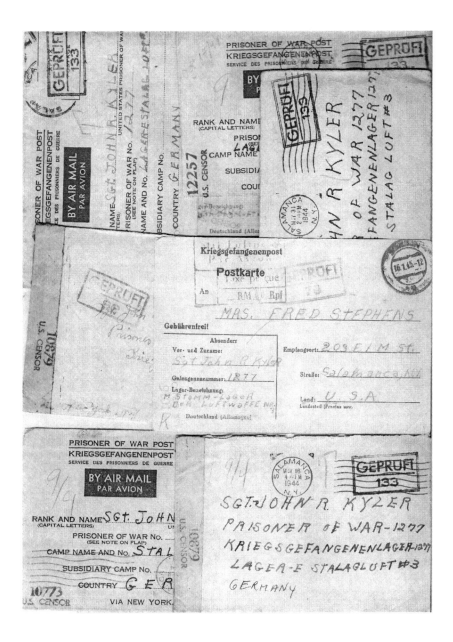

Salamanca, New York
May 8, 1944

My Darling,

We were so relieved to hear from you and know you are O.K. We hear from Morris quite often. I mean Ruth mostly. She has been here since March. She quit her work on account of her health. Jim asks for his Uncle Roland. In fact all our friends do. Am waiting for a sticker to send a package to you Dear. Tony was home for ten days. Jean is home for good. Expects soon. I hope it won't be twins. Wish for hair the color of Jean's and the type of the dad – curly. We are all as well as possible. We of course miss our honey. Take care of yourself dear and have lots of courage. We love you. Don't forget that. All My Love, Mom

*   *   *

Salamanca, New York
June 12, 1944

Darling,

Hope you have been receiving our mail. Was delighted to get your three. The first one came last. Jean had letters from Tony today. He is where John S. is. Ruth has been here since March 12. Has no place else to stay since her mother passed away. She is company for Jean and they take walks together every day. We have very cool nights around here. Morris is well also Helen, Jim and Fred. Did Kathleen write you as yet? Had a letter from Lawrence C. mother, California, today. I was so happy to get it. Wrote to the orderly but have had no response as yet. Jim sends you a hug. We are all as well as can be expected and hope you continue to be brave. All our love, Mom

*   *   *

Salamanca, New York
June 14, 1944

Dearest Johnnie,

How are you fine I hope. Mom had a letter from Cook's mother. She hasn't heard from him at all. Fred is making Jim a sand box. Jim played in the sand all day. He's got a nice suntan by the time summer is over he will be black. Jean had four letters from Tony that's the first she's had for six weeks. Maybe he can get your watch. Theresa Sartori is going to graduate from the eighth grade and Rose from high school. Rosey works in a drug store. Lloyd and Bea bought a trailer to travel in style this summer. Morris expects to come home soon. Ruth looks for him every day. Jim is sitting next to me. I asked him if I should tell you he's a bad boy and he began crying and said to tell you he is a good boy. Lots and lots of love. Your sister, Helen

*   *   *

10/11/44
Dearest brother John,

How are you? We are all praying that everything is ok. Everyone here is fine but very much concerned over you. Mom is still quite a trooper as she has hopes the same as the rest of us that you will be home soon. We had two letters from you last week. One was written in May the other in June. I wonder if you know we had an increase in our family. You are now uncle to a little niece. She was born August twenty-sixth. We named her Toni Marie. Tony hasn't seen her and I imagine it will be some time before he will. She looks just like him. Her hair was dark but is getting reddish like mine. Jim is a bigger doll then ever and always talks about his uncle John. His hair is still snow white and he has beautiful eyes. We all think he looks like you when you were young. Helen and Fred bought the house they were living in. Morris was home in August. Rose Sartori is going to business school in Olean. Carol works at the bakery. I believe Elinor does also but I never see her. Everyone sends their love and best wishes. Love, Jean

*   *   *

Stalag Luft IV
[Gross Tychow]
October 15, 1944

Dear Helen,

Very happy to get your letter. I had almost given up hope. I was glad to hear you're all well and Jim is coming along so fine. You should send pictures. Give my love to all. Take care of mom and Bizzaro family. Love, J

*   *   *

Stalag Luft IV
{Gross Tychow}
November 11, 1944

Dear Helen,

I hope you, Fred and (little bit) are well. Did Jim get that tan? I can hardly wait for those pictures. So Jim is going to lose a little lime-light. Or did he lose it already. I hope Jean makes out OK. Love, John

*   *   *

Poems by John Kyler as a POW:

A GOOD PILOT

by John Kyler

A pilot is a well trained chauffeur,
And is bossed by the entire crew.
But when it comes to pinches,
(He'll tell you what to do!)

He keeps the plane in formation,
Way up there in that blue.
And when the fighters start coming in,
He calls them off to you.

He sets up there so helpless,
With no gun to fire back.
But when it comes to courage,
That's something he doesn't lack.

To him his crew's welfare
Is foremost in his mind,
And when it comes to bailing out,
You can bet he'll be last in line.

GUNNER'S WISH

I wish to be a pilot
And you along with me
But if we all were pilots
Where would the air force be

The pilot's just a chauffeur
It's his job to fly the plane
But its we who do the fighting
Though we may not get the fame.

It takes guts to be a gunner,
To set in the lonely ball,
When the Messerschmitts are coming,
And the FW's give you their all.

So if we must be gunners,
Then let us make this bet:
We'll be the best damn gunners
That have left the U.S. yet!

FATE

(In memory of W/O Raymond Stephen,
RAF killed in camp by lightening)

What fate has man when close at hand
Was freedom, liberty, and his land
What fate this young flyer,
Who went out each day to die or do.
He lost his plane but not his life
In prison camps for years he fought
For strife.
What fate had he who flew so high
When peace so near but to die.

TS

So you want to be a gunner, huh?
You will regret those words.
Buddy you're plumb crazy.
Flying was meant for birds!

I was told the same story once,
But as most I did not heed.
I was flying high and mighty,
Until the 190's got their bead.

But no use complaining,
All is over and done.
Combat was a son of a bitch,
But the phases were lots of fun.

Other Poems taken from John R. Kyler's notebook...

A GOOD GIRL

Please don't ask me to marry you,
Mother would just have a fit.
Good gosh it was just today we met
Can't you be patient a bit?

You know how people would talk about things,
I mean if they're not in good taste.
Besides I don't think a girl if she's nice
Would marry a man in such haste.

I'll wed you tomorrow if you like,
And share your toothbrush and comb.
But if you keep teasing me darling,
I'll get up, get dressed and go home.

MARGIE

Her name was Margie, she was one of the best,
But there came the night I gave her the test.
I looked at her with joy and delight,
For she was mine the whole of the night.
She looked so pretty, so neat so slim,
The night was dark, the lights were dim.
I was so excited my heart missed a beat,
I knew that night I was in for a treat.

I saw her stripped, I saw her bare,
I felt all around her, I felt everywhere.
We started off, she screamed with joy,
For this was her very first night with a boy.
I got as high as quick as I could,
I handled her well—the response was good.
I turned her over, then right on her side,
Then on her back, every way I tried.

It was a great thrill,
She was the best in the land,
That four-engine bomber
Of Bomber Command

A LOVELY HAND

Last night I held a lovely hand,
A hand so sweet and neat
I thought my heart would burst with joy
So wildly did it beat.

No other hand into my heart
Could greater solace bring
Than the dear hand I held last night,
Four aces and a king.

KRIEGSGEFANGENEN HARRIS

"Harris get your barracks bag,
The shipping list is here!
We are sailing on the first tide,
For home and yesteryear."

But Harris stirred no muscle
To join the homing flocks
He was parked before a tiny stove,
Beside a Red Cross box.

"Harris we are sailing
The bitter war is done
Its off to the States boy
To our sweethearts and fun."

But Harris turned a deaf ear
His stubbornness uncleft.
"Why should he sail for anywhere
With all those groceries left?"

'Tis a sad tale they tell these days,
Along the lonely streets
Of Kriegsgefangenen Harris
With his parcel full of meats.

Some love adventure
Some love curly locks
But Kriegsgefangenen Harris
Loves a faithful Red Cross Box.

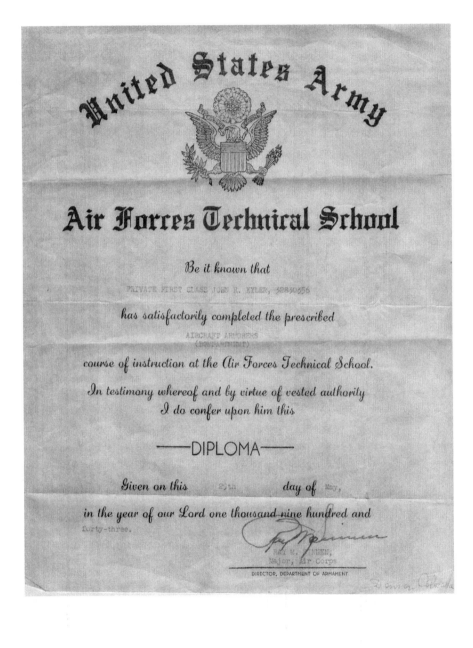

ACKNOWLEDGMENT

Loan no.

Date.

Received from American Red Cross $ .... as a loan which I promise

to repay ....
Date

John R. Kyler
Signature

Red Cross station or office

TRIPLICATE

TO BE GIVEN TO RECIPIENT OF LOAN

STATEMENT OR REPORT OF INTERVIEW OF RECOVERED
PERSONNEL

Last Name   First Name   Middle Initial   Army Serial Number   Grade

As of date of loss to United States Control Under "Remarks" on
reverse side give signed, complete statement in narrative form of
the circumstances leading up to and immediately following his capture
or other separation from his unit or organization.
UNIT OR ORGANIZATION

Name and Grade of immediate Commanding Officer and any other members
of his organization who are familiar with the circumstances.

Position occupied or duty being performed

FOR PERIOD OF ABSENCE FROM UNITED STATES MILITARY CONTROL
prisoner of War
Name of Prisoner of War Camp or Camps in which imprisoned, and
length of time served in each.

Names of Senior/United States Army Officers in each such Prisoner
of War Camp.

Duties performed while in Prisoner of War Camp or Camps

Army of the United States

SEPARATION QUALIFICATION RECORD
SAVE THIS FORM. IT WILL NOT BE REPLACED IF LOST

This record of job assignments and special training received in the Army is furnished to the soldier when he leaves the service. In its preparation, information is taken from available Army records and supplemented by personal interview. The information about civilian education and work experience is based on the individual's own statements. The veteran may present this document to former employers, prospective employers, representatives of schools or colleges, or use it in any other way that may prove beneficial to him.

1. LAST NAME—FIRST NAME—MIDDLE INITIAL			MILITARY OCCUPATIONAL ASSIGNMENTS		
Kyler, John R.			10. MONTHS	11. GRADE	12. MILITARY OCCUPATIONAL SPECIALTY
2. ARMY SERIAL NO.	3. GRADE	4. SOCIAL SECURITY NO.	5	S/Sgt.	Armorer Gunner - 612
32 830 356	S/Sgt.				
5. PERMANENT MAILING ADDRESS (Street, City, County, State)					
197 Elm St. Salamanca, N.Y.					
6. DATE OF ENTRY INTO ACTIVE SERVICE	7. DATE OF SEPARATION	8. DATE OF BIRTH			
3 Feb 43	28 Nov 45	23 Feb 23			
9. PLACE OF SEPARATION					
Separation Base Rome AAFld., Rome, N.Y.					

SUMMARY OF MILITARY OCCUPATIONS

13. TITLE—DESCRIPTION—RELATED CIVILIAN OCCUPATION

Armorer gunner - In charge of guns and turrets on ship - made checks of guns and turrets to make sure of working conditin.

WD AGO FORM 100
1 JUL 1945

This form supersedes WD AGO Form 100, 15 July 1944, which will not be used.

MILITARY EDUCATION

14. NAME OR TYPE OF SCHOOL—COURSE OR CURRICULUM—DURATION—DESCRIPTION

L/F Colo.   9 weeks - AP.
LAAF - Tex. 6 weeks

CIVILIAN EDUCATION

15. HIGHEST GRADE COMPLETED	16. DEGREES OR DIPLOMAS	17. YEAR LEFT SCHOOL	OTHER TRAINING OR SCHOOLING	
			20. COURSE—NAME AND ADDRESS OF SCHOOL—DATE	21. DURATION
10	G.S.	1941	3/12 Aircraft sch. Olean, N.Y.	

18. NAME AND ADDRESS OF LAST SCHOOL ATTENDED

Salamanca, N.Y.

19. MAJOR COURSES OF STUDY

Acad.

CIVILIAN OCCUPATIONS

22. TITLE—NAME AND ADDRESS OF EMPLOYER—INCLUSIVE DATES—DESCRIPTION

5-03.500   Aircraft Assembler

Bell Aircraft
Buffalo, N.Y.
6/12 Year.

ADDITIONAL INFORMATION

23. REMARKS

24. SIGNATURE OF PERSON BEING SEPARATED	25. SIGNATURE OF SEPARATION CLASSIFICATION OFFICER	26. NAME OF OFFICER (*Typed or Stamped*)
John R. Tyler		

U. S. GOVERNMENT PRINTING OFFICE—O-657477

ENLISTED RECORD AND REPORT OF SEPARATION
HONORABLE DISCHARGE

1. LAST NAME - FIRST NAME - MIDDLE INITIAL	2. ARMY SERIAL NO.	3. GRADE	4. ARM OR SERVICE	5. COMPONENT
Kyler John R	32 830 356	S/Sgt	AC	AUS
6. ORGANIZATION	7. DATE OF SEPARATION	8. PLACE OF SEPARATION		
92nd Bomb Gp 407th Bomb Sq	28 Nov 1945	Rome AAF1d Rome New York Separation Base		
9. 197 Elm Street	10. DATE OF BIRTH	11. PLACE OF BIRTH		
Salamanca New York	23 Feb 1923	Salamanca New York		
12. ADDRESS FROM WHICH EMPLOYMENT WILL BE SOUGHT	13. COLOR EYES	14. COLOR HAIR	15. HEIGHT	16. WEIGHT	17. NO. DEPEND
See 9	Hazel	Brn	5'8½"	146	0

18. RACE	19. MARITAL STATUS	20. U.S. CITIZEN	21. CIVILIAN OCCUPATION AND NO.
WHITE NEGRO OTHER(specify) X	SINGLE MARRIED OTHER (specify) X	YES X NO	Aircraft Assembler 5-03,500

MILITARY HISTORY

22. DATE OF INDUCTION	23. DATE OF ENLISTMENT	24. DATE OF ENTRY INTO ACTIVE SERVICE	25. PLACE OF ENTRY INTO SERVICE
27 Jan 1943		3 Feb 1943	Ft Niagara New York
SELECTIVE SERVICE DATA X	26. REGISTERED	27. LOCAL S.S. BOARD NO. 646	28. COUNTY AND STATE Cattaragnus Co NY	29. HOME ADDRESS AT TIME OF ENTRY INTO SERVICE See 9

30. MILITARY OCCUPATIONAL SPECIALTY AND NO.	31. MILITARY QUALIFICATION AND DATE (i.e., infantry, aviation and marksmanship badges, etc.)
Armorer Gunner 612	AAF Air Crew Member Badge AAF Tech Badge W/GnrBar

32. BATTLES AND CAMPAIGNS

Normandy   Rhineland
Northern France   Central Europe   Air Offensive Europe

33. DECORATIONS AND CITATIONS

American Campaign Medal World War II Victory Medal 3 Overseas Service Bars
European African Middle Eastern Campaign Medal W/5 Bronze Stars Good Conduct Medal

34. WOUNDS RECEIVED IN ACTION

None

35. LATEST IMMUNIZATION DATES				36.	SERVICE OUTSIDE CONTINENTAL U.S. AND RETURN		
SMALLPOX	TYPHOID	TETANUS	OTHER (specify)	DATE OF DEPARTURE	DESTINATION	DATE OF ARRIVAL	
7Feb43	12Sep45	17Aug43	See 55	6 Nov 1943	ETO	13 Nov 1943	
37. TOTAL LENGTH OF SERVICE				38. HIGHEST GRADE HELD	10 Jun 1945	USA	17 Jun 1945
CONTINENTAL SERVICE			FOREIGN SERVICE				
YEARS	MONTHS	DAYS	YEARS	MONTHS	DAYS		
1	2	14	1	7	12	S/Sgt	

39. PRIOR SERVICE

None

40. REASON AND AUTHORITY FOR SEPARATION

Conva of Govt RR 1-1 Demobilization AR 615-365 15 Dec 44

41. SERVICE SCHOOLS ATTENDED	42. EDUCATION (Years)	
Lowry Colo 9 wks Armorer LAAF Texas 6 wks Aerial Gnr	Grammar 8	High School 2	College 0

PAY DATA

43. LONGEVITY FOR PAY PURPOSES	44. MUSTERING OUT PAY	46. SOLDIER DEPOSITS	46. TRAVEL PAY	47. TOTAL AMOUNT, NAME OF DISBURSING OFFICER
YEARS 2	MONTHS 10	DAYS 2	TOTAL $ 300	THIS PAYMENT $ 100	none	$ 12.45	195.55 PERCY W NEWTON Major AC

INSURANCE NOTICE

IMPORTANT If PREMIUM IS NOT PAID WHEN DUE OR WITHIN THIRTY-ONE DAYS THEREAFTER, INSURANCE WILL LAPSE. MAKE CHECKS OR MONEY ORDERS PAYABLE TO THE TREASURER OF THE U. S. AND FORWARD TO COLLECTIONS SUBDIVISION, VETERANS ADMINISTRATION, WASHINGTON 25, D. C.

48. KIND OF INSURANCE	49. HOW PAID	50. Effective Date of Allotment	51. Date of Next Premium Due	52. PREMIUM DUE EACH MONTH	53. INTENTION OF VETERAN TO
Nat. Serv.	U.S. Govt.	None	Allotment	Direct to V. A.			EACH MONTH	Continue	Continue Only	Discontinue
X			X		30 Nov 1945	31 Dec 1945	$ 6.50	X	

54. REMARKS (This space for completion of above items or entry of other items specified in W. D. Directives)

Lapel Button Issued
ASR Score (2 Sept 1945) 76
ADD Immunization Dates
Typhus 3 Sep 1943
Cholera 14 May 1945
Yellow Fever 4 Sep 1943

55. SIGNATURE OF PERSON BEING SEPARATED	57. PERSONNEL OFFICER (Type name, grade and organization - signature)
John R. Kyler	A A ANDERSEN Capt AC

WD AGO FORM 53-55
1 November 1944
This form supersedes all previous editions of WD AGO Forms 53 and 55 for enlisted persons entitled to an Honorable Discharge, which will not be used after receipt of this revision.

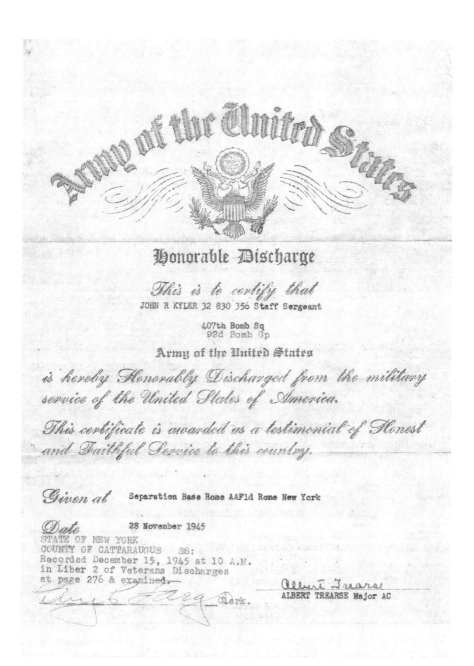

ARMY AIR FORCES

Certificate of Appreciation

FOR WAR SERVICE

TO

JOHN R KYLER 32 850 356 S/SGT

𝕴 CANNOT *meet you personally to thank you for a job well done; nor can I hope to put in written words the great hope I have for your success in future life.*

Together we built the striking force that swept the Luftwaffe from the skies and broke the German power to resist. The total might of that striking force was then unleashed upon the Japanese. Although you no longer play an active military part, the contribution you made to the Air Forces was essential in making us the greatest team in the world.

The ties that bound us under stress of combat must not be broken in peacetime. Together we share the responsibility for guarding our country in the air. We who stay will never forget the part you have played while in uniform. We know you will continue to play a comparable role as a civilian. As our ways part, let me wish you God speed and the best of luck on your road in life. Our gratitude and respect go with you.

COMMANDING GENERAL
ARMY AIR FORCES

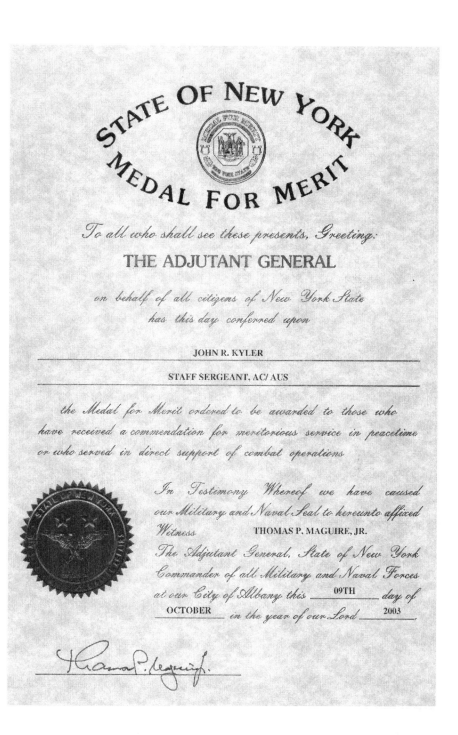

STATE OF NEW YORK
MEDAL FOR MERIT

To all who shall see these presents, Greeting:

THE ADJUTANT GENERAL

*on behalf of all citizens of New York State
has this day conferred upon*

JOHN R. KYLER

STAFF SERGEANT, AC/ AUS

*the Medal for Merit ordered to be awarded to those who
have received a commendation for meritorious service in peacetime
or who served in direct support of combat operations*

*In Testimony Whereof we have caused
our Military and Naval Seal to hereunto affixed
Witness* THOMAS P. MAGUIRE, JR.
*The Adjutant General, State of New York
Commander of all Military and Naval Forces
at our City of Albany this* 09TH *day of*
OCTOBER *in the year of our Lord* 2003

The United States of America

honors the memory of

John R. Kyler

This certificate is awarded by a grateful
nation in recognition of devoted and
selfless consecration to the service
of our country in the Armed Forces
of the United States.

President of the United States

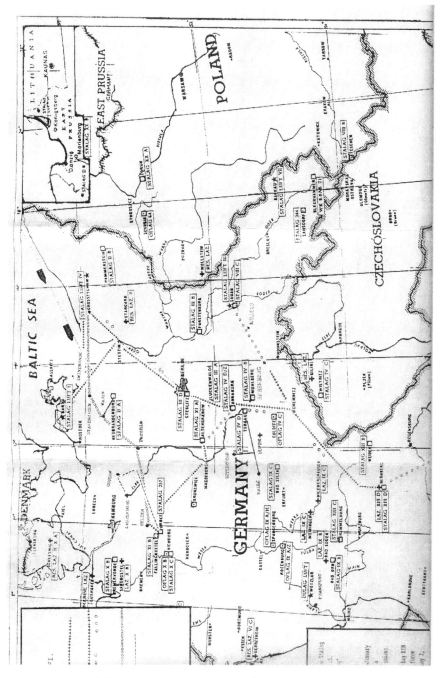

Map indicating Stalag Luft VI, IV and I.

LIFE AND DEATH OF A GERMAN TOWN

TENSE MOMENTS WHILE ALLIES TAKE CONTROL

An air of tension hung over the camp for many days. The presence of the English and American armies on the Elbe and the Russian encirclement of Berlin made everyone feel that the end must be near. The commencement of a new Russian drive across the lower Oder toward the Baltic ports finally increased the tension to an almost unbearable pitch. Panic reigned in the Vorlager. No German had any more interest in guarding the prisoners, but only in saving his own life. Confidential reports were hurriedly burnt — and copies of "Mein Kampf" went to swell the flames.

Conference with the Kommandant

Finally, late in the afternoon, the Senior British and American officers were called to a conference with the German camp Kommandant Colonel Warnstedt. They were told that orders had been received to move the whole camp westward. Colonel Zemke stated he was not willing to move at all, and asked in that case what the German attitude would be. The Commandant replied that he would not tolerate bloodshed in the camp; if we did not intend to move, he and his men would evacuate themselves and leave us in sole possession of the camp. When the Germans left it would be up to us to take over the camp peacefully and assume full control.

At approximately 1 A.M, on April 30 Major Steinhauer informed Group Captain Weir and Colonel Zemke that the Germans had evacuated the camp, leaving it in our charge. When the camp woke up in the morning it was to find itself no longer under armed guard and comparatively free.

Where are the Russians?

Our next problem was to establish contact with the Russian forces. It was decided to send out something in the nature of a recco patrol. An American Major, a British Officer speaking German, and an American Officer speaking Russian, set out with the German in the auto which was equipped with an American flag on one fender and a white flag on the other, to investigate the real situation in Barth and then proceed to the main Stralsund—Rostock and some 15 kilometers south of the camp — was there for any signs of Russian spearheads or of the proximity of the front line. The first patrol returned in the early evening. Still no sign or news of the Russian Army, but had been driving.

Russian Contact (con. from Page 1)
Every house draped with red flags (who said the Germans weren't chameleons?). Suddenly, there was Uncle Joe —— or one of his ambassadors: a chunky little Dead End guy who loomed up and flashed a variety of lethal weapons and a cacophony of Slavic language.

"Engliski", shouted the scouts.

"Never mind the words", said Joe's man, "this isn't Dulug" or something like that in Russian And without ceremony they went to the nearest Russian officer. It was 1st Lt Alec Nick Karmyzoff, infantryman from Tula, you can see that written in Russian! He'd fought his way from Stalingrad — three years across Russia, Poland and Germany — to the relief of Stalag Luft I.

Toasts are Drunk.
Karmyzoff came in the main gate. Commanding Officers Zemke and Weir received him. Schnapps seared kriegie throats — glasses smashed Hitler's picture, the barracks jiggled with cheering and back-pounding. Toasts were drunk: " To the destruction of Germany — she will never rise again! And to our solid and enduring friendship." Karmyzoff went to the Russian barracks (our co-kriegies) — told them about himself, their army and the new life that was beginning. Thus the first contact, Karmyzoff bedded down on the floor — "Rather the floor than a German bed," said he. BBC announced Hitler dead; kriegies heard the "Hit Parade" from home; the excitement was overwhelming — But what an experience

QUAKING BARTH BURGHERS BOW BEFORE REDS

As Russian tanks rumbled Northwards on the cobblestoned roads from Stralsund, as Russian cavalry and guerilla troops tore hell-bent for the Baltic, as the spluttering German radio flashed a message of place names that had gone under in the Red rip tide, Barth became an open city and an open grave. The few Americans who had been in town on camp duties from Stalag I knew that the life of Barth was a living death. We had seen the streets peopled by children and octogenarians; we had noticed that all males were either lame, halt or blind; we had stared into empty shop windows and watched with the sodden wives of the master race straggle back from the bombed land, whipped, half-hungry of the war that stalked the streets of German towns. By April 30, this year of grace, the good burghers of Barth turned their faces to the wall and stopped hoping.

LET 'EM EAT CAKE

Life had not been good to the bakery shop where the camp bread was made; there was little cake and not sold to Jews or Poles. It did not explain that cake was the real power of supermen either. There was no cake. But there were good things in the larders of Barth baking powder requisitioned from Holland. Needles more commandeered from Denmark, wines looted from the cellars of France, sparkling and noodles hijacked from Italy, Worcestershire sauce which had trickled through mysteriously from England, olive oil drained from Greece, in short, all types of blood from the turnip of Europe. If Mussolini considered the Mediterranean his sea, Hitler considered the world his oyster and was trying to serve it up to the Reich on the half shell.

A House of Cards

As the first explosions from the flak school reverberated under the sullen Baltic sky, the new order toppled on Barth like a house of cards. Red flags and white sheets began to appear in the windows of the ginger bread houses. Flight was futile and the old stood queriously on their door steps, wringing gnarled hands and weeping. Pictures of Hitler were torn down and scattered like confetti. Two German children came wailing into the bakery shop. They had heard American airmen ate little boys and mother said the day of reckoning was at hand.

Barth, like the whole of Deutschland—err-alles Germany, was on its knees, interior. But mayhem did not materialize. We got drunk.

BARTH HARD TIMES

Vol 1 No. 1 LAST 1 SATURDAY MAY 5th 1945 PRICE 1 D- BAR.

Editor: F.L. E. R. INKPEN Assoc: 1st Lt N. GIDDINGS Publisher: 1st Lt D. MacDONALD Printing: F/LT J. D. WHITE

RUSSKY COME!

RELIEVED!

Colonel Zemke intended to write this appreciation of the relief of Stalag Luft I, but [illegible] duties have made this impossible. He has, in his own words, "taken a powder" to make final arrangements with the relieving Soviet forces.

It is therefore my privilege to introduce this Memorial Edition of the BARTH HARD TIMES.

During the [illegible] during this struggle our newspaper has faithfully recorded the German war communiques and [illegible] upon them in capable editorials.

With the redemption of a continent, our exile is ended. Our barb-bound community will soon be a memory. So, on behalf of Colonel Hubert Zemke and myself, to all our fellow-kriegies: GOOD LUCK!

G.C. C. T. Weir.

WHAT D'YE KNOW- JOE!!

BRAITHWAITE FINDS UNCLE JOE

Contacts Russian Infantryman at Crossroads Five miles South of Stalag One.

Major Braithwaite and Sgt Korson, our Stalag scouts, raced out to a cross-roads 5 miles south of Barth with the order, "find Uncle Joe". This was 8 p.m., May 1.

They searched southward, defying a rumored Russian curfew which was about as brief and emphatic as their own order: "EVERYONE stay put; anyone seen moving will be shot on sight."

Meanwhile, Wing Commander Blackburn's telephone crew were ringing numbers in Stralsund, hoping a Russian would answer the phone and we could break the big news of our presence. "Try the mayor," they asked the girl (who was still working Barth's phone exchange). "Not a chance," said she. "Barth's mayor poisoned himself and Stralsund's mayor has sprouted wings."

Scouts Braithwaite and Korson pushed on 3 miles. The scenery: thousands of people everywhere, sitting down, waiting.

Barth Hard Times Newspaper

Terug op de plaats van crash

BERINGEN/KOERSEL - Een grote dag voor de Amerikaanse Candy Brown (55) en haar moeder Sarah (85): de twee dames werden op het stadhuis van Beringen ontvangen. Hun overleden vader en echtgenoot, sergeant John R. Kyler, maakte op 4 februari '44 een crash mee boven Koersel. De Amerikaanse gasten bezochten nadien de plaats van de ramp.

Candy Brown en haar moeder Sarah (hier met Richard Heyligen) werden op het stadhuis ontvangen.

De Amerikaanse bommenwerper B-17, met als bijnaam Margriet, werd die dag door Duits afweergeschut uit de lucht gehaald. Het vliegtuig keerde terug van een bombardement boven Frankfurt en vloog naar de Britse basis Podington. Het had een tienkoppige bemanning aan boord. De brandstoftank werd geraakt en het toestel stortte naar beneden. De bemanning kon zich redden met parachutes. Toen het vliegtuig de grond raakte, brak het in stukken. Sergeant John R. Kyler, de buikkoepelschutter van het toestel, werd opgevangen in een naburige boerderij. Al snel werd hij echter opgepakt door de Duitsers. Richard Heyligen, aanwezig op de officiële ontvangst, zag het allemaal gebeuren. Hij was twaalf jaar oud en ging net naar school. "De B-17 werd aangevallen door Duitse jachttoestellen. Het toestel werd geraakt en verloor hoogte. Met loeiende motoren kwam het naar beneden. Ik zag parachutisten uit het vliegtuig springen. Het toestel landde in de weilanden in de vallei van de Zwarte Beek. Door de verse sneeuw en met behulp van speurhonden konden de Duitsers de bemanningsleden snel oppakken. Slechts twee van de tien, Mikulka en Blakely, konden ontsnappen met behulp van burgers, zo bleek later. De anderen, waaronder Kyler, zijn krijgsgevangen gemaakt en naar Duitsland gebracht."

PVM

Belgium Newspaper Article

Amerikaanse familie bezoekt plaats waar vliegtuig tijdens oorlog crashte

BERINGEN

Echtgenote Sara en dochter Candy Brown van de intussen overleden Amerikaan John Kyler zijn speciaal naar Beringen gekomen om de plaats te bezoeken waar zijn vliegtuig tijdens de oorlog neerstortte. Kyler maakte deel uit van de bemanning van de B17 die op vrijdag 4 februari 1944 door de Duitse luchtafweer werd neergehaald boven Koersel.

De B17 die de Vlaamse naam "Margriet" droeg, keerde huiswaarts na een lading bommen gedropt te hebben boven Frankfurt. Boven Koersel werd het toestel door de Duitse luchtafweer getroffen. Richard Heyligen, die toen nauwelijks was, zag het allemaal gebeuren. "Het vliegtuig werd aangevallen door Duitse jachttoestellen en er ontstond een vuurgevecht," herinnert hij zich. "Plots begon het hoog te verliezen en kwam het met loeiende motoren naar beneden. De inzittenden waren er met hun parachute uitgesprongen. De B17 kwam daarop neer in de weilanden van de vallei van de Zwarte Beek."

Door de verre uitschouw en met de hulp van een speurhonden hadden de Duitsers niet veel tijd nodig om enkele bemanningsleden gevangen te nemen. Twee van hen, McCulkin en Blakely, slaagden erin te ontsnappen met de hulp van enkele burgers.

Richard Heyligen met de vrouw en de dochter van de Amerikaan Kyler die boven Koersel neerstortte.

Foto RV

Article in Belgium Newspapers explaining "our" visit.

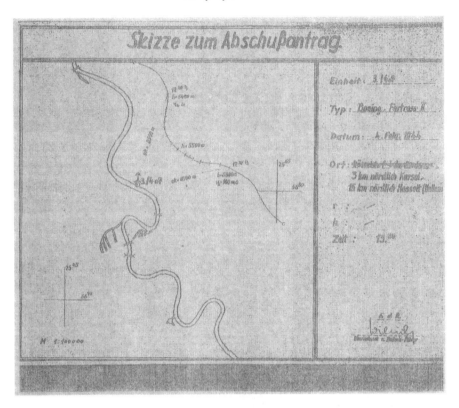

Page from Missing Air Crew Report indicating Crash Site

THE MYSTERY OF MARGRIET

In her e-mails Candy was asked if she knew what the nickname "Margriet" meant. It was not the name of the B-17 or the Frankfurt mission and she could not get an explanation. Before Candy left Belgium, Guy gave her the following information which was translated from the book *Markante Feiten*, solving the mystery of the name "Margriet":

"04-02-44

The *Margriet* had dropped her bombs above Frankfurt and wanted to return to her base in England, yet the German anti-aircraft guns decided different. One of the German missiles (FLAK) exploded below the left inside engine. This direct hit caused a lot of damage to the plane, and because the German anti-aircraft post reported a fire on the plane we may conclude that one of the fuel tanks was blown into pieces, which caused the conflagration outside the plane but which also extinguished as the fuel was used up.

The information that M Blakely mentioned were problems with the oil pressure, the oxygen, intercom and the propeller, which couldn't be [fixed].

The question that stays: Was Caylor, in a position in the plane where the explosion occurred? Was Caylor already wounded then?

That the pilots Cook L and Bangs R stayed levelheaded is sure because they brought the plane to a level where there was enough oxygen. The free spinning propeller and left engine that was blown to pieces [created drag] on the left wing [which necessitated constant correction by the pilots]. Also a possibility is that [excess] fuel in the right wing could be a problem, and had to be pumped over to the left wing to keep the plane controllable.

The *Margriet* suffered a loss of power and the formation was an easy prey for the German hunters. According to Blakely they put the landing gear down as a sign of surrender. But this attack left behind a track, a 20mm German bullet was found among some pieces of wreckage where the plane crashed and was loaded onto a truck.

Probably [it] was this bullet [that] caused the fire and got stuck somewhere in the plane. Because of the explosion…of the bullet, flaps the back part, the phosphorus out and starts to burn as soon as it comes in the air. Supposing this bullet ended up in the cockpit, that would have been the end of the *Margriet*. Where this attack took place we don't know. Certain is that the *Margriet* her last straight line flew from East to West, just beside or in the center of the German anti-aircraft defense sector Helchtern, Hasselt. Was there a prohibitory clause to fire that Day because of the visibility? And were the Germans allowed to fly everywhere? We don't know.

What we do know is that the first who jumped out of the plane, land in the area of the German watchtower that stood on higher lying ground, at the alleged "fonteintje" (fountain).

The security service of the army (before the war it was the biggest security service of Europe) was standing by every day, and it was sure that they knew about a plane in trouble by the radar ground stations. As soon as the first crewman, Caylor came down direction West (STAL) the Germans received a signal and could determine from where Caylor jumped out. Helped by the fresh snow and equip with bloodhounds, the Germans didn't give the crew much time to escape. But 3 of them managed to escape thanks to the quick action from a few Civilians. When Cook jumped as last he saw J Joys drop with his parachute. That means that when he came down 3 or 4 kilometers further than Joys, Cook managed to stay free for 26 days. The *Margriet* that flew on an automatic pilot began to turn clockwise, because of the 2 right engines that developed more power then the one left engine. And the left propeller from the broken engine served as a brake on the left wing. When the fuel was used up the engines stopped.

The *Margriet* went down with driving force, the left wing tilting. Its protruding landing gear got stuck into soft ground, broke and remained somewhere in the field. The left wing also broke off and because of that the *Margriet* moved to the left came down beside a verge almost lifted out of the ground, the right wing pulled down some birches. The *Margriet* lay intact, except the left wing and the landing gear.

It was an image of pride, strength and hope for a few who saw this enormous plane lying there. But also a thorn in the flesh of the Germans, who on 5/02/44 already in the early morning started to demolish the plane and loaded the big parts onto trucks and left the rest with the intention that the civilians saw the wreckage as a pile of misery. The Germans took the weaponry and the radio material and the rest served as German propaganda.

Yet, this German stunt got undermined very soon through the inhabitants. They spread the rumor that the crewmember blew up the plane them selves. This thesis is still told, after 62 years. But, also raised stories about the escaped crew, the given help and betrayal. These stories got bigger and bigger and they tided over some generations. There are those who kept quiet, the silent ones who provided Mikulka with an other name and passport and didn't spoke to anyone. Bert Boelanders, he who let the descendants look up astonished because he died and almost never talked about the war. It is because of these stories that we could find out some facts.

The history of the *Margriet* and her crew.

The *Margriet*, a pure Flemish name of a flower, marguerite or daisy. Janet S. Cox from Utah chose these flowers for the memorial of the crashed Allied planes in Houthalen. The white daisy a symbol, an end of a true story."

Significantly, the bouquets of flowers that Guy and Willy gave to Candy and Sara contained daisies.

Interrogation Form for Thomas Mikulka, Tail Gunner
Courtesy of Yvonne Daley-Brusselmans

PAGES FROM DAD'S NOTEBOOKS...

Stalag Luft 6 & 4 Notebook Cover – notice the shading of the B-17

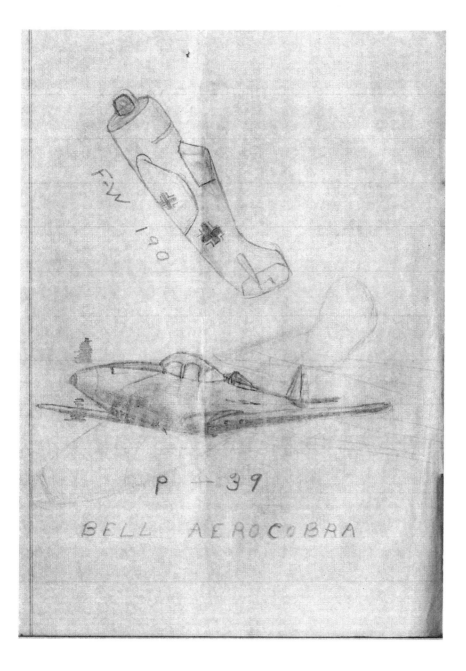

Dreams of liberation

The parachutist (you can see the outline of the parachute and an upside-down house)

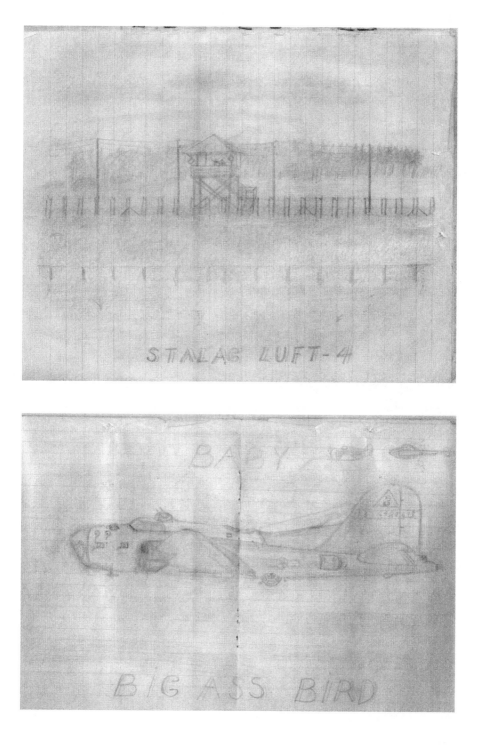

Gunners   Wish

I wish To be a pilot
   And you along with me
But iF we all were Pilots
   Where would The air Force be

The pilots just a chaffeur
   Its his Job to Fly The Plane
But its we who do the Fighting
   Though we may not get The Fame

It takes guts To be a gunner
   To set in the Lonely ball
When The Messesschmitts are coming
   And The Fw's give you their all
                                    (OVER)

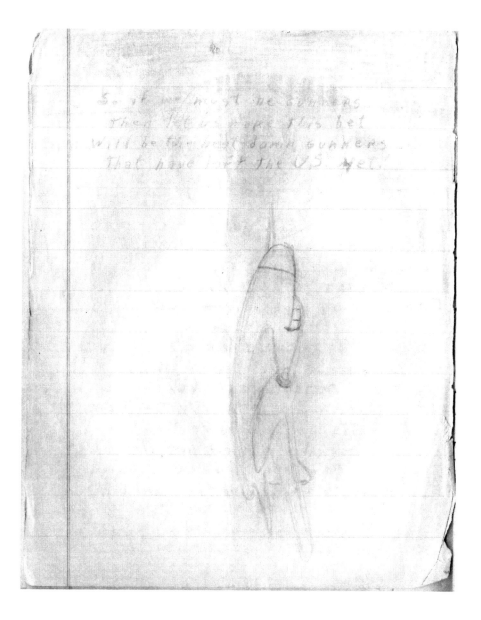

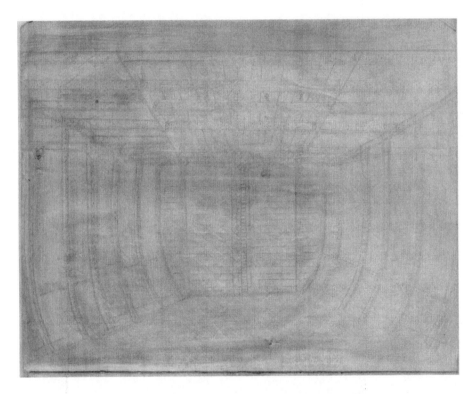

**Hold of the boat that transported POWs from
Stalag Luft VI to Stalag Luft IV**

Camps and dates

POEM FROM JAY JOYCE'S NOTEBOOK

(Courtesy of Bea Joyce)

MY LAST FLIGHT

by S/Sgt. Jay Joyce, POW #1365, (as written in his POW notebook)

It was early in the morning
When we were called from bed,
You are going on a mission
To us the Sergeant said.

We jumped into our clothing
Outside we did go.
The sky was black and stormy
And nary a star did show.

We ate and went to briefing
To learn a thing or two.
They said your going to Frankfurt
And his words were oh so true

They talked about this
And they talked about that.
He said that we were all going
But there's a few who won't come back.

There's a hundred and fifty flak guns
Which can be brought to bead on you,
Then there is five hundred fighters
You'll meet up there in the blue.

The snow was lightly falling
As we walked out to the plane,
And in our minds we're wondering
Just what the day will bring.

Our guns were set and ready
To spit their deadly juice.
The sky still dark and gloomy
It didn't seem much use.

Then came time for takeoff
Up into the sky we flew.
On through those dark stormy clouds
Up to the beautiful blue.

We climbed up to the altitude fast.
The pilot said, "Put on your mask."
At nineteen thousand, we formed the formation
Then off we sped to free our nation.

We are over the channel now
So test your guns, for soon we meet the huns.
The enemy coast boys we are now there
Keep on your toes and we'll have some fun.

Flack to the front flack to the rear
Over the interphone, that's all I can hear.
A call from the tail my guns have quit
Then from the ball, my turret is hit.

We are over the target now
We watch the bombs go down,
We wonder what they're hitting
A factory, shipyard maybe a town.

Then a call from the ball
Number two has been hit.

What I Never Told You

The pilot tries to feather
But the engine won't quit.

We drift from formation
We fly out all alone
We are dodging the fighters
We are trying to get home.

Then all of a sudden, from out of the sun
The fighters are coming, give her the gun.
They come from the north, and from the west
The gunners are game, they're doing their best

Suddenly we hear bail out, get gone
I headed for the door the wind very strong.
I grabbed the rip cord as I went through the door
I landed in Belgium right on the shore.

The people they came from all around
To see what the Jerry's had shot down.
Then the soldiers came and took me away
Now in Stalag 4, I'm forced to stay.

Written by Lindsay Brown about "Someone Special"

Someone special is my Grandpa Kyler. He takes me places and plays soccer with me. He takes me swimming up to my Aunt's house and he watches my soccer and basketball games. He buys me lots of things. He works really hard to watch me and all of my cousins. When my mom and dad both go to work at the same time we go over to his house. He was in World War II. He flew in a plane called a B-17 bomber. My grandpa loves planes. I wish I could take him to an exhibit in New York where a man has restored a B-17 bomber. My grandpa is a very special and interesting person. He has lots and lots of friends. Everybody likes him. He helped me with some social studies and math that I didn't understand. He does everything he can for me. He is the best.

(Lindsay's grade was "A" on this paper)

Grandpa John and his following

**My family: Dawn, Clair ("Buster"), Sara,
John, Sandra, Candy, Angel**

REMEMBERING DAD

Candy Kyler Brown

[In loving memory of my father, John R. Kyler, POW #1277, who passed away May 4, 2004. Read and remembered with my friends on the 2005 trip to Stalag Luft I.]

I knew not a soul but I knew my own heart.
I needed to journey out of the country to Barth.
No doubt in my mind, it was the right thing to do.
So much about dad as gunner & POW that I hadn't a clue.
A few facts that I'd gathered, important to pack;
With God's grace and some luck – to collect info to bring back.
Back and forth at the train station – I stepped all over the place.
I left confident that at some point I'd stepped in dad's space.
I can only imagine and picture him here:
So young and courageous – full of suffering I fear.
I wanted someone to remember – to recall his face.
I wished to hear stories of him from roomies – but it would not be the
    case.
But it really didn't matter because of everyone here.
I heard stories of you and your dads, and felt my own dad was near.
Uncertain of dad's compound – I walked South's edge and North 1, 2,
    and 3.
I ventured cross the field certain that he could see.
I stared to the heavens slowly turning around – not sure why.
But I was thinking all these years later – I'm seeing the same sky.
I was mesmerized by the steeple and glanced from every direction.
I'm sure I caught the same angle as dad from one of the sections.
I accomplished what I'd hoped for – I felt fulfilled.
For brief moments I became him – feelings that I cherish still.
One year ago today – just like that – dad was gone.
But what a tribute to remember him with you Ex-Kriegies of Stalag Luft I.

MY MISSION

Candy Kyler Brown

[This Poem was written and read by the Author on the tour in 2006.]

I ask myself "how did he feel?"
But why do I need to know?
I did not even know him then
As it was a lifetime ago.

I could not discern for I was not there
My feelings could never be like his
To witness as my father did
An impossibility is what it is.

My walk freely across the empty grounds
That now are open as can be
It's nothing like the crowded compounds
Caged by wire as far as the eye can see.

The wretched confinement, hunger and cold
Extreme hardships most will never know.
I can only imagine the deprivation
Of all those courageous men so long ago.

My leisurely ride in a B-17
On a bright and beautiful day
To being shot at in a ball turret
Cannot compare in any way.

Many thought I was crazy
When I jumped out of a plane
But it was in memory of dad's bailout,
So it was heartfelt not insane.

I am compelled to persevere
And trace his route the best I can
The path of a boy who went to war
And returned home a man.

The vague depiction in my mind
Is a delineation of each trial.
Although it is during different times
I feel admiration and love in every mile.

In my pursuit of my father's story
I do not know what I hope to find
For it was not me and I was not there
But I play his role in my mind.

I am so proud of all the heroes
And the sacrifices they made.
To win for us our freedom
A gift I would never trade.

Forever heroes to future generations
This is the goal in which I strive
To assure these brave now weary men
That in our memory they will survive.

THE FINALE

Candy Kyler Brown

[Written before, during and completed after my return from my final efforts to retrace my father's complete route as a POW in camps Stalag Luft VI, Stalag Luft IV and Stalag Luft I.]

This trip was called the "finale"
So I'm certain it was my last.
My final attempt in my heartfelt quest -
My desire to seek my father's past.

With only remnants to build from
In the treasured notebooks that he kept,
I read between the lines feeling his pain
For all the tears I sense he wept.

The tears for his loneliness
And for the loved ones he left behind.
The tears for the freedom that he lost
And the fear that he may lose his mind.
The tears for the intense emptiness
And the wonder of what hardships were ahead.
The tears for the starvation that he suffered
And the freezing weather he would dread.

The soil on the grounds that I've dreamt to walk
It is so sacred to a daughter such as me
As I realize the blood sweat and tears
Absorbed in these revered grounds for liberty.

I wanted to see the area my father walked
It is his past that I hope to find.
It is as if I look through his eyes
And visions of him there invade my mind.

Each camp area that I visit
Is a significant stop in his route.
A path that has also become mine
And that I have traveled in my pursuit.

What motivates me I'll never know
I just feel my father's drive.
I wish to tell his story
And how he managed to survive.

He never would complain
And he would keep busy this I know
He would want to go home some day
To the place he left so long ago.

He surely dreamt of his future
Just as I dream of his past
As I cover areas he traveled as a POW
From his first camp to his last.

I know that my unwavering inspiration
Will help me to achieve my goal.
For in my mission to write my father's story
I've indulged my heart and soul.

Sources

INTERNET SOURCES

www.b24.net

www.merkki.com

www.armyairforces.com

www.accident-report.com

www.aviationarcheology.com

www.controltowers.co.uk./P/Podington_B-17.html

www.92ndma.org

www.stalagluft4.org

www.archives.gov/research/tools/index.html

inquire@arch2.nara.gov

www.axpow.org

www.angel45-2b.com

BOOKS

Bussels, J., *De doodstraf als risico (Death Penalty as a risk)*, Belgium publication, 1981.

Cupp, William L., *A Wartime Journey – Bailout Over Belgium, World War II*. Manhattan Kansas: Sunflower University Press, 2002.

Daly-Brusselmans, Yvonne, *Belgium Rendez-Vous 127—Anne Brusselmans, M.B.E., Resistance World War II*. Manhattan, Kansas: Sunflower University Press, 2001.

Dillon, Carrol F., *A Domain of Heroes*. Sarasota, Florida: Palm Island Press, 1995.

Ekwall, Ralph W., *Brother Bob's War--There were many heroes in the Great War – this is the story of one of them*. Copyright 2006.

Freeman, Roger A., as told by Hubert Zemke, *Zemke's Stalag-The Final Days of World War II*. Shrewsbury, England: Airlife Publishing Ltd. 1991.

Janis, Charles G., *Barbed Boredom, a Souvenir Book of Stalag Luft IV*. Irvingston, NJ:1950

O'Donnell, Joseph P., *the Shoe Leather Express*. Trenton, New Jersey: Joseph P. O'Donnell Publisher.

Book I *The Evacuation of Kriegsgefangenen Lager, Stalag Luft IV Germany*, 1982

Book II *Luftgangsters Marching Across Germany*, 1986

Book III *The Pangs of the Thorn*, 1989

Book IV *A History of Stalag Luft IV*, 1995

Book V *A Time of Great Rewarding*, 1999

Book VI *Talent Behind Barbed Wire,* 2002

Rennell, Tony, Nichol, John, *The Last Escape – The Untold Story of Allied Prisoners of War in Europe 1944-45.* New York: Penguin Books 2004.

Roy, Morris J., *Behind Barbed Wire.* New York: Richard R. Smith 1946.

Rutten, Mathieu, *Markante Feiten (Oorlug 17 Limburg).*

Turner, *92nd Bomb Group (H)—Fames Favored Few.* Paducah, Kentucky: Turner Publishing Company 1996.

Sloan, John S., *The Route as Briefed—The history of the 92nd Bombardment Group-USAAF 1942-1945.* Cleveland Ohio: Argus Press 1946.

Walker, John B., *A Guide to Airplanes of the U.S.A.* Racine, Wisconsin: Whitman Publishing Company 1943

MANUSCRIPTS, MILITARY DOCUMENTS, REPORTS., ETC.

Angele Mathile Kneale, Unpublished Memoirs, *"Children, Go, I will tell thee…." (Nana's Life)*. October 1996

Oscar "Mick" Wagelie, *My Story*, Unpublished journal.

Michel Careme, *Le Biblio c/doc du MRA/KLM, de la Section Air et Espace*. Royal Army Museum (Brussels).

Richard Bing, *Train Ride to Barth, Article in Ex-POW Bulletin*: October 1993.

American Prisoners of War in Germany, 15 July 1944. Report prepared by Military Intelligence Service War Department.

Christopher McDermott, M.A., M.Phil. *J223 Report JPAC 242-Internal; Stalag Luft VI; Prisoner of War isolated burials; Silute, Lithuania:*Joint POW/MIA Accounting Command, Hickam AFB, HI 96853, 21 April 2005.

Missing Air Crew Report 2237

CONVERSATIONS, CORRESPONDENCE, E-MAILS, ARTICLES, MISCELLANEOUS...

Marge Ballard

Arthur "Bud" Bodie

Lester Bishop

Piet Brouwer

John Bryner

Bob Bueker

Lloyd Burns

Walter Grotz

Joseph Leo

Milton Klarsfeld

Carolyn McGory

Donald Menard

William Moore

Vicki Morgan

Joseph Reus

Robert & Helen Seidel

Leland Story

John Tayloe

About the Author

Candy Kyler Brown was born and raised in New York State, and was always close to her father, John R. Kyler, a World War II veteran, and her mother, Sara Kyler. The third eldest of five children, Candy learned very little from her father about his wartime experiences, knowing not much more than he was a ball turret gunner in B-17s flying from England, that he was shot down in 1944, captured by the Germans, and held as a POW until VE day in the Spring of 1945. When in 2004 her father died unexpectedly, she quickly realized that there was a great deal that she did not know about her father's wartime experiences, simply because, like many veterans, he chose never to speak about them. Thereafter, and for the next six years, Candy Kyler Brown undertook the mission to retrace her father's entire wartime history, from enlistment in New York State, through training, to his old airbase in England, and then on to follow his movements in Belgium, Lithuania, Germany and Poland. With painstaking effort she compiled the history, and met many of the people who had played a large part in her father's dangerous existence as he tried to survive in a Germany that was literally collapsing before the World.

Candy Kyler Brown presently lives in Kill Buck, New York, with her husband Bradley, not far from her mother Sara, and her children, Lindsay and Nicholas.

CPSIA information can be obtained
at www.ICGtesting.com
Printed in the USA
FFOW02n1107251115
18921FF